D1446678

The African Diaspora and the Study of Religion
Edited by Theodore Louis Trost
(2007)

Aesthetic Formations: Media, Religion, and the Senses
Edited by Birgit Meyer
(2009)

Aesthetic Formations

Media, Religion, and the Senses

Edited by

Birgit Meyer

AESTHETIC FORMATIONS
Copyright © Birgit Meyer, 2009.

First published in 2009 by
PALGRAVE MACMILLAN®
in the United States—a division of St. Martin's Press LLC,
175 Fifth Avenue, New York, NY 10010.

Where this book is distributed in the UK, Europe and the rest of the world,
this is by Palgrave Macmillan, a division of Macmillan Publishers Limited,
registered in England, company number 785998, of Houndmills,
Basingstoke, Hampshire RG21 6XS.

Palgrave Macmillan is the global academic imprint of the above companies
and has companies and representatives throughout the world.

Palgrave® and Macmillan® are registered trademarks in the United States,
the United Kingdom, Europe and other countries.

ISBN: 978–0–230–60555–8

Library of Congress Cataloging-in-Publication Data is available from the
Library of Congress.

A catalogue record of the book is available from the British Library.

Design by Newgen Imaging Systems (P) Ltd., Chennai, India.

First edition: August 2009

10 9 8 7 6 5 4 3 2 1

Printed in the United States of America.

Contents

Illustrations

Series Editor's Preface

RELIGION/CULTURE/CRITIQUE is a series devoted to publishing work that addresses religion's centrality in a wide range of settings and debates, both contemporary and historical, and that critically engages the category of "religion" itself. This series is conceived as a place where readers will be invited to explore how "religion"—whether embodied in texts, practices, communities, and ideologies—intersects with social and political interests, institutions, and identities.

Aesthetic Formations goes to the very heart of these questions. The book is the culmination of several years of intensive ethnographic fieldwork in Africa, Asia, and Latin America and the Caribbean, focusing on the question of technological mediation in the consolidation, transmission, and transformation of religion. Each chapter of the book invites readers into worlds where media—cinema, television and video, radio, audio cassettes, and the Internet—provide, not merely modes of representation for religious ideas, but spaces where religious communities make their homes and articulate themselves. But the notion of mediation is more capacious yet in *Aesthetic Formations* and so what counts as media expands beyond the conventional modalities (film, television, etc.) into the body itself as a space of mediation. Indeed, religion is reframed by the authors of this book, not undertood as an object of representation but rather as mediation itself.

Reading *Aesthetic Formations* can be a dizzying experience as images and sounds overwhelm the reader from all sides: televisions blare, radios blast, cinematic images flash across the screen. The book produces a sort of religious vertigo as the reader is transported from one scene of spiritual fervor to the next. Religious worlds overlap and compete for adherents, both using conventional media in new formats as a strategy of outreach but also offering themselves up as more effective modes of mediation for spirits and the divine. The cacophony and visual overload of *Aesthetic Formations* achieves a sort of mimetic charge, moving beyond reportage and analysis and toward a different kind of ethnographic representation.

The contributors to this volume have worked together for several years in close collaboration, and as a consequence they have produced a work that is richly textured with details from the ethnographic field but also theoretically coherent. Each chapter in the book can stand on its own, but when read together, the chapters that comprise *Aesthetic Formations* make a compelling argument for a transformed academic approach to religion in the contemporary, globalized world. This book stages precisely the kind of discussion this series was created to promote.

ELIZABETH A. CASTELLI
Religion/Culture/Critique Series Editor
New York City
December 2008

Preface

At the beginning of the twenty-first century one cannot fail to notice the marked presence of religion throughout the globe. Electronic and digital media have become more easily available for new expressions of identity and politics of belonging. This has offered possibilities for religious groups to assert their public presence and to appeal to new audiences. However, there is also a remarkable display of religious forms and elements in public culture outside the domains of institutionalized religion. Diverse phenomena such as the skilful adoption of television and video by Pentecostal-Charismatic churches, the efficient use of audiocassette sermons for the spread of Islamic reform movements, the appearance of spiritual sites of veneration in cyberspace, the emergence of new charismatic prophets whose fame spreads via the media, or the representation—and for some viewers: presence—of spirits and divine power in movies, challenge us to develop new perspectives on religion, and religious modes and moods of binding and belonging in our time.

The cover image, painted by the Ghanaian artist Gilbert Forson, evokes many of the questions that are now provoked, in a time when modern devices such as video cameras have become part and parcel of religious practices. How does the eye of the camera affect the image of Jesus? Does the cloudy substance that emanates from the camera suggest that his image remains invisible, or does this substance rather suggest a new aura that the image of Jesus achieves by being mediated and circulated via a video-film? Furthermore, given that Forson's image emerged in a setting in which Pentecostal-Charismatic churches make skilful use of the new availability of media as video-film, television, radio, and print, it also raises questions such as: What happens when religions adopt new media? How does this affect the message, the ways in which believers are reached and addressed, and the role of religion in the public realm?

This volume explores the rearticulation and concomitant transformation of religion as it occurs through the negotiation and incorporation of newly accessible mass media and the specific styles of binding that go along with them. It focuses on neotraditional religions such as Candomblé in

Brazil and Afrikania in Ghana, on Pentecostal churches and the Catholic Charismatic Renewal in Brazil, Venezuela and Ghana, on Islamic movements in Northern Nigeria, and on the global Raelian Movement, as well as the migration of religious repertoires into the sphere of entertainment— radio on the Caribbean Island of Sint Maarten, and film in Bangladesh and South India. The volume is based on a long-term cooperation of 10 researchers and myself in the framework of a research program titled *Modern Mass Media, Religion and the Imagination of Communities. Different Postcolonial Trajectories in West Africa, South Asia, Brazil and the Caribbean,* which took place at the Amsterdam School for Social Science Research at the University of Amsterdam between 2000 and 2006 and has been generously sponsored by The Netherlands Foundation for Scientific Research (NWO) and the University of Amsterdam in the framework of a PIONIER grant.

Situated at the core of our research, this volume addresses the role of religion and new and old media in the emergence and sustenance of new kinds of communities or formations, which generate particular notions of self and others, modes of religious experience, and of being and acting in the world. In the first chapter, I present, by way of introduction, my perspective on the religion-media-community nexus, which I developed in the context of our intense collaboration, during the course of which I have been able to visit most of the research venues. The volume is organized into three parts, each of which addresses key aspects of the central theme: the question of boundary politics in the formation of religious subjectivities and communities (Part 1), the implications of the presence of religion in the public realm for the relation between the religious and the secular (Part 2), and the paradoxical relation between mediation and immediacy (Part 3). Each of these parts contains a set of chapters from the researchers who have been cooperating in our program: Maria José de Abreu; Marleen de Witte; Francio Guadeloupe; Lotte Hoek; Stephen Hughes; Brian Larkin; Carly Machado; Martijn Oosterbaan; Rafael Sánchez; and Mattijs van de Port.

Anthropological research is usually understood to be a quite individual endeavor. This is grounded in anthropologists' particular methodology and attitude regarding knowledge production, in that anthropologists view themselves as the key research "instrument." As ethnography is necessarily embedded in intersubjective encounters between researchers and their interlocutors that generate unexpected findings, amazement, and fascination, anthropologists tend to be suspicious of carrying out research within conceptual and methodological straitjackets that already presuppose and guide certain outcomes. This has consequences for the way in which a research program, such as the one on which this volume is based, takes shape. Directing this program, it was my key concern to maintain a balance between the virtue of anthropological knowledge production as grounded in unique intersubjective research settings and the value of working together on a common theme. The PIONIER grant made it possible for me to gather a number of imaginative, enthusiastic researchers who were passionate fieldworkers in their respective research locations, and shared an urge to grasp the role of media in shifting the place and role of religion. We used this unique opportunity to develop a new intellectual space for conceptualizing key issues that arose from our research, as well as interrogating our research in the light of new, exciting questions. Practically, we organized a weekly seminar, which took place throughout the six years of the program's duration, and which attracted a number of additional researchers and guests. In our seminar, which took place on Monday mornings in my office, we gathered around a rather too small table and discussed relevant literature in the fields of anthropology and media, religious studies, media studies and visual culture, and postcolonial studies, as well as each other's work in progress.

As the theme of religion and media appeared to be a hot topic at the time of our program taking shape, we also engaged in intense conversations with upcoming initiatives such as the establishment of the Center for Religion and Media directed by Faye Ginsburg and Angela Zito at New York University, the research project Indonesian Mediations directed by Ben Arps and Patricia Spyer under the auspices of the Royal Dutch Academy of Sciences at Leiden University, the International Study Commission on Media, Religion and Culture chaired by Stewart Hoover, Peter Horsfield, Jolyon Mitchell, and David Morgan, the Deus in Machina project directed by Jeremy Stolow at Concordia University, and the NWO-sponsored research program The Future of the Religious Past, Religious Forms and Elements in the 21st Century directed by Hent de Vries. In the course of the duration of our program, we organized a number of international workshops and conferences in which we involved participants affiliated with the above-mentioned initiatives, as well as individual scholars working in the emergent field of religion and media. I am particularly happy that we were able to invite Charles Hirschkind, Meg MacLagan, and Jeremy Stolow to participate in our conversations as visiting fellows, which made it possible for them to join us in Amsterdam and enrich our discussions for about three months.

The research program on which this volume is based was a truly collective endeavor that allowed us to address new questions and develop new concepts and terms in an intellectually enticing, constructive, and convivial sphere. I would like to thank all the authors for their deep, ongoing commitment to the project, and our international partners and visiting fellows for their genuine interest in and support of our work. José Komen, Miriam May, and Anneke Dammers from the ASSR offered incredible logistical support, without which our program initiatives would not have materialized. Erik van Ommering assisted me in preparing the manuscript for publication. In addition to the scholars already mentioned, I also grate-fully acknowledge the substantial intellectual input into our inquiries of Miriyam Aouragh, Kwabena Asamoah-Gyadu, Gerd Baumann, Patricia Birman, Elizabeth Castelli, David Chidester, Sudeep Dasgupta, Ken George, Rosalind Hackett, Webb Keane, Peter Geschiere, Annelies Moors, David Morgan, Chris Pinney, Esther Peperkamp, Brent Plate, Peter Pels, Joel Robbins, Herman Roodenburg, Vincent de Rooij, Benjamin Soares, Vivian Sobchack, Irene Stengs, Thijl Sunier, Dorothea Schulz, Peter van der Veer, Karin Willemse, Rijk van Dijk, and José van Santen. Since my move from the University of Amsterdam to the VU University Amsterdam in 2006, I have also gained greatly from discussing the central ideas gener-ated by this program with, in particular, André Droogers, Ruard Ganzevoort, Linda van de Kamp, Kim Kibbe, Miranda Klaver, Johan Roeland, Oscar Salemink, Regien Smit, Jan van der Stoep, Marjo de Theije, and Peter Versteeg. Particular thanks go to Jojada Verrips for his enduring and reliable intellectual and practical support, and his sparking inspiration throughout this endeavor.

BIRGIT MEYER
Amsterdam, September 2008

Introduction

From Imagined Communities to Aesthetic Formations: Religious Mediations, Sensational Forms, and Styles of Binding

Birgit Meyer

Over the past decade, a host of studies probing into the relation between religion and media emerged in the interface of anthropology, sociology, media studies, religious studies, philosophy, and the arts. Moving beyond a view of religion and media in terms of a puzzling antagonism, in which two ontologically distinct spheres—the spiritual and the technological—collide, scholars now develop new approaches that regard media as intrinsic to religion. Rather than interpreting the at times spectacular incorporations of new media by religious groups as an entirely new phenomenon, the question raised is that of how a new medium interferes with older media that have long been part of religious practice. This understanding moves our inquiry out of the limiting field of binary oppositions, in which religion features as the Other of modernity and technology, whose eventual disappearance is presumed. The shift toward a new postsecularist vantage point from which to explore the rearticulation of religion in specific contemporary settings (Asad 2003; Taylor 2007) proves to be far more productive than debates about the decline of religion or its withdrawal from the public sphere undertaken from the paradigm of secularization. It allows us to take a fresh look at the salient appeal and public presence of diverse forms of contemporary religious expressivity (De Vries 2008).

The rearticulation of religion necessarily implies some kind of transformation, which entails shifts of its position in relation to the state and the market, as well as the shape of the religious message, structures of authority, and modes and moods of binding and belonging. In other words, one of the reasons why religion remains a vital, appealing force lies exactly in its propensity to transform by incorporating new media and addressing and linking people in new ways. Of course, this transformation does not stand by itself, but occurs within broader processes, such as the much-discussed reconfiguration of postcolonial nation-states that struggle to bind citizens into "the imagined community" of the nation (Anderson 1991), the concomitant emergence of alternative religious, ethnic, and life-style communities (Appadurai 1996; Castells 1996–1998; Ginsburg, Abu-Lughod, and Larkin 2002), and the global spread of neoliberal capitalism (Comaroff and Comaroff 2000; Ferguson 2006). These processes effect, and are up against, a pervasive sense of distraction and fragmentation (aptly captured by the German term *Zerstreuung*, Benjamin 1999[1936]), which entails a dissolution of the taken-for-grantedness of lifeworlds, yielding experiences of loss of certainty and security, as well as new opportunities (Bauman 2001) and a pertinent quest for truth and authenticity (Houtman 2008; Lindholm 2008; Taylor 1989; Van de Port 2004).

The purpose of this introduction is to map out the intellectual space in which the contributions to this volume evolved in the context of our collaborative research program on the relation between media, religion, and the making of communities (as mentioned in the preface).[1] I use the notion intellectual space so as to emphasize the fact that our research program was not intended to develop one overarching theory and methodology. Our concern was to build a new conceptual setting from which to interrogate theoretical notions relevant to the religion-media-community nexus in the light of our research findings, and vice versa. While the ten chapters address different, albeit closely interrelated, aspects of the role of media and religion in the making of communities in our time, I will here spell out the central ideas that characterize the approach that I have developed in the course of directing this program. Discussing the potential and limitations of Anderson's notion of the "imagined community" (Section I), introducing the alternative term "aesthetic formation" (Section II), and pleading for an understanding of religion as a practice of mediation that is centered around distinct "sensational forms" (Section III), this introduction stresses the importance of taking into account the role of bodies, the senses, media, and things in the making of religious subjects and communities (see also Meyer 2008a). While both media and religion have long been located in the sphere of the imagination and virtuality, I advocate an alternative approach that takes their material dimension seriously, so as to grasp how religion and media touch ground and yield tangible forms and formations in social life. By virtue of being mediated via modern media that offer unprecedented possibilities to reach out and articulate religion in the public realm, religious modes of binding and making community transform, and this implies new opportunities, paradoxes, and tensions (Section IV).

I   Imagined Communities:
Potential and Limitations

Emile Durkheim's question "What are the bonds which unite men one with another?" has not lost actuality since it was raised more than 110 years ago (1984[1893]). While the ways in which communities are formed is subject to change, it is nonetheless clear that in our contemporary world community is much in demand—even the term itself, as Zygmunt Bauman remarks, "feels good: whatever the word 'community' may mean, it is good 'to have a community'" (2001, 1). Although it is debatable whether religion etymologically relates to *religare* (to bind again), it is clear that the quest for—and question of—community plays out even more markedly in the field of religion. Indeed, for Durkheim, social cohesion depended on shared collective representations of a "sacred" and its communal ritual worship.

Seeking to grasp the making of (religious) communities in the framework of the research program on which this volume is based, it has been impossible to neglect the pioneering proposition of Benedict Anderson to view the nation as an imagined community, existing in the minds of its members and called into existence via a new reading public generated by the rise of "print capitalism." As many scholars have noted, one of the attractions of this proposition lies in the fact that it moves beyond earlier understandings of communities as depending on face-to-face communication, which were contrasted with modernity's prime social formation—*Gesellschaft*—and expected to vanish eventually in the face of individualization. In Anderson's perspective, communities evolve around mediated imaginations that are able to substitute the (spatial) distance between members with a feeling of togetherness (see also Cohen 1985).[2] This view of communities as not given but imagined and, by implication, mediated has been a major source of inspiration for our research program and this volume. It suggests that a focus on media, and the new publics—whether these may be readers, listeners, spectators, or other kinds of audiences—generated by them is a suitable starting point for studying the making of community, as is also suggested by Michael Warner (2002; see also Hofmeyr 2006; Sumiala 2008). In this understanding, a community is not a preexisting entity that expresses itself via a fixed set of symbols, but a formation that comes into being through the circulation and use of shared cultural forms and that is never complete (Latour 2005; see also de Abreu and Guadeloupe in this volume).

While Anderson was interested in the implications of the shift from premodern large-scale religious imagined communities to the rise of nationalism and the nation-state as the prime module of the modern era, this volume explores the rise and appeal of religious, mass mediated communities at a time in which the nation-state is found to be somewhat in disarray (partly because it faces the emergence of religious communities that challenge the capacity of the secular state to maintain the primacy of the nation over religious identities). Even though our research is located at another historical moment, Anderson's analysis of the rise of the modern nation-state in the wake of the decline of large-scale religious communities united by a sacred language is a productive starting point for further reflection about the potential and limitation of the notion of the modern imagined community.

As is well known, Anderson attributed the possibility of imagining the nation in the first place to the "half fortuitous, but explosive, interaction between a system of production and productive relations (capitalism), a technology of communication (print), and the fatality of human diversity" (1991, 42). This interaction yielded an entirely new mode of experiencing the world and imagining community. The decisive difference between the imagination of community in premodern and modern times can be grasped by focusing on the shifting status of language. In the past, the sacred languages of Latin, Arabic, Greek, and Chinese were "the media through which the great global communities of the past were imagined." What was said in these sacred languages "were emanations of reality, not randomly fabricated representations of it." As ontological reality was apprehensible only through the "truth-language of Church Latin, Quu'ranic Arabic, or Examination Chinese" (14), the imaginations of community that were conveyed by these languages could be experienced as true.

Modern imaginations of community, by contrast, are formed on the basis of a modern understanding of language that rests on the idea of the arbitrariness of the sign (43). From this perspective, language is a referential code that is separated from that which it bespeaks, and that has lost an earlier ontology of truth inextricably bound up with the legitimacy of divinity, and the worldly power backed by it. Anderson emphasized that in Europe print capitalism lay the basis for a new modern national consciousness by creating new spheres of communication (above the many vernaculars and below Latin) that yielded more or less fixed languages associated with new national centers of power. He posited that this process was facilitated by the "very arbitrariness of any system of signs for sounds" (43). At this point our criticisms come in. If the language in which modern imagined communities are expressed is basically arbitrary, the question arises as to how these communities face the burden of featuring as in principle "randomly fabricated representations" that are no longer rooted in a "truth-language" and manage to be taken as real, rather than just imagined, by their members.[3] How, in other words, are the languages on which modern imagined communities depend reinvested with a sense of truth and reality? A theoretical focus that remains limited to the "imagination" is unlikely to help us answer this question, the problem being that such a focus calls for the theoretical exercise of (de)constructing imaginations by revealing the mechanics of their construction. While the usefulness of constructivist approaches is beyond doubt, certainly when it concerns the unmasking of power claims that posit essentialized truths, in order to understand how imaginations become real for people we must move a step further (Latour 2005, 88ff.; Geschiere 2009).[4] How can we grasp the rigor with which members of imagined communities (long to) experience these imagined bonds as authentic repositories of truth beyond questioning in our time?[5] Anderson himself asserted that the nation, despite being a figment of the imagination, has the power to invoke strong, emotional affects in and bonds between people, preparing them to die—or kill—in its name. The imagined community of the nation, thriving as it does on strong feelings of attachment and commitment, strives to command citizens' confidence in the truthfulness of its fictionality.

Persuading people of the truthfulness of fictions is a process that we also encountered in our research on the power and appeal of religious messages, even though they may well be characterized as simulacra that successfully convey "reality-effects" (Schwartz 1995, 316; see especially van de Port in this volume). Indeed, in order to achieve this and be experienced as real, imaginations are required to become tangible outside the realm of the mind, by creating a social environment that materializes through the structuring of space, architecture, ritual performance, and by inducing bodily sensations (see also Meyer 2008a). In brief, in order to become experienced as real, imagined communities need to materialize in the concrete lived environment and be felt in the bones. The point is that although Anderson acknowledged the importance of emotional attachment and embodiment, this is not fully accommodated by his theoretical notion of the modern imagination. Stuck in asserting the essentially arbitrary character of all signs, this notion is of limited use to show how imaginations become tangible by materializing in spaces and objects, and by being embodied in subjects. Anderson's remark, made somewhat in passing, that communities are to be distinguished "by the *style* in which they are imagined" (1991, 6, my emphasis), hints at the importance of scrutinizing how the binding of people into imagined communities actually occurs and is realized in a material sense. More attention needs to be paid to the role played by things, media, and the body in actual processes of community making. Indeed, in order to grasp the particular modes through which imaginations materialize through media and become manifest in public space, generating sensorial sensibilities and aptitudes that vest these imaginations with a sense of truth, we need to move into the broader sphere of what I call *aesthetic formations.*[6]

II   Aesthetic Formations

As I have just explained, I launch the notion of "aesthetic formation" so as to overcome the limitations of "imagined community," while retaining Anderson's view that the making of bonds in modern times depends on media and mediation. This raises the question as to what can be gained by substituting "imagined" with "aesthetic," and "community" with "formation."

Let me begin with the former. My understanding of aesthetics is not confined to the now common meaning that it acquired at the end of the eighteenth century (largely through Immanuel Kant), when it became limited to the beautiful in the sphere of the arts and its disinterested beholder. Instead, I suggest returning to its roots in Aristotle's much older and more encompassing notion of *aisthesis*, which designates "our corporeal capability on the basis of a power given in our psyche to perceive objects in the world via our five different sensorial modes (...), and at the same time a specific constellation of sensations as a whole" (Meyer and Verrips 2008, 21). Understood in this way, *aisthesis* refers to "our total sensory experience of the world and our sensitive knowledge of it" (ibid.; see also Verrips 2006; de Abreu, Hoek in this volume). This appreciation of a more encompassing, embodied understanding of aesthetics as rooted in *aisthesis* is now beginning to be more widely shared among scholars so as to better account for the affective power of images, sounds, and texts over their beholders. Especially in the study of the relation between religion and media, and in the field of visual culture at large, scholars seek to move beyond a representational stance that privileges the symbolic above other modes of experience, and tends to neglect the reality effects of cultural forms. The coinage of new terms such as "corpothetics" (Pinney 2004), "somaesthetics"

(Shusterman 2002, see also Hirschkind 2006), or the "cinesthetic subject" (Sobchack 2004; see also Hoek in this volume) signals a shift from the study of imaginations in terms of representations toward more visceral and material approaches of cultural forms in processes of binding (Morgan 1998, 2005; Meyer 2006a).

The fact that imaginations, most certainly in the sphere of religion, are able to touch beholders and induce in them a sense of being true and powerful—as many chapters in this volume show (see especially van de Port, Hoek, de Witte, and Machado)—is well captured by the move toward aesthetics as proposed here. At stake are, in other words, the modes through which imaginations materialize and are experienced as real, rather than remaining at the level of interchangeable representations located in the mind. Imaginations, though articulated and formed through media and thus "produced," appear as situated beyond mediation exactly because they can be—literally—incorporated and embodied, thus invoking and perpetuating shared experiences, emotions, and affects that are anchored in, as well as triggered by, a taken-for-granted lifeworld, a world of, indeed, *common sense*.

Why aesthetic *formation*, however, rather than aesthetic *community*? I certainly do not discard the notion of community per se, but indicate that we need to move beyond understanding community as a fixed, bounded social group. In order to get a better grip on the making of communities as a process, it is helpful to invoke the term formation, because it is more encompassing and dynamic. Formation refers both to a *social entity* (as in social formation)—thus designating a community—and to *processes of forming* (see also Mahmood 2005, 17ff.).[7] These processes of forming mold particular subjects through shared imaginations that materialize, as explained above, through embodied aesthetic forms. The term aesthetic formation, then, highlights the convergence of processes of forming subjects and the making of communities—as social formations. In this sense, "aesthetic formation" captures very well the formative impact of a shared aesthetics though which subjects are shaped by tuning their senses, inducing experiences, molding their bodies, and making sense, and which materializes in things (see also de Abreu in this volume, and de Abreu 2009). Again, my concern here is not so much to replace the term community, but to launch a dynamic—indeed, per*form*ative—understanding of community as an aesthetic formation. This is the way in which the notion of community is used in the contributions to this volume.

Another reason for opting against the notion of "aesthetic community" lies in the fact that it is invoked in a confusing and, in my view, problematic manner. Many authors attribute this notion to Kant, yet define it in their own way, as a particular type of community aligned with Western consumer culture. For instance, in his book *Community. Seeking Safety in an Insecure World* (2001[1790]), Zygmunt Bauman claims that the aesthetic community is "brought forth and consumed in the 'warm circle' of experience," yet faces a problem of endurance and is doomed to disappoint because of its lack of "binding power" (65).[8] This type of community is, according to Bauman, closely linked with the entertainment industry that seduces people through elaborate spectacles, featuring celebrities and short-lived idols who "conjure up the 'experience of community' without real community, the joy of belonging without the discomfort of being bound" (69). He draws a sharp distinction between aesthetic communities that produce "bonds without consequences," and ethical communities that entail, as conceptualized by Durkheim, "ethical responsibilities" and "long-term commitment" (71ff.). In a similar manner, Veit Erlmann describes aesthetic communities as grounded in an epistemology of appearance (*Erscheinung*) rather than substance (*Wesen*), and as a "hallmark of a worldview without synthesis, of an age of contingency and ambiguity," to be found in "societies without the security of tradition, but also without the claims to universal truth of former eras" (1998, 12).

Here, aesthetic community is devoted to pleasure and beauty, and smacks of postmodern superficiality and lack of substance. While it is debatable as to how far these authors stay close to Kant's original notion of *sensus communis aestheticus*,[9] they do still carry the legacy of his narrowing down of aesthetics to beauty and the arts, and a rather crude distinction between concepts and feelings, mind and body, appearance and substance (Meyer and Verrips 2008, 22ff.). While I appreciate the fluidity entailed in the notion of aesthetic community, invoking a sense of being always in the making, I have severe reservations about its equation with mere pleasure and consumer culture, and the, albeit implicit, disdain with regard to experience and emotions. The undeniable existence of the kind of instant, easily dissolvable communities that Bauman and Erlmann have in mind should not yield a generalized view of aesthetic communities as necessarily superficial and short-lived, and opposed to a more genuine kind of community. In sum, against the backdrop of my plea for a broader understanding of aesthetics in terms of *aisthesis* that is not predicated on a dualism of body and mind and acknowledges the role of all senses in experiencing, and making sense of, the world, it is clear that the notion of aesthetic community as it has so far been employed is of limited use for our purposes: grasping the dynamics of the transformation and binding capacity of religion in our contemporary world.

My notion of aesthetic formation resonates well with Michael Maffesoli's proposition of a new understanding of community in our time (1996), which takes seriously the importance of media (in particular images), their bodily impact, and the forming power of a shared "aesthetic style" (31ff.). Taking as a point of departure a post-structuralist understanding of images as hyperreal simulacra that create a reality of their own rather than referring to a world out there (see also Baudrillard 2001), Maffesoli is in favor of what he calls a "figurative sociology" (not to be confounded with the figuration sociology instigated by Norbert Elias), which explores the nexus of images and society in our contemporary "imaginal world." The central feature of this imaginal world concerns the role of shared images in forging links between individuals, organizing them into communities. While this echoes Anderson's notion of imagined community, Maffesoli pays far more attention than Anderson to the ways in which shared images mobilize and thrive upon shared sentiments, inducing modes, and moods, of feeling together.

Writing in the late twentieth century, Maffesoli notes an increasing reenchantment that occurs around televised, mass-produced images that gain the status of icons and idols around which new, cultic communities are formed. No longer confined to a separate sphere, religiosity is spreading out, "contaminating, step by step, all of social life" (88). His thinking is clearly indebted to Durkheim's notion of collective consciousness as constituted by "the idea that [society] has of itself" (89). As is well known, for Durkheim this collective consciousness was a cause and effect of effervescence, in that it offers a synthesis *sui generis*, "giving rise to sentiments, ideas and images that 'once born, obey the laws proper to them'" (89). Maffesoli posits that the mass-produced images around which people congregate in our time have gained a quasi-religious status, in that they generate the effervescent sentiment of sharing and taking part in a larger social ensemble. As this sentiment is induced via a common aesthetic, the *Homo religious* and the *Homo aestheticus* converge: "the sharing of the image, the aesthetic that this gives rise to, generates relations, engenders linkages and, in short, favors religion" (92).

This aesthetic (which Maffesoli also grounds in the broad understanding of *aisthesis* advocated here) induces a shared sensory mode of perceiving and experiencing the world that produces community.[10] Community thus evolves around shared images and other mediated cultural forms (see also Morgan 2007, 165ff.). This sharing, it needs to be stressed, does not merely depend on a common interpretation of these forms and an agreement about their meaning (as asserted by interpretative or symbolic anthropology), but on the capacity of these forms to induce in those engaging with them a particular common aesthetic and style. Understood as "the essential characteristic of a collective sentiment," style operates as a "'forming form' that gives birth to whole manners of being, to customs, representations, and the various fashions by which life in society is expressed" (5).

Maffesoli thus coins the notion of "aesthetic style," which he locates at the "conjunction of the material and the immaterial" (33) so as to indicate the importance of bodies, things, and images in bringing about new communities and even communion. Such an "aesthetic style" produces a particular subjectivity and habitus.[11]

As I have already remarked, the emphasis Maffesoli places on the relevance of aesthetics, and the concomitant importance of style, resonates well with the concern of this volume to grasp the emergence of new kinds of religious communities that evolve around mass mediated images and other cultural forms by paying due attention to the material dimension. Although his work is limited to images, it can be extended to include other cultural forms that appeal via sound, smell, or touch.[12] However, whereas Maffesoli observes a process of general reenchantment in which anything that binds people to images and other cultural forms via a shared aesthetic already qualifies as religion, the chapters in this volume are based on research in settings in which actual religious groups assert their public presence against other religious and nonreligious groups, or where specific religious repertoires—or "sensational forms," see next section—are employed in addressing people. This implies that we need to pay close attention to the specific ways through which particular religions and religious forms and elements feature in the making of communities via distinct aesthetic styles.

Although from a more conventional perspective it may seem counterintuitive to bring together religion and style, I suggest moving beyond a view of religion as primarily associated with content and style as primarily associated with form. Such distinctions, Talal Asad has argued, echo the modern dualism of outward forms and inner self, according to which form is inferior to substance and meaning (1993; see also Mahmood 2001; Engelke and Tomlinson 2006). Privileging belief over objects and practices, and spirit over matter, modern understandings of religion became "dematerialized" (Chidester 2000; Keane 2007). By calling attention to aesthetics and style I seek to overcome such unproductive distinctions, so as to grasp the material dimension of religious modes of forming subjects and communities (see also Meyer 2006a).

As I have outlined in an earlier publication (Meyer 2004a), an emphasis on style liberates us researchers from a sole focus on meaning—for a long time one of the prime concerns of the anthropology of religion—and opens up a broader field of inquiry that alerts us to the importance of appearance and modes of doing things without dismissing them as mere outward, and hence secondary, matters. Style is at the core of religious aesthetics exactly because the adoption of a shared style is central to processes of subjectivation, in that style involves particular techniques of the self and the body that modulate—and, indeed, "hone" (Hirschkind 2006, 82, 101)—persons into a socio-religious formation. Operating as a marker of distinction (as Anderson also suggested), style is central to the making of religious and other kinds of communities. Understood as a "forming form," style thus operates in the making of aesthetic formations, both by shaping persons and by lending them a shared, recognizable appearance—and thus an identity (see also Benjamin 2006, 43).

III Religious Mediations and Sensational Forms

As I mentioned earlier, a shift occurred in the study of religion and media from studying, as Jeremy Stolow put it, "religion *and* media" toward an understanding of "religion *as* media" (2005). The view of religion as mediation has been persuasively argued by the Dutch philosopher Hent de Vries (2001, see also Plate 2003; van der Veer 1999; Zito 2008, 76–78) who critiques the conceptualization of media and religion, and technology and the transcendental, as belonging to two ontologically different realms. Instead he proposes to understand religion as both positing, and attempting to bridge, a distance between human beings and a transcendental or spiritual force that cannot be known as such. From this philosophical perspective, religion can best be analyzed as a practice of mediation, to which media, as technologies of representation employed by human beings, are intrinsic. It is important to note that this perspective extends the notion of media, which implies modern devices such as film, radio, photography, television, or computers—the usual focus of scholars studying media—toward the inclusion of substances such as incense or herbs, sacrificial animals, icons, sacred books, holy stones and rivers, and, finally, the human body, which lends itself to being possessed by a spirit. Such a view of media as mediators puts in perspective the adoption of typically modern media into religion, and cautions against a deterministic view of modern media as technologies that act by themselves (see also Verbeek 2005). Conversely, this approach also implies that the transcendental is not a self-revealing entity, but always effected by mediation processes, in that media and practices of mediation invoke (even "produce") the transcendental in a particular manner.[13] Indeed, adopting a view of religion as mediation makes it possible to raise entirely different questions from those asked by earlier studies of media *and* religion.

If, as an understanding of religion as a practice of mediation suggests, religion and media need to be understood as coconstitutive, it makes little sense to claim that there is a religious essence that exists prior to, and independent of, the medium through which this essence is subsequently expressed (see also Mazzarella 2004). As content cannot exist without form, a message is always mediated. It is formed by the technologies through which it is expressed, yet—contra Marshall McLuhan's "The Medium Is the Message"—not to be reduced to these technologies. Interestingly, in many of the religious settings we encountered in our research, no clear separation is being drawn between medium and message, form and content. What looks like media from an outsider's perspective may be fully embedded in religious practice, such as, to name just a few examples, icons in Byzantine Catholicism (James 2004), the Torah in Judaism (Stolow 2007, forthcoming), photographs in spirit possession (Behrend 2003; Morris 2000), audiocassettes and other audiovisual media in new Islamic movements (Eisenlohr 2006; Hirschkind 2001, 2006; Schulz 2003, 2006a, 2006b), photographs and lithographs in Hinduism (Pinney 2004) or television and computers in Pentecostal Churches (de Abreu, de Witte, and Sánchez in this volume). The media that are involved in invoking and getting in touch with the transcendental and in binding and bonding believers are usually rendered invisible through established and authorized religious structures. By the same token the media intrinsic to religious mediation are exempted from the sphere of "mere" technology. In so doing, media are authenticated as being part and parcel of the very transcendental that is the target of—and from a more skeptical perspective: invoked by—mediation. In other words, mediation itself is sacralized (see also Chidester 2008) and attributed with a sense of immediacy through which the distance between believers and the transcendental is transcended (Mazzarella 2006; see also Eisenlohr n.d.; Engelke 2007). Paradoxically, immediacy thus depends on mediation *and* its denial.

The conceptualization of religion as mediation was a major step in our research program. Once media are understood as being intrinsic to religion, it becomes of central concern to explore the ways in which people negotiate and possibly adopt new media. We found that media by and large only become an issue when they are new and the possibility of using them is considered.[14] This raises exciting empirical questions as to how new media relate to—for example, fit in with, reinforce, challenge, affect, transform—established practices of mediation. Instead of studying how religious practitioners adopt modern media, and media broadcast religion, as was the case with earlier approaches in the field of religion and media, our program focused on shifts in religious mediation. We did so by exploring how religious groups negotiate new (or at least newly accessible) media, and the formats, styles, and possibilities for public exposure as well as the modes of binding and bonding that go along with them.

In order to better grasp the ways in which religious mediations address and mobilize people and form them aesthetically—the main concern of our research and this volume, as explained in the previous section—I have coined the notion of "sensational form" (Meyer 2006a).

These are relatively fixed, authorized modes of invoking and organizing access to the transcendental, thereby creating and sustaining links between believers in the context of particular religious power structures. Sensational forms shape both religious content (beliefs, doctrines, sets of symbols) and norms. Including all the media that act as intermediaries in religious mediation practices, the notion of sensational form is meant to explore how exactly mediations bind and bond believers with each other, and with the transcendental. These forms are transmitted and shared; they involve religious practitioners in particular practices of worship, and play a central role in modulating them as religious moral subjects. It needs to be stressed again that I do not use form in opposition to content and meaning, or ethical norms and values, but as a necessary condition without which the latter cannot be conveyed. Sensational forms can best be understood as a condensation of practices, attitudes, and ideas that structure religious experiences and hence "ask" to be approached in a particular manner.[15] Religious sensational forms work in the context of particular traditions of usage, which invoke sensations by inducing particular dispositions and practices toward these forms. In other words, such forms are part and parcel of a particular religious aesthetics, which governs a sensory engagement of humans with the divine and each other and generates particular sensibilities that "are not something purely cognitive but are rooted in the experience of the body in its entirety, as a complex of culturally and historically honed sensory modalities" (Hirschkind 2006, 101).

Exploring the implications that the availability of new media has for religious groups, the question is how these new media impact on established sensational forms, and hence the aesthetic styles that form subjects and communities. We found that the question of the adequacy of old and new media to mediate the transcendental may give rise to vehement disagreements, as for instance in the case of Candomblé in Salvador de Bahia, where priestesses such as the renowned Mae Stella have taken up an "iconophobic" position, insisting that the secret truth-knowledge at the heart of Candomblé does not lend itself to any other form of mediation than the body of the spirit medium. In other words, religious knowledge can only be acquired through the experience of the "real time" of the lengthy initiation process. However, at the same time television formats enter into the *terreiros*—for example, when initiates demand a video-recording of their initiation ceremony, preferably in the *telenovela* style (van de Port 2006), and priestesses engage in asserting their presence and

power in Bahia's mediascape while celebrities in the world of arts and politics also stress their affinity with Candomblé. Van de Port argues that
Candomblé indulges in a "public performance of secrecy" (Chapter 1),
which testifies to its deeply ambivalent attitude toward new media. A similar stance prevails in the neotraditional Afrikania Movement in Ghana
that struggles to rescue "African Traditional Religion" from the assaults of
Pentecostal churches that have become hegemonic in Southern Ghana.
Comparing the media practices of Afrikania and the International Central
Gospel Church (ICGC), Marleen de Witte (Chapter 8) shows that
Afrikania finds it difficult to accommodate itself to the predominance of
visibility that prevails in Ghana's current public sphere. While Afrikania
seeks to master its own representation in the mass media, paradoxically
the traditional priests whom it claims to represent wish to maintain an
aura of secrecy, insisting that the gods and their abodes do not lend themselves to be captured through the eye of the camera, and reproduced on
screen (see also Meyer 2005a; see also Ginsburg 2006, Spyer 2001). Brian
Larkin (Chapter 5) investigates how the availability of print and radio,
which were coded as prime media of colonial modernity, became central
to conflicts about the modalities through which Islam was supposed to be
present in public. He shows that the embracement of these modern media
by Sheik Abubaker Gumi was part of reformulating Islam, a project
through which Islam was aligned to a more rational religious practice that
fits in with the modern, secular state. Showing how this rearticulation
yielded conflicts with Sufi movements, which had hitherto been dominant in Northern Nigerian Islam, but which now also started to engage
with radio, Larkin shows that debates and conflicts about media, and the
new forms of public presence allowed by them, is central to religious
transformation.

The point is that the availability of new media may ensue critical delib-
erations about their potential to generate and sustain authentic experiences
and forms of authority within existing religious traditions.[16] Technology
thus never "comes in a 'purely' instrumental or material form—as sheer
technological possibility at the service of the religious imagination" (van de
Port 2006, 23), but is to be embedded in the latter through an often complicated negotiation process in which established authority structures may
be challenged and transformed (see also Eisenlohr 2006; Kirsch 2007;
Schulz 2003, 2006a). Of crucial concern here is the question of how the
aesthetics and styles that particular new media forms imply clash or can be
made to merge with established religious aesthetic styles. In other words,
as message and medium, content and form, only exist together, the big
question is how earlier mediations are transformed by being remediated via
new media (Bolter and Grusin 1999; see also Meyer 2005b, Hughes in this

volume), and whether and how these remediations are authenticated as acceptable and suitable harbingers of religious experience.

Other contributions to this volume spotlight how new audiovisual media are being incorporated into religious mediation practices, generating new sensational forms. Maria José de Abreu (Chapter 7) shows that for the Catholic Charismatic Renewal (CCR), television is regarded as a modern technology that is suitable to render present the Holy Spirit. Analyzing Charismatics' richly somatic experiences of contact with the Spirit, she discerns a telling homology between the Holy Spirit and an "electricity generator" that "infuses energies," and the association of the bodies of believers with "antennas of retransmission." Therefore, television is not considered as a *Fremdkörper*, but as exceptionally suitable to screen the message of the CCR to a mass public. A similar idea of direct transmission underpins Rafael Sánchez' analysis of Pentecostal squatters in Caracas (Chapter 10), who have their bodies seized by the Holy Spirit as Its prime medium and, in turn, seize whatever houses or goods the Spirit tells them to take. Sánchez analyzes Pentecostal church services in the Monarchical Church in Caracas as a "televisual context" in which participants raise their arms, not unlike a "forest of antennas," eager to transmit "live" the power of the Holy Spirit. In the Ghanaian ICGC, pastor Mensa Otabil has his image, and the footage of his recorded service, carefully edited so as to appear as a charismatic icon to his nationwide and international audiences (Chapter 8), eager to touch them even by transmitting the Holy Spirit via the television screen. Indeed, as also Carly Machado (Chapter 9) shows, cameras and screens are indispensable for the creation of fame and charisma, as in the case of the prophet Raël, who appears as most powerful and present not by being actually there, but via his screened "live" image. All these examples suggest remarkable elective affinities between religious modes of representation and new audiovisual technologies (see also Pinney 2004; Stolow 2008).[17] At stake is, in other words, a confluence of media technologies, on the one hand, and the transcendental that they claim to make accessible and the modes through which they address and mold subjects via sensational forms, on the other. In this sense, spiritual power materializes in the medium, and is predicated to touch people in an immediate manner.

This entanglement of media and gods and spirits in religious sensational forms is not limited to religious groups per se, but also occurs in broader realms, such as entertainment (e.g., Hoover 2006). My own research on "pentecostalite" video-films in Ghana (Meyer 2003a, 2004a, 2005a, 2005b), for example, investigates the intersection of these films with the tremendous popularity of Pentecostal-Charismatic churches. Intriguingly, audiences understand technology as acting in the service of revealing the whereabouts of the "powers of darkness," which include demonized indigenous gods and spirits, as well as witchcraft and occult forces such as mermaids and Indian spirits. Although most spectators were fully aware that certain spectacular supernatural apparitions were produced by computer-designed special effects, they did not dismiss these images as fake or make-believe, stating rather that "technology shows what is there." A similar conclusion can be drawn regarding the visualization of gods in Tamil cinema in the 1930s. Stephen Hughes shows that the genres of the mythological and devotional were inscribed in ongoing processes of remediation through which the appearance of gods on screens was framed as a unique transcendental experience (Chapter 4, see also Hughes 2005; Vasudevan 2005). Such intersections between religion and film offer powerful evidence for the mobilization of media technologies in inducing belief via—and even in—cinematic or televised images. In this way technology becomes part of a broader project of "make-believe" in which belief is vested in the image, and not an invisible beyond (De Certeau 1984, 186–187). Or, as Derrida put it succinctly, "There is no need any more to believe, one can see. But seeing is always organized by a technical structure that supposes the appeal to faith" (2001, 63). Importantly, such religious mediations in the sphere of entertainment are relevant to politics of belonging. While Hughes shows that the projection of mythologicals and devotionals was central to the articulation of new religious agendas in the public sphere, Francio Guadeloupe (Chapter 6) focuses on the ways in which popular radio DJs in the Caribbean island of Sint Maarten mobilize Christian repertoires in invoking an inclusive politics of belonging that goes against local, exclusivist, and xenophobic articulations of identity. Even though these "sonic architects" and their listeners are not staunch, churchgoing Christians, they mobilize Christian language so as to bring into being a more encompassing Caribbean community and identity.

Still, certainly in the sphere of entertainment, the relation between religion and the sphere of media need not be as smooth as the examples of Ghanaian videos and Tamil cinema suggest. For instance, in Bangladesh (Hoek in this volume; Hoek 2008) popular film and the visibility it lends to women, who are "unveiled" down to appearing nude in pornographic scenes, is heavily contested. Here the public appearance of women, which was unleashed by their incorporation into paid industrial labor, is subject to a moral debate launched by members of the middle class, in which visibility and obscenity appear as closely related. Lotte Hoek shows how women in the film industry negotiate religious and social constraints on their public presence by staying aloof from the filmic image of the nude woman that depicts their bodies and speaks through their voices. The fact that this filmic image is created by dubbing, in that the takes of one actress are underlain with the voice of another, eases this process of disassociation. Hoek understands this as an adaptation of the practice of *porda*—that is, the modes through which woman become present in public—to the specific dynamic of the Bangladeshi film industry. While in Bangladesh actresses involved in film making negotiate middle class and religious moral standards in such ways that they continue to participate in obscene films, in Northern Nigeria Hausa video movies are heavily critiqued by the Muslim establishment because they display too much of the female body (Larkin 2008; see also Krings 2005)—so much so that current censorship requirements make it virtually impossible to still shoot a movie (Larkin personal communication). Such critiques not only touch upon allegedly obscene images, but also dismiss the medium of film as such, and its link with the allegedly immoral space of the cinema. Of course, actual viewers may have a different idea about this kind of movie. As Martijn Oosterbaan (2003; see also Chapter 2) shows, born-again audiences in the *favelas* of Rio de Janeiro do not only evaluate (and possibly dismiss) televised entertainment on the basis of their Pentecostal worldview: they even put their faith to test by observing to what extent watching obscene images still has a bodily impact (sexual arousal being a sign of too much worldliness). The point here is that both in the sphere of the production and consumption of films, people mobilize a religiously underpinned ethics of acting, listening (Hirschkind 2001, 2006) and watching (see also Bakker 2007).

Many more examples from the research conducted in our research program (and other researchers in the field) could be invoked, but the point should be clear: This volume demonstrates that the accessibility of (new) media offers a strong potential for religious transformations, while at the same time media themselves are subject to religious mediation practices. As the incorporation of new media may entail significant changes in established sensational forms, authority structures, and the public presence of a given religion, a study of the negotiation of media offers deep insights into processes of binding and bonding in our time. This is the key concern that drives the various contributions to this volume.

IV   Religion in the Public Realm

The contributions to this volume show that new possibilities for religions to go public, and to assert their presence in the public sphere, involve paradoxes and tensions. While within religious circles, such processes often are subject to ongoing concern and reflection—expressed, for instance, by fears of "watering down"—scholars need to be wary of simply echoing such views of media and public exposure in terms of the erosion of "real" religion and "real" social bonds. This is why, in Section II, I argued against contrasting aesthetic and ethic communities in terms of superficial versus true, as suggested by Zygmunt Bauman, and pleaded for a close analysis of the actual modes and sensational forms through which bonds are made in religious practice. For the same reason, I am critical of Manuel Castells' ideas about the erosion of religion in "the information age" (see also Meyer and Moors 2006b, 5). In his view the adoption of modern mass media technologies into religion is supposed to ultimately destroy religion's legitimacy: its claims to point a way out of "the system." This volume disagrees with his view that in this process, "societies are finally and truly disenchanted because all wonders are online and can be combined into self-constructed image worlds" (1996–1998, 1: 406).

As explained in the previous section, the contributions to this volume show that the adoption and use of new media is subject to negotiation and eventually incorporation into religious mediations. While certainly the adoption of modern media has intentional and unintentional consequences, it is problematic to analyze this process in terms of disenchantment, as if these media, like a Trojan Horse, would erode religion from within. The point is not the gradual vanishing of religion, but its transformation. As Hent de Vries succinctly pointed out in a critique of Castells, "[w]hat seemed to dry up the resources of religion can equally be viewed as religion's most effective and resourceful continuation" (2001, 13). Indeed, the successful public presence of religion today depends on the ability of its proponents to locate it in the marketplace of culture, and embrace audio-visual mass media so as to assert their public presence (see also Moore 1994), whilst still being able to feature as religion, and hence not reducible to the ordinary. Instead of grounding our analysis on an essentialist view of either community or religion as being in danger of corruption by the forces of mass mediatization, entertainment and the logic of the market, it is more productive to explore how the use of electronic and digital media actually shapes the transformation—and hence continuation—of both communities and religion in our time.

Importantly, the implications of the adoption of new media into religious traditions need to be evaluated in the light of the broader social order, in particular by examining the ways in which states (are able and willing to) regulate the place and role of religion in society. As Brian Larkin shows in his discussion of the use of radio by Muslim reformers in Northern Nigeria (Chapter 5), preaching via the radio entailed the adaptation of Islam to colonial modernity. Sheikh Abubakar Gumi's concern was to relieve Islam from being an inherited set of practices that underpin everyday life and affirm the power of Sufi sheiks and their magical-mystical rituals. Instead, he urged Muslims to read and understand the Hadith and the Qur'an by themselves, instead of relying on Sufi sheiks' mediations. This implied a rationalization of Islam as well as an intensification of religious experience. In this way, Islam was embedded and rearticulated within in a secularizing project that remained, however, messy and replete with paradoxes. Similarly, Stephen Hughes (Chapter 4) points out how in early Tamil cinema in the 1930s, mythologicals and devotionals became central to debates about the emergent categories of secular and religious, which ultimately proved impossible to disentangle. In so doing, Hughes gives historical relief to current debates about the contribution of televised versions of the *Mahabharatha* and *Ramayana* to the rise of Hindu religious nationalism, and the reconfiguration of the relation between religion and politics in India (Mankekar 1999; Rajagopal 2001; see also Dwyer 2006).

While the chapters by Larkin and Hughes address the historical antecedents of the complicated relation between media, religion, politics and entertainment, other contributions concentrate on settings characterized by a salient public articulation of religion and the appeal to religious forms in contemporary public culture. The boundaries between religious and secular, and religion, politics and entertainment have become ever more difficult to draw, and this impinges on the manner in which people are addressed and bonds are formed. In Ghana, the spectacular rise of Pentecostal churches as a public force would have been unthinkable without the retreat of the state from dominating the public sphere in the early 1990s in the wake of the adoption of a democratic constitution. This implied not only a Pentecostal hegemony in public culture, but also made politicians tap into Pentecostal resources so as to appeal to these Christian constituencies (Meyer 2004a; de Witte in this volume, de Witte 2008). In Brazil, the CCR and the new Pentecostal Churches that are in search of publicity and credibility make deliberate use of mass media which had become commercialized already in the period of dictatorship, yet were dismissed by Liberation Theology as being indebted to American cultural and political imperialism (de Abreu in this volume). The public presence of this kind of inspired religion, which easily embraces television and the modalities of stardom, in Ghana, Brazil, Venezuela and elsewhere, signals overlaps in the styles that are deployed in religion, politics, and the sphere of entertainment in addressing people and in processes of binding. An instance of ultimate overlap is the example of Caribbean DJs who use Christianity as a suitable public language to express and claim commonalities (Guadeloupe in this volume), even though people are quite critical about Christian religion per se. All these examples pinpoint the tremendous capacity of especially Christianity, as a world religion par excellence, to spread out and leave its mark in the public sphere, thereby affecting all domains of society. A similar argument can be made, I believe, with regard to other "world religions" that spread by virtue of developing portable sensational forms, which can be transposed on a global scale (see also Csordas 2007). Processes of reaching out by incorporating new media, and the formats and styles that go along with them, challenge our understanding of religion "as we know it" in high modernity. This concerns not only the collapse of boundaries between a secular, public realm and the private sphere, but also the paradoxes with regard to the making of communities which arise with religious transformations.

The central paradox discerned in our research concerns the logic of expansion into the public sphere by incorporating new media and modes of representation, as mentioned earlier. As I explained in the previous section, the new possibilities for public exposure may be found to threaten longstanding modes of binding participants, as in the case of the aforementioned Mae Stella who fiercely opposes the public representation of forms and elements derived from Candomblé, and insists on keeping what really matters out of the limelight of cameras. As van de Port shows (Chapter 1), Mae Stella's dismissal of the migration of Candomblé's expressive forms into folkloristic entertainment exemplifies a politics of boundary maintenance. Interestingly, however, this does not draw Candomblé into full seclusion, as the very act of drawing such boundaries is itself a media performance: claiming difference occurs in public, and is part and parcel of a project of asserting the importance of Candomblé, certainly at a time at which Pentecostal and charismatic Christianity is on the rise.

While for Candomblé, as for Afrikania, public outreach is problematic, this is central to Pentecostal proselytization, which entails its own ambivalences and paradoxes. As Martijn Oosterbaan shows, encroachment upon the public realm is haunted by the danger of polluting the message. Churches such as the Brazilian neo-Pentecostal Igreja Universal run their own media studies with high-tech church services, talk shows and soaps, news and politics, and as the world is regarded as a theatre for the struggle between God and the Devil, they also launch and support Pentecostal candidates in elections. They seek to create a Pentecostal sphere that is different from "the world," yet by necessity depends on the use of media and techniques of representation that also operate outside of Pentecostalism. Spreading out thus paradoxically not only implies an encroachment upon "the world," but also its incorporation (see also Spyer 2008).[18] For these media-savvy Pentecostals, it hence becomes ever more difficult to draw a boundary between being *in* the world, but not *of* the world. The more the born-again community spreads out and takes in, the more it faces the challenge to stay apart by drawing boundaries that are always already destabilized by its drive to expand. Similarly, as Marleen de Witte (Chapter 8) points out, the ICGC faces the difficulty of converting the broad public to be reached out there into audiences, and to touch these audiences in such a way that they are prepared to become part of the church community, rather than merely attending church services as clients in search of health and wealth. Clearly, also here outreach seriously challenges older Christian models of organizing believers, such as that of the congregation. Maria José de Abreu (Chapter 7) also stresses the particularity of charismatic community making as an enduring performance that is never complete—a breathing body—and hence impossible to fix and control within set boundaries (causing much headache to the Catholic Church). This mode of making community—truly in the sense of an aesthetic formation—resonates with the styles of binding mobilized by the Raelian Movement, which also works by calling on the body and the senses, and a strong aesthetic appeal (Machado in this volume). Notwithstanding the strict Raelian leadership structure, the Raelian conventions generate modes and moods in ways that have much in common with dance events such as White Sensation and similar shows.

All these examples give insight into paradoxes and ambivalences involved in the making of religious formations in our time. Many contributors to this volume discern a continuous balancing act between reaching out and staying apart, between embracing the world and staying aloof, between addressing and appealing to the public and imposing some kind of boundary through which believers are set apart. While this involves complicated negotiations within religious groups, this balancing act cannot, however, be simply reduced to the erosion of religion, let alone secularization. Instead the public realm itself is affected—or, to recall Maffesoli's terms: "polluted"—by religion. I understand the term pollution here as signaling, in the sense of Mary Douglas (2002[1966]), a "matter of out place," in that religion is not supposed to be present in the ideal image of the public sphere as it has been articulated famously by Jürgen Habermas (1990[1962]). Indeed, the theoretical and political implications of the spread of religious forms and elements into the public sphere, which was long held to be a secular realm, and yet obviously entails a quite messy mix of religion, entertainment and politics, thus questioning the possibility of drawing boundaries between religious and secular, are just beginning to be addressed from a global (rather than merely Western) perspective and need our attention (Salvatore 2007; Schulz 2006b; Willford and George 2004). The fact that it is increasingly difficult to say where religion stops, and begins, has serious implications for our understanding of the relation between religion and "the world" in our time.

In this context, the striking importance of aesthetics and the body that is emphasized not only in the practice of religion, but also in the sphere of politics, entertainment, and the public realm at large, raises critical questions. Reflecting on the lure of the body in contemporary politics and religion, Rafael Sánchez (Chapter 10) situates Venezuelan Pentecostals in a broader development of the political order toward an erosion of the demarcation between private and public and the concomitant "return of bodiliness, viscerality, and the senses to center stage." The practice of politics, he observes, becomes more and more analogous to the mode of operation of the Holy Ghost, who sensuously grips believers in his crusade to possess the world. Not unlike Pentecostal church services, the Venezuelan public sphere has become a site in which a politics of representation, with its own registers of critical reflection predicated on distance, is being replaced by a striving for the immediate "live" presence of political power, which, in turn, is heavily indebted to registers from televisual entertainment (Sánchez 2001). Discerning throughout the world similar processes of collapsing the political into a spiritual struggle between God and the Devil, Sánchez closes his chapter wondering whether "something good is ever to come out from such an unsettling state of affairs, so redolent with viscerality."

Despite being difficult to answer, the question itself is immediately relevant to the central proposition made in this introduction: the need for a conceptual shift from the notion of imagined communities to aesthetic formations. As I pointed out in Section I, in earlier work on the making of communities, the bodily dimension has been quite neglected. Of course, this neglect did by no means imply that this dimension did not actually matter in social life: the point is that it did not capture much scholarly attention. However, the strong interest in the body, the senses, experience and aesthetics in the social and cultural sciences today signals an increasing awareness that the emergence and sustenance of social formations depends on styles that form and bind subjects not only through cognitive imaginations, but *also* through molding the senses and building bodies. It is no wonder that this interest comes up at a time in which many religions move toward a strong, deliberate emphasis on spectacular sensuous experiences, the public realm becomes a stage for self presentation and display of identity (as signaled by Warner [1992] in his critique of Habermas's disembodied view of the public sphere as constituted by talking heads), and politicians ever more frequently play the personal card and are pushed to prove their authenticity. In the *Erlebnisgesellschaft* (Schulze 1993), the body and the senses that are stimulated so as to provoke grand sensations, certainly demand reflection and research.

Scholarly attention paid to the body and the senses, however, should not yield a straightforward celebration of embodiment and an uncritical adoption of the body as the real ground of experience. This point is made perceptively by Lotte Hoek (Chapter 3) who explicitly looks not only at how the viscerality of bodiliness seduces, but also how it may be eschewed. As she points out, it is exactly because female actresses are aware of the visceral power of cinematic images that they seek to exempt themselves from being eaten up through male desire. They seek to do so by adopting a practice of *porda* that severs the link between their own voices and bodies and the cinematic image. Far from taking the body as the ultimate, as it were natural, resort of truth, this volume emphasizes that the body itself is not just there, but inscribed via religious and other sensational forms, and via structures of repetition. The point is that as scholars we need to understand how and why the body has become such a powerful repository of truth and authenticity in our time (see also Shusterman 1997), which can be mobilized against experiences of loss and insecurity by being loaded with spiritual power. Thus we seek to grasp, on the one hand, the appeal of bodiliness and viscerality in appearing as harbingers of truth beyond discourse, and, on the other hand, the actual mobilization of the body into social formations and projects of binding and bonding. In short, this volume strives to understand how the body is subject to formation, and yet vested with an aura of ultimacy that denies being formed—just as immediacy also depends on mediation and its denial.

V This Volume

As stated at the beginning, our research program was not intended to produce one binding framework or paradigm to be adopted by all researchers. Instead, our collaboration created a highly stimulating intellectual space for engaging in conversations, whilst also leaving ample room for the specificities of the research locations and individual research interests. In this Introduction I have sought to reveal myriad connections and resonances between the ten chapters, and to draw out my perspective on the relation between aesthetic formations, religious mediations, sensational forms and styles of binding. While this perspective has been generated by digesting all the research taking place under the auspices of our research program, it should be pointed out that the authors themselves do not necessarily employ exactly the same conceptual terms. Engaging in common research together need not, and indeed should not, imply that everything is placed in the same framework. In this sense, this introduction can best be read as a discussion, which seeks to pull out certain threads that link the work of scholars who work together on a similar theme.

The volume is organized in three parts. Part 1 evolves around "Boundary Politics," and addresses the difficulty in drawing boundaries between Candomblé, as a religion predicated on secrecy, and the public realm (Mattijs van de Port, Chapter 1), the chronic instability of the boundary between being born again and moving out into the world in a *favela* in Rio de Janeiro (Martijn Oosterbaan, Chapter 2), and the personal strategies adopted by Bangladeshi film actresses to retain a distinction between personal identity and cinematic image (Lotte Hoek, Chapter 3). Part 2 focuses on how the articulation of "Religion in the Public Realm" questions the possibility of maintaining stable distinctions between secular and religious. While Stephen Hughes (Chapter 4) locates the emergence of film as a new medium that is easily appropriated to visualize the gods in the interface of emergent debates of colonial modernity, and Brian Larkin (Chapter 5) discusses to what extent the transmission of *tafsir* via the radio is part of a project of modernizing Islam, Francio Guadeloupe (Chapter 6) introduces the setting of Sint Maarten, in which religious affiliation is downplayed, yet Christian forms circulate all the more and are key to encompassing politics of belonging. Part 3 is devoted to various instances that involve the complicated "Mediation of Immediacy," as in the case of the CCR studied by Maria José de Abreu (Chapter 7), the Afrikania Movement and the ICGC researched by Marleen de Witte (Chapter 8), the Raelian Movement that stands central in Chapter 9 by Carly Machado, and finally Rafael Sánchez' chapter (Chapter 10) on the elective affinities between Pentecostalism and politics in Venezuela.

Notes

I wish to express my heartfelt thanks to Mattijs van de Port, Jeremy Stolow, and Jojada Verrips for their critical questions, stimulating comments, and constructive suggestions on earlier versions of this text, and Harriet Impey for her perceptive editing.

1. The key proposition of the initial program proposal was that the relationship between the postcolonial nation-state, media, and religion has been significantly reconfigured since the mid-1990s, and has entailed the emergence of a new public sphere characterized by a blurring of neat, modernist distinctions between public and private, religion and politics, debate and entertainment. The main concern of the program, as formulated in the original proposal, was to chart the emergence of such new arenas in concrete locations on the basis of thorough empirical investigations, and at the same time, to question and rethink the rather normative, Western concepts that are usually employed as analytical tools. Seeking to appreciate cultural particularities and yet to yield generalizable analyses, the program proposal made a plea for detailed historical

and ethnographic exploration in the framework of a comparative perspective. For more information see www.pscw.uva.nl/media-religion. Next to a host of articles authored by the program participants, the program also yielded five dissertations: Guadeloupe 2006a, published in 2008; Oosterbaan 2006; de Witte 2008; Hoek 2008; and de Abreu 2009, as well as four publications derived from conferences we organized (Meyer and Moors 2006a; Hughes and Meyer 2005; Meyer 2008b; Hirschkind and Larkin 2008).

2. In his groundbreaking book, Cohen pointed out that the recourse to fiction and symbolism occurs when geographic, natural boundaries become insecure. The perceived threat of the erosion of the local, be it via the homogenizing force of states or the processes of deterritorialization associated with globalization, means that community becomes increasingly a fiction existing primarily in people's minds. In this view, a social formation qualifies as a community if people feel a strong emotional attachment to a shared set of forms and images that do not necessarily derive from "natural," spatial boundaries.

3. Anderson's view, of course, resonates with modern theories of language and the symbolic as systems or codes of representation. As many scholars have noted, the modern attitude toward language and the world is based on a rift between the sign or symbol and its referent in the world. Thinkers from de Saussure to Lacan took as a point of departure this basic separation of language and reality, symbols and experience, representation and the world, implying that the modern imagination hovers around the perception of a loss of reality that can never be recaptured. An intriguing position that questions a view of language as based on an arbitrary system of signs is offered by Peirce, who introduced a differentiated array of signs, among them index and icon, which are understood to render present what they represent, thus overcoming the rift between sign and reality that goes with Saussurian approaches (Keane 2007).

4. Latour's *Reassembling the Social* (2005) has been a major source of inspiration. I agree with Latour that "it is not enough for sociologists to recognize that a group is made, 'reproduced,' or 'constructed' through many means and through many tools" (39). The Social is not constructed around a preexisting set of collective representations (as an all too simple reading of Durkheim might suggest—ibid., 38), but is being "reassembled" in a dynamic process of ongoing mediation.

5. This question stands central in a new NWO-sponsored research program directed by Mattijs van de Port, Herman Roodenburg, and myself, titled *Heritage Dynamics. Aesthetics of Persuasion and Politics of Authentication in Brazil, Ghana, South Africa and the Netherlands.*

6. The particular aesthetic through which the Nazi regime sought to draw citizens into its vision of a Germanic superpower (see Benjamin 1999[1936]) is just an extreme example of the use of aesthetic resources by nation-states to envelop citizens in the imagined community of the nation. Scholars have been suspicious about the political use of aesthetics, regarding it as a supreme demagogical tool. While it is of course important to be critical about the ways in which states, and other power regimes, address and form people by appealing to their senses and shaping the material environment, it is high time for social scientists

to pay more attention to political aesthetics—understood in the broad sense advocated in Section II—so as to better understand how power works (see also Rancière 2006).

7. Taking inspiration from Michel Foucault and Judith Butler (1999) on the process of subjectivation through which modern subjects are formed, Mahmood closely examines the formative power of the Islamic piety movement in the making of embodied female religious subjectivities. In so doing, she moves beyond a dualistic understanding of religious regimes and individual persons, and calls attention to the importance of formation in the double sense advocated here.

8. He states: "As long as it stays alive (that is, as long as it is being experienced), aesthetic community is shot through with a paradox: since it would betray or refute freedom of its members were it to claim non-negotiable credentials, it has to keep its entrances and exits wide open. But were it to advertise the resulting lack of binding power, it would fail to perform the reassuring role which for the faithful was their prime motive in joining in" (2001: 65).

9. "Aesthetic community" is the—rather misleading—English translation of Kant's (2001 [1790]) notion of *sensus communis aestheticus* (*aesthetischer Gemeinsinn* in the German original). Kant presupposed the subjective universality of aesthetic experience and judgments of taste as solely based on feelings, not concepts. The *sensus communis aestheticus* does not refer to an actual community, but to a universal faculty to judge taste and experience beauty, the main point being that this faculty can be assumed to exist. Not only is this understanding grounded in the problematic limitation of aesthetics to beauty, it also separates concepts and feelings and locates the faculty of experiencing pleasure in a disinterested beholder.

10. Perception, it needs to be noted, always involves a kind of concentration, filtering out what disturbs the intensity of a particular experience. Indeed, as Jojada Verrips argues (2006), *aisthesis* always implies some kind of *anaesthesia*. See also Crary (2001).

11. Obviously, this resonates with Bourdieu's work on habitus, as an embodied disposition, and taste and style as modes of distinction.

12. Until recently, the study of visual culture was highly ocular-centric. However, in the past decade, even in the study of media that are closely associated with the eye—such as pictures, photographs, and films—scholars have been concerned with taking into account the interplay of the senses, and the visceral, affective dimension of visual culture (Sobchack 2004; Pinney 2004; Morgan 1998, 2005, 2007; Mitchell 2005; Freedberg 1989; Howes 2003; Verrips 2002).

13. I use "transcendental" with some hesitation and for lack of a better term, in the sense of a power that is framed to be beyond the ordinary and in this sense "other" or "*alter*" (see also Csordas 2004). I explain at some length in another publication that my understanding of the transcendental does not postulate the existence of a Numinous Power out there, but is grounded in the here and now, in that my interest lies in how religions induce experiences of the transcendental in the here and now (Meyer 2006a). I also opt for using the notion

of the transcendental because I share Vivian Sobchack's proposition that human beings, as lived bodies, "have the capacity for *transcendence*: for a unique exteriority of being—an *ex-stasis*—that locates us 'elsewhere' and 'otherwise' even as it is grounded in and tethered to our lived body's 'here' and 'now'" (2008, italics in the original). While I acknowledge that defining religion is deeply problematic because definitions tend to freeze contingent historical factors into universal features (Asad 1993), I deem it important that we can still speak about religion and make comparisons. In my understanding, the transcendental (in the sense of an "other" or "*alter*" that exceeds the ordinary) is key to most understandings of religion, even if scholars do not spell this out explicitly. Certainly at a time in which, against the expectations of secularization theory, gods and spirits appear to have so much appeal, instead of remaining stuck in asserting the impossibility of defining religion, we need to explore what kinds of religion and religiosities emerge in our era of globalization and mediatization (see also Csordas 2007, 261). This is the prime concern of the present volume.

14. Of course, this approach is not new per se. It resonates with a large body of works by media historians, which moves beyond technological determinism and grounds new technological inventions in the field of communication (such as the bicycle, the train, the telegraph, radio, television, etc.) in specific social fields, teasing out how at a given time new media relate to already existing "old" media. For a well-argued plea in favor of such historically grounded understandings of media and technology that also take into account the dimension of aesthetics, style and design see Verbeek 2005.

15. My notion of sensational form is indebted to David Morgan's seminal work in the field of religious visual culture, which can well be extended to the broader field of religious mediations. As he put it, "images and how people look at them are evidence for understanding belief, which should not be reduced to doctrines or creeds of a propositional nature. Belief is embodied practice no less than a cerebral one. Revelation is a constellation of seeing, speaking, and writing (as well as other media)..." (2005, 21).

16. This may also entail a rejection of certain media as being unsuitable to be incorporated. As argued by Michele Rosenthal (2007), many studies of religion and media have paid too little attention to the emergence of deliberate critics and nonusers, for whom rejection of particular media becomes a distinctive marker. See also Matthew Engelke for a thoughtful analysis of how the Zimbabwean Friday Apostolics' rejection of media (such as books) that render the Christian message tangible is part and parcel of a broader practice of mediation that faces the Protestant problem of how God can be present and yet unmediated (2007). Rejecting certain media is thus not a question of staying aloof, but needs to be analyzed as a negotiation of media in terms of their negation.

17. The religion-technology nexus is explored in the *Deus in Machina* project directed by Jeremy Stolow (http://www.ghostlymachine.com/~stolow.html, Stolow 2008) and in the Religion and Technology project launched by the Dutch Stichting Toekomstbeeld der Techniek (Foundation for the Future

Image of Technology) (van Well 2008). My own thinking about religion and technology has gained much from my involvement in these projects.

18. Of course this is prefigured in Clifford Geertz' famous distinction between religious "models of the world" and "models for the world" (1973), which is also based on the drive to create the world in the light of the ideal image believers have of it. However, whereas in Geertz' exposé the transformation of the world is to occur by following a set of norms, in the cases that stand central in this volume, we encounter a strong drive to capture and as it were colonize the world as a space, which is seen as a stage for the final struggle between God and the Devil, and which implicates all domains of society.

Part 1

Boundary Politics

Chapter 1

"Don't Ask Questions, Just Observe!" Boundary Politics in Bahian Candomblé

Mattijs van de Port

When I got stuck in a traffic jam in São Gonçalo do Retiro, a peripheral neighborhood in Salvador in which the *terreiro* (temple) called Ilê Axé Opô Afonjá is situated, I began to realize that my assumptions about the upcoming event had been wrong. From what I had read in the announcement, the Semana Cultural da Herança Africana na Bahia (Cultural Week of the African Heritage in Bahia), was going to be yet another one of these rather boring meetings of Salvador's Candomblé elite, who organize a never ending cycle of (often highly self-congratulatory) seminars, debates, fairs, and *homenagems*. However, judging from what I saw through the window of my car things might well be different this time. Hundreds of cars were trying to make it to the opening night of the Cultural Week, impatiently honking their horns, clutching up ill-lit roads, and floodlighting the street vendors who ran from one car to the next to sell their cashew nuts and beer and silicone bra strings. Policemen were all around, trying to control the traffic and monitor the crowds, who, in a steady stream, entered the central square of the terreiro's compound.

Yes, the Candomblé elite was there. I recognized some of the dread-locked activists from UNEGRO[1] and Casa de Oxumaré, a Candomblé house with an activist profile; the *chique* ladies with their expensive afro-print dresses and turbans who always seem to be around; just as these men who—whatever the color of their skin—dress up in Nigerian fashion, with wide, colorful pants, caftan like shirts, and a little hat in matching print. I soon spotted some of the intellectuals and anthropologists who frequently show up at these events (the latter probably commenting on my eternal presence in their field notes). I also identified some of the girls from the terreiro choir, who all boosted new, elaborately braided hairdos and wore identical wine red dresses, the color of Xangô. The rest of the audience must have been made up of a significant portion of the clients, members, and affiliates of Ilê Axé Opô Afonjá and—judging from their Bermudas and plastic flip-flops—a great number of people from the local neighborhood. As always, the place was full of gays, people like my hairdresser Adilson (who had alerted me to the event) and his friends, who had come here to have an evening out, to pay their respect to the terreiro, meet up with friends and flirt a bit with strangers.

On a raised platform, behind a long table decorated with African fabrics, raffia, palm leaves, and dried pumpkins on a string, sat Mãe Stella de Oxóssi, high priestess of Ilê Axé Opô Afonjá, with her honored guests. The priestess was all dressed up for the occasion. Her white turban, many-colored necklaces, and white crinoline dress sparkled in the spotlights—an exotic, queen-like figure, which dulled the appearance of the elderly gentlemen in tie-and-suit who sat to her right and left: Gilberto Gil, the minister of culture in the recently elected leftist Lula government, Antonio Imbassahy, the mayor of Salvador, and two well-known local anthropologists, Julio Braga and Vivaldo Costa da Lima.

The latter was droning up a text he had written for the occasion. It was something about the *obá*'s of Xangô, a council of twelve "ministers"—a honorary function this particular terreiro has introduced in the internal terreiro hierarchy. Costa da Lima had made it his task to highlight the authenticity of that move with detailed ethnographic accounts from Africa, where similar institutions seem to exist. It went on and on and on, a stream of words that no one really listened to, but that, as a play of sounds—Portuguese sounds mingling with African sounds—sufficed to convey that Bahia's link with Yoruba culture was being celebrated here.

When Gilberto Gil finally took over the microphone, the chatting and muttering of the audience quieted down. The brand new minister in the Lula government—flown in by helicopter just for the occasion, as I was told—reminded the audience that he too was an obá, a minister of Xangô. Accepting his new job in Brasília, he said, had been greatly facilitated by the fact that he already was a minister "at this primary, that is, the spiritual level" long before his current position as a minister of state. He praised Xangô, that "great saint," and expressed his deepest respect and the respect of all the ministers and members of parliament in Brasília to Mãe Stella, to the Candomblé community, to the *Roma Negra* that is Salvador, and to his beloved Bahia, the "blessed land of the Orixás." Time and again, he received a standing ovation from the audience. TV-cameras pushed forward, trying to get as close as possible to the speaker. People in the audience took pictures as well.

The opening of the Cultural Week ended with a presentation of "Xangô Awards" to people whose outstanding support for the community of Candomblé needed to be highlighted. It turned out to be a veritable celebrity show as artists, scholars, actors, and TV personalities from within the Candomblé community handed over the sculpted statues to artists, scholars, actors, and TV personalities from the society at large.

All the while, Mãe Stella remained seated, nodding her turbanted head appreciatively when the merits of the winners were proclaimed, distributing vague smiles to no one in particular. At one point she whispered something in the ear of Gilberto Gil, who was sitting to her right. And she also communicated something to the mayor of Salvador, who was sitting to her left. But that was for us to see, not to hear. For she never addressed the audience. No word of welcome and no word of gratitude. Nothing. Not a single word came from her lips.

"She's very humble" is what Adilson told me when I asked him about her not saying a word. I knew what he was talking about. People would always tell me, time and again, that Mãe Stella is such a humble woman. Common, plain—*humilde e simples*—were the terms they would use. But that was not what I was looking at during this opening night. Amidst the hollow phrases and worn out clichés that make up the soundscape of officialdom, Mãe Stella remained silent, Queen of an Ineffable Sacred, radiating a power and potency that far exceeded the ministers, mayors, and academics.

In Bahia, the term Candomblé refers to multiple religious traditions of African origin, all of which are centered on the worship of spiritual entities called orixás. The task of individual terreiros is to oversee the initiation of spirit mediums and to organize the yearly cycle of rituals and festivities in honor of the orixás. In addition to such religious tasks, terreiros operate in what Brazilian scholars have aptly called the *mercado dos bens de salvação* (the market for salvation commodities): they generate an income by providing spiritual, divinatory, and curative services to a clientele made up of both cultists and noncultists.[2]

Such overall similarities among the different traditions notwithstanding, the Candomblé universe is a heterogeneous field. Cultists recognize the traditions of different *nações* (nations), such as Nagô-Ketu, Jeje, and Angola, and within these traditions the autonomy of the individual terreiro is such that considerable variation is found in doctrine as well as in ritual (Capone 1999; Santos 1995; Wafer 1991; Matory 2005). The autonomy of individual terreiros is further increased by the absence of a central institution with enough power to impose a canon of Candomblé orthodoxy. This multifariousness of religious practices does not mean, however, that the Candomblé universe is heading toward ever greater fragmentation. Cultists retain a strong sense of community, especially now that the cult is threatened by increasingly powerful Pentecostal churches, which have designated Candomblé as the prime site of "devil worship" (see also Oosterbaan in this volume). Another force that seems to work toward homogenization, rather than fragmentation, comes from a relatively small number of terreiros belonging to the Nagô-Ketu tradition. With historical records that go back to the first half of the nineteenth century; with a highly prestigious clientele of artists, intellectuals, media celebrities, and local politicians; and with the "certificates" of purity and authenticity conferred by generations of anthropologists who have studied them, the Nagô-Ketu terreiros have managed to acquire so much prestige and status that their particular understanding of the "religion of the orixás" is highly influential among the more peripheral terreiros in Salvador. Many of the latter try to mimic the rituals, ceremony, and aesthetics of the more prestigious cult houses and seek to incorporate some of their doctrinal rigor and orthodoxy (on the ascendancy of the Nagô cult in Candomblé, see Capone 1999; Dantas 1988; Parés 2006).

Ilê Axé Opô Afonjá is one of these prestigious terreiros in Salvador. Of all the terreiros, it is probably most actively engaged in reconstructing a public face for Candomblé. The Cultural Week was very much part of this effort.

A Polite Request to Please, Shut Up

Long before the Cultural Week took place, Mãe Stella wrote a booklet called *Meu Tempo é Agora* (My Time Is Now, 1993): a curious mixture of autobiography, religious guidebook, and etiquette manual for terreiro life. She wrote:

> Our religion is so strong and so mysterious that it raises the curiosity of those who are outside. They seem to think that a host of curious questions, sometimes even impertinent ones, is synonymous with knowledge. But I tell you, those ways are dangerous, leading into true labyrinths, and with dire results. I therefore advise the visitors and friends of the Axé:[3] don't ask questions, just observe! (Azevedo 1993, 88)

Mãe Stella's proud assertion that her religion is so "strong" and "mysterious" as to garner the attention of outsiders signals the assertiveness of some members of the Bahian priesthood. The opening scene to this chapter illustrates that there are grounds for her pride: from a forbidden and persecuted religious practice of African slaves and their descendants, Candomblé has become a highly prestigious and well-respected religion, which ranks as the prime cultural heritage of the Bahian state, and attracts ever more variegated audiences (cf. Santos 2005; Van de Port 2005a). However, Mãe Stella's performance of silence in front of a huge audience, as well as her explicit call "not to ask questions," is emblematic of a deep concern in certain Candomblé circles that, for all of the successes that have been booked in Candomblé's long struggle for social and political recognition, another kind of threat looms large at the horizon that urges the priesthood to police the boundaries of their imagined religious community ever more rigorously.

Due to the overwhelming interest in Candomblé, the cult has become the object of literary interpretation, artistic elaboration, philosophical meditation, and anthropological explanation (not to mention commercial and political exploitation). There is, in other words, a hyperproliferation of discursive knowledge about Candomblé, and ever more people (and prestigious ones at that) are involved in the production of this knowledge as to what is Candomblé. In the eyes of the priesthood, this development poses a serious threat to what they call the cult's "deep truths": its *segredos* (secrets), *mistérios* (mysteries), and *fundamentos* (fundaments). In Candomblé, it is understood that "deep truth" only reveals itself during the time-consuming path of initiation. Deep truths "come to you with time," as one initiate phrased it succinctly: with submitting one's body to the initiation procedures and the yearly cycle of rituals; with the observation of the many do's and don'ts of terreiro life; and finally, with opening up the body for divine possession. "Deep truth" is an understanding of things that is, in its essence, inarticulable.

Both Mãe Stella's silence and her call "not to ask questions" seek to express this inarticulability: it is a demonstration of the belief that there is an incommensurable difference between saying "the initiation cycle lasts seven long years" (a phrase of seven words, which produce their meaning in a split second) and the experience of living those seven long years of energies given and energies received. Highlighting that difference, instructing outsiders "not to ask questions," is a refusal to surrender to the proliferation of discursivity, to other people's interpretations, explorations, meditations, and explanations of the cult. What should be discussed in this chapter, then, is how the notion of nondiscursive "deep truths," grounded in a prolonged immersion in the ritual cycle, has come to play a crucial role in the attempts of Ilê Axé Opô Afonjá to police the boundaries of its imagined religious community; how the performance of silence (which paradoxically requires a constant breaking of the silence) seeks to contain noninitiates in the role of ignorant yet awestruck spectators, and how priestly power over religious meaning can thus be regained.

The Public Life of Candomblé

In Bahia, Candomblé has always been a public presence, but, for reasons that I have elaborated elsewhere, from the 1920s onward Candomblé has become the "mastercode" of contemporary Bahian culture politics: its symbols, images, myths, philosophies, rhythms, and aesthetics have been endlessly reworked and publicly displayed to signify Bahia's unique cultural character (Dantas 1988; Johnson 2002; Santos 2005; Van de Port 2006, 2007). Huge statues representing the orixás have been erected at central points in the Bahian capital Salvador, Candomblé terreiros have been put on the list of the state's historical monuments, and—as can be deduced from the opening night of the Cultural Week—politicians regularly appear in front of the cameras with Candomblé priestesses to make sure that their links with the Candomblé universe are publicly known. On the commercial front, Bahiatursa, the state tourist organization, is fully involved in the dispersion of Candomblé imagery so as to create a recognizable and marketable profile on the global market for exotic travel: a visit to a nightly ceremony of Candomblé is now an obligatory element in the Bahian tourist program. Shopping malls, hotels, streets, and condominiums have been named after the orixás. Advertising agencies time and again seek recourse to Candomblé imagery to sell products as varied as typewriters, apartment buildings, garden furniture, and insurances.

As stated, this overall interest in the cult, and the ubiquitous presence of Candomblé imagery in the Bahian public sphere, has produced a steady stream of visitors to the terreiros, seeking knowledge by asking questions: tourists, journalists, artists, intellectuals, and a large number of anthropologists. Consequently, the cult is inscribed into an ever more colorful fan of narratives as to its meaning and significance. Social movements—blacks, gays, ecologists, feminists, progressive Catholics—have "discovered" the expressive potential of Candomblé, recognizing it as a proto form of their emancipatory struggles and politics, and have come to understand Candomblé as the "exemplary gay friendly religion," a "site of black resistance," and "a form of ecological consciousness." In other circuits Candomblé has been interpreted as a kind of astrology, as the immaterial cultural heritage of the

Figure 1.1   Statue of Iemanjá, Candomblé goddess of the deep seas, in serial production. Photo by Mattijs van de Port.

Bahian state, as an ideal blueprint for the reorganization of business organizations (Vergari and Helio 2000), as a proto particle theory (Correia 1999), and—with the booming of Pentecostalism—as devil worship.

Responses in the Candomblé community to these developments are deeply ambivalent. As the opening of the Cultural Week already indicated, there is a lot to gain by all the attention. The prestige that comes with visiting statesmen, professors, and celebrities opens up alleys for material profit and political influence. Terreiros like Ilê Axé Opô Afonjá openly court these possibilities. In fact, the text that was read by anthropologist Vivaldo Costa Lima at the opening night discussed "the council of the twelve *oba's*" and the honorary title of the *oloiês* or *ojoiês* (Yorubá for "friend of the house")—inventions (or "restorations," depending on one's perspective) that help to link ever more influential and affluent outsiders, "writers, deputies, painters, university professors, merchants, industrials, medical doctors and foreigners who live in Bahia," in da Costa Lima's words (Lima 1966, 101) to the religious community. Next to these prestigious bonds, terreiros like Ilê Axé Opô Afonjá successfully profit from revenues that follow from being labeled "cultural heritage": state subsidies to keep up the premises, NGO funding for "social" activities, and revenues from tourists visiting the terreiro compound.

Yet there is also a deep concern about what the new audiences in the public sphere seek to make out of the cult. With indignation Mãe Stella notices that "Candomblé became fashion: the *búzios* (cowry-shells) are thrown [a divinatory practice, MP] in shops and bookstores, the strings of beads and the *ferramentos* (iron symbols of the orixás) are used only because they are 'beautiful'" (Azevedo and Martins 1989, 20). Worse, at the time of carnival "sacred objects of our rituals are paraded down the avenues, and people behave as if they are possessed" (ibid.). Insisting that Candomblé should be restored to sovereignty, that the cult can only be understood its own terms, she wrote

> Since slavery, black is considered to be synonymous with poverty, ignorance, and knowing no other right than to know not to have any rights; the black man has always been the toy of the culture that stigmatizes him, and thus his religion became a play as well. Let us be free, let us fight against what humbles us and disrespects us, against that which only accepts us if we dress in the clothes they gave us to wear. (Mãe Stella, in Campos 2003, back cover)

While this critique concerns society at large, Mãe Stella's fiercest critiques are directed toward terreiros and Candomblé practitioners who stray from the aforementioned "purity of propositions and rituals":

> There are those who dress up in the garments of the orixá, who improvise, merely "give it a go" (*dá um jeitinho*), who use *garçons* to serve fancy drinks, offer candle light dinners while the Candomblé is taking place and watch on video the latest celebration in honour of the orixás. At present, we even have "computerized priests"...[we too] love candlelight dinners with a good glass of wine, but everything has its place and its time. And this place, most certainly, is not a Candomblé terreiro at the time of a public celebration in honour of the orixás. (1989, 21)

She continues that "in the face of so many barbarisms (*barbaridades*) acted out by people who say they are initiated—some of them being priests—we can't blame non-adepts for their disbelief" (20). The extent of her worries is probably best captured in a statement that I found in a recently published "profile" of her religious leadership, written by one of her *filhas*:

> The worst enemies of Candomblé today are those who practice it in a fluttering way. Those who have no knowledge of the secrets (*fundamentos*), who have no basis or certainty as to what it is that they are doing. They disfigure everything. They are unscrupulous. The police, the state, the church, they are no longer the enemies of Candomblé. Our enemies are the so called adepts, who disfigure everything and destroy Candomblé. [There

are] fanatics in other religions also, but they do not attack us. (Mãe Stella, in Campos 2003, 60)

One can easily see what lies at the heart of Mãe Stella's concerns. In her perception the Candomblé of the public sphere is moving eerily close to what Jean Baudrillard (2001) would call a *simulacrum*. Not only has the omnipresence of Candomblé imagery outside the terreiro walls severed this imagery from priestly control over the production of meaning; the power of the public forms of Candomblé is such that these forms cannot be dismissed as "mere imitations." They have become a reality on their own, producing—in the way of the simulacrum—their own reality effects.

Numerous examples come to mind: Joãozinho da Goméia, a priest from Salvador who already in the 1950s stirred up the nightlife in Rio de Janeiro by taking his troupe of initiates to perform their rituals and dances in fancy nightclubs (cf. Lody and Silva 2000); the popular TV talk show in the 1970s, where a possessed medium was invited over, which then sent the whole studio audience—including the talk show host—in trance in front of a nationwide TV audience (cf. Maggie 1992); the initiates who were found singing sacred texts copied from an ethnographic book (cf. Silva 1995); the woman who told me she became possessed by a spirit when listening to a carnival song on the radio in which the name of an orixá was mentioned; the awe-instilling artworks of the Bahian photographer Mario Cravo Neto who makes ample use of Candomblé as a source of inspiration, and who, in the words of one critic, is a "magician" himself, "capable to capture the imponderable mystery beyond the mere images of an initiation religion" (Ildásio Tavares, in Cravo Neto 2004).[4]

In all of these instances, distinctions between "true" and "false," "original" and "copy," "real" and "imaginary," "sacred" and "profane" lose their meaning, causing havoc in the regimes of truth that buttress Mãe Stella's religious views (Baudrillard 2001, 171).

Seeking to Undo the Work of the Simulacrum

In *Simulacras and Simulations* (2001), Baudrillard describes the responses of societies where the dynamics of simulation are at work as follows:

> When the real is no longer what it used to be, nostalgia assumes its full meaning. There is a proliferation of myths of origin and signs of reality; of second-hand truth, objectivity and authenticity. There is an escalation of the true, of the lived experience; a resurrection of the figurative where the object and substance have disappeared. And there is a panic-stricken

production of the real and the referential, above and parallel to the panic of material production. (174)

It is astonishing just how much of this can be pointed out in Ilê Axé Opô Afonjá's answer to the perceived threat of the simulacrum. Time and again, the terreiro shows vigorous attempts to "draw the line," to instruct the public at large that "Candomblé is not a matter of opinion" but "a religious reality that can only be realized within the purity of its propositions and rituals" (Mãe Stella, in Campos 2003, back cover).

This striving for "purity" takes the form of an antisyncretistic ideology that seeks to restore Candomblé to its African origins. Thus, in 1983, Mãe Stella initiated the penning of a public manifesto to break with syncretism, which she dismissed as "a relic of the past," which may have been necessary to help the cult survive under slavery but is no longer useful in the present time. She called for the removal of all catholic saints from the terreiro's altars (in the little museum at the terreiro's compound, I found them, rather unceremoniously, stored in an old fashioned, glass paned kitchen cupboard). She encouraged the use of Yorubá in liturgy, naming practices, and education; and in the design of the terreiro's Web site, publications, and video productions, icons signaling "Africa" (wax-prints, wood-carvings, shields and spears, leopard skins, etc.) produce an African look. All of this to impress the public at large that "... the religion that we practice is an African religion, it's essence is African. We are Brazilians, but we have a religion of Yorubá origin. African" (Mãe Stella, in Pretto and Serpa 2002, 33).

"Purity" also means calling a halt to the blurring of boundaries between Candomblé as "religion" and Candomblé as popular culture. As will be elaborated below, Mãe Stella is not only crusading against earlier understandings of Candomblé as a "cult," "sect," or "animistic practice," but most of all against the label of "folklore." She repeatedly fulminated against the profanation of sacred symbols from Candomblé in the field of entertainment, commerce, and carnival.

The "second-hand truths, objectivity and authenticity" that—following Baudrillard—are in such high demand when simulation abounds are delivered by a great number of anthropologists who have put themselves at the service of the priesthood. With the prestige of the written word (in what is largely an oral tradition), the prestige of their scientific methods, as well as the prestige of their belonging to the white middle classes, they have become important arbiters in an attempt to shift the "true" from the "false," and the "authentic" from the "degenerated." Their books are widely known by the Candomblé priesthood—especially the work of Pierre Verger, a French anthropologist and photographer who makes explicit comparisons between Bahian Candomblé and the "original" cults in West Africa.

These attempts, however, only exacerbate the dilemmas Ilê Axé Opô Afonjá is facing in its claim to be the one-and-only authentic voice of Candomblé. Mãe Stella seems to be well aware that the public sphere is the arena where the fight for sovereignty has to be fought and although a visibly media-shy figure, she does seek publicity to pursue her politics. She has published a number of books, gives public speeches, appears on TV and in the newspapers, organizes debates and scholarly meetings, has initiated a museum on the terreiro's compound, and has participated in international conferences on the religion of the Orixás. This move to the public sphere forces the terreiro to explain itself in the terms, media formats, and styles that govern the public sphere. In other words, to make her arguments and demands understood to a public at large, she will have to seek recourse to vocabularies and media images she imagines to be understandable for that public at large. And this is where sovereignty sought becomes sovereignty lost. In its attempt to make itself understood, the terreiro constantly resorts to comparisons of Candomblé with a Christian blueprint of religion ("It is clear that we are a religion, because we have a theology, we have a liturgy, and we have dogmas. These are three characteristics of all religions," Mãe Stella, in Pretto and Serpa 2002, 26; see also De Witte in this volume); conceptualizes the orixás in a New Age vocabulary as "ancient energies"; and stresses the importance of education and knowledge (Ilê Axé Opô Afonjá founded a school on the terreiro grounds, and is highly active in organizing seminars and scholarly meetings).

Ilê Axé Opô Afonjá is certainly successful in foregrounding itself as the legitimate representative of Afro-Brazilian religion ("we are now always invited to religious meetings," Mãe Stella says, "we may not always go, but we are always invited!"). Yet the prize that is being paid for public recognition is that the public understanding as to what Candomblé is all about does not transcend the horizons of what the public finds imaginable. This is well illustrated in the following *laudatio* for Mãe Stella that I found in a Bahian newspaper. The text mentions, among other things, that

> ...the priestess was chosen by the United Nations to represent the tradition of the Orixás in Rio de Janeiro, next to the most diverse religious leaders such as the Dalai Lama of Tibet and Rabbi Henry Sobel. As a recognition of the utmost importance of the cultural and social work that Mãe Stella has done in Bahia and in Brazil she has been invited to conferences at universities and international institutions such as the Brazilian Contemporary Arts in London, Harvard University in Washington, and the Caribbean Institute in New York. The priestess also received the medals "Maria Quitéria" and the "Ordem do Cavaleiro," the trophies "Esso" (a

prize for black writers) and "Clementina de Jesus," and a great *homenagem* (tribute) by the Bahian people in 1995 (…) To foreground her dedication and activities to strengthen the Candomblé religion with its traditions of thousands of years, Mãe Stella has now received from the Federal Government the medal of the "Order of Cultural Accomplishment," and will see her terreiro of Ilê Axé Opô Afonjá be declared to be part of the National Historical Patrimony. (Tribuna da Bahia, 20 November 1999)

I can hardly think of a better demonstration of how the simple fact that Candomblé has accessed the public sphere profoundly changed the symbolization of priestly authority—indeed, just how much Mãe Stella became dependent on public criteria to argue her authority as a religious leader beyond the walls of her terreiro: in ethnographies (as well as in Mãe Stella's own publications) the sources of sacerdotal power and prestige—and consequently, authority—are always explained in terms of the seniority and genealogy of a terreiro, the reputation and stature of the priestly lineage, and the length of someone's initiation: authority is with *os mais velhos*—"the oldest," that is, those who are in the know (see Castillo 2005).

In the public sphere, however, the authority of the priestess can no longer be solely based on her having lived up to such religiously defined criteria. If a priestess like Mãe Stella wants to be *publicly* recognized as an authoritative voice, she needs to have recourse to a form of "impression management" that stresses values that a much wider audience is able to recognize and appreciate. And thus we are served this "cocktail of fame" that mixes "worldwide recognition" (Mãe Stella's election by the United Nations, and invitations to travel to places around the world) with academic prestige (Harvard and other universities), state decorations, and the full weight of Culture. Furthermore, the juxtaposition of Mãe Stella with the Dalai Lama and Rabbi Henry Sobel is another clear instance that the resources to construct a public notion of Mãe Stella's authority differ hugely from those that make up the display of authority in her own terreiro: in the *laudatio*, the priestess comes to represent ethnic, traditional, cultural, and socio-political values, rather than religious ones (cf. Van de Port 2005d).

It is hard to miss the irony in all of this. More than anything, it was Mãe Stella's vision to "restore" Candomblé to its status of "African religion" that drove her to the public sphere. Out in the public sphere, however, she had to mobilize all kinds of extra religious qualities so as to create a publicly recognizable profile of authority: what we find, then, is that her authority as a religious leader is rooted in the culture politics of the Bahian state, in her representing Afro-Brazilian culture, and—more and more—in her being simply "famous."

Eloquent Silence

What we find, then, is that, on the one hand, the truth-unsettling work of the simulacrum produces a call for an assertion of the boundaries of the true and authentic community of Candomblé. On the other hand, however, all attempts by the priesthood to produce such an assertion in the public sphere force them to "translate" their religious knowledge in publicly accessible terms, thus fuelling the simulacrum even further.

The call "not to ask questions" is an attempt to deal with these issues: attacking discursivity to bypass the "labyrinths" (as Mãe Stella phrased it succinctly) of meaning production; just as Mãe Stella's authoritative silence in the face of the anthropologist's endless stream of words at the opening night of the Cultural Week was highly suggestive of the priestess having access to greater, deeper truths. And this was indeed the suggestion made by all the priests that I encountered: getting to know us is getting to know our "deep truths," and these can only be accessed through initiation. A closer look at these "deep truths" may be necessary here.

The fact that Candomblé is a religion based on initiation means that its performance of secrecy is crucial. This performance of secrecy is guided by a great many rules and regulations, which determine who has access to what knowledge, and at what time; who is allowed to speak and who is to remain silent; who has the right to tread certain areas of the terreiro; who is allowed to see sacred objects or witness ritual practices and who is not. Breaking these rules and regulations may cause the wrath of both priests and spirits (cf. Johnson 2002; and for Bahia, Castillo 2005).

The performance of secrecy is inextricably linked with—or rather expressive of—a very particular understanding in Candomblé circles as to what constitutes religious knowledge and how religious knowledge can be transmitted. Candomblé holds that knowledge can only be obtained through the "lived experience of interpersonal and group relationships, through transmission and absorption of a *força* (force), and a gradual development of symbolical and complex knowledge about all the collective and individual elements of the system at all levels" (Elbein dos Santos 1989, 17). What this means is that year in, year out, the cultists go through the motions of the ceremonies and ritual obligations, and it is only with the passing of the ritual cycles, with feeling the density of time itself, that the experiential knowledge that Candomblé seeks to instill in its adepts "sinks in." Knowledge, in other words, comes with doing: with observing the taboos, participating in the rituals, subjecting oneself to the rigid terreiro hierarchy, respecting one's commitments to the orixás. People from Candomblé are resolute in saying that there is no other road to religious knowledge than this lengthy, time-consuming path and adepts told me that they were instructed, time and again, not to be curious, not to ask questions, not to sneak to one of the city's libraries to read ethnographies, not to try to run ahead of time, *quemando etapas* (skipping stages). Knowledge would come to them when the time was right for it. Giselle Binon-Cossard, a French anthropologist who became a priestess, explained it thus:

> In Candomblé it is believed that nothing done in a hurry turns out right. By asking, people will only understand this much of a certain notion but they will not assimilate it. It is only time that will make knowledge sink in. Let's say, it is as with French wine: it gets better by *decanter* [...]. Intellectually it is the same thing. Things have to get to rest. You learn, but then you leave it at that. And when it has ripened you go back to it, structuring it, balancing it out. (Binon-Cossard, in Silva 2001, 44)

William James' classic description of mystical states as ineffable, noetic, transient, and passive helps to clarify the specific quality of this knowledge. With ineffability, James means that the experiential knowledge of the mystic defies expression. Its "quality must be directly experienced; it cannot be imparted or transferred to others" because "[n]o adequate report of its contents can be given in words" (1904, 371). Adding to the ineffable the "noetic" quality of mystical states, James sought to highlight that while mysticism is a state of being, and the mystic's experiences are insights "unplumbed by the discursive intellect," these experiences are nonetheless to be understood as knowledge. "They are illuminations, revelations, full of significance and importance, all inarticulate though they remain; and as a rule they carry with them a curious sense of authority for after-time" (ibid.). The notion of "transiency" signals the fact that mystical states cannot be sustained for long: they fade out, after which their quality can but imperfectly be reproduced in memory. James stressed that transiency does not imply that mystical states are merely interruptive. "Some memory of their content always remains, and a profound sense of their importance. They modify the inner life of the subject between the times of their recurrence" (372). "Passivity," the fourth quality attributed to mystical states of consciousness, expresses that "although the oncoming of mystical states may be facilitated by preliminary voluntary operations...the mystic feels as if his own will were in abeyance, and indeed sometimes as if he were grasped and held by a superior power" (ibid.).

Inarticulate yet deeply meaningful, inseparably linked to experiences in the here and now, mystical states do not lend themselves for remediation. Immediacy is their alpha and omega. To cast this knowledge in texts, images, or whatever other expressive forms is—as Mãe Stella maintains—"dangerous, leading into true labyrinths, and with dire results." She certainly does not stand alone in her dismissal of all abstractions from direct experience. A Candomblé priestess told anthropologist Luis Nicolau Parés:

> No one can ever really talk with certainty about the mysteries. The mysteries are the mysteries. The secrets are the secrets, and no one will ever know anything. Those who study, those who come to observe, they are observing, but they don't know the deep knowledge. For one says one thing, and another says another thing, and so they only leave one confused. I always leave the researchers dangling... (1997, 2)

This specific understanding of religious knowledge—with its stress on religious practices, rather than exegesis—privileges the human body as the prime site of what Mircea Eliade (1959) has called hierophany, the appearance of the sacred. Initiation rituals, animal sacrifice, spirit possession—in all these activities the human-body-in-performative-action is the medium to gain access to the mysterious *fundamentos*, the "deep knowledge" (Johnson 2002; cf. Van de Port 2005b) that Candomblé holds in high esteem. Statues and images only become meaningful after the bodily intervention of the priest in ritual acts. Words—as Juana Elbein dos Santos made clear—do not have power because of their explicatory potential, but because they are utterances of the body, involving breath, saliva, bodily temperature (1989, 46). Visual and discursive registers of mediation are explicitly declared to be inadequate for the transmission of "deep knowledge"—"mere images, mere words," as one of my interlocutors phrased it.

The performance of silence clearly serves to uphold the primacy of this conception of knowledge over other forms of knowing. Of course, there is other knowledge about the cult, as Mãe Stella's frequent media appearances testify. Terreiros have opened Web sites, published books, launched CDs with sacred chants and rhythms, have worked with documentary makers, and have produced videos. They organize study meetings and festivals to which they invite the press, hoping to get (and often getting) media coverage. There is also an emergent "tradition" of making photo albums and home videos of the important ceremonies that mark the progress of a cultist in the initiation process. Yet all of that is indeed understood as "another kind of knowledge." When asked why Ilê Axé Opô Afonjá opened up a Web site on the Internet, Mãe Stella replied:

> As far as the Internet is concerned, we only did it to make public, even abroad, that there is an *Axé* in the way that we understand it, and what it is

that we offer in terms of education, culture, science, all of which can of course also contribute to a person's understanding of things. (Mãe Stella, in Pretto and Serpa 2002, 46)

Yet when I asked the manager of the terreiro's Web site to explain the choices underlying its content, I received a very brief response

> We opted for this kind of information on our website. All other knowledge can only be acquired through initiation. References to the orixás, their colors, the days of the week consecrated to them, etc., that is a kind of knowledge that is already widely available. We initiated this webpage to participate on the Web, the importance is to be there. The question of the audience we address, the number of people we reach, our aims, all of that is secondary. I don't know whom you could contact for further information.

When Mãe Stella orders visitors to her terreiro not to ask questions, but simply observe the activities unfolding before their eyes, she voices a concern over a shift in mediation: with ever more people knocking on her terreiro's doors wanting to hear her out—shoot pictures, make documentaries, write books and dissertations, hold interviews, be informed—discursive, rational forms of understanding threaten to outclass the bodily, experiential forms of knowledge that Candomblé valorizes. What is at issue is an attempt to safeguard a passive, time-bound, bodily order of knowledge acquisition geared toward immersion in a world where learning is understood as a fast, active, and efficient process of knowledge exchange geared toward "getting the picture."

The one example I will explore in greater depth so as to better grasp the troubling aspects of Candomblé having become a simulacrum concerns the Balé Folclórico da Bahia, the state folklore ensemble that puts on stage a spectacularized version of the dances of the orixás. I can't think of a clearer case of the working of the simulacrum as the sheer effervescence that is produced by this dance group, and unsurprisingly—there is no group subject to more venomous critiques from Mãe Stella and her ideological company than the Balé.

The Controversy around the Balé Folclórico da Bahia

The Balé Folclórico da Bahia exists since 1988. The company recruits its dancers "from the street," as Zebrinha, the company's choreographer and instructor, told me in one of our interviews. If they prove to be talented they are subjected to a tough regime of training and rehearsal. There is never a shortage of candidates, Balé Folclórico da Bahia is an international success, and travels all over the world. On Pelourinho, the historic center of Salvador, they have a show every night in Teatro Miguel de Santana, where, next to such dances as *samba de roda*, *maculêlê*, and *capoeira*, they give a demonstration of sacred dances from Candomblé. Dressed in the sacred attire of the orixá, the dancers perform the dances of the possessed in a spectacularized way. Another production, called The Court of Oxalá, tells the stories of the orixás, and has a central role for the trickster god Exú, here presented in the figure of a madman.

In Candomblé circles, these programs are highly controversial. Time and again, Mãe Stella attacked the Balé Folclórico in the strongest terms

There are these folklore show that exploit what is most serious in Candomblé: the manifestation of the orixá in his sons and daughters. So the tourist will see the show, sees the youngster "dressed as the orixá," imitating the battle cries [of the warrior spirits], dancing the sacred dances. Then this tourist will decide to go visit a ceremony, and who knows, will find that same handsome lad truly transformed in Xangô, Oxossi or Ogum. What will he think? If he has a bit of good sense, he will conclude that Candomblé is nothing serious, that it belongs to such things as the *samba de roda*, that it is folklore. (1989, 20)

Candomblé is a religion. It has nothing to do with the folklore shows that can be seen in nightclubs, where they put on the orixá's dance, as if the dancer were a filho-de-santo....These shows are vulgar imitations. Having to witness how the sacred is profaned on stage, how these dances are performed in a sequence that includes maculelê, capoeira, or samba de roda is saddening to all serious people, regardless of whether they are priests or laymen. (1993, 34–35)

Twenty years later, she hasn't moved her position on these productions.

This folklorization is a lack of knowledge and understanding! I once talked to one who dances (or danced) in the Balé Folclórico da Bahia. I said: "You dress like Iansã?" and she: "But Mãe Stella, this is only to pay tribute to my *santo*." Little does she know, does she? Goes there dressed as Iansã, to dance on stage, and afterwards goes out to have a beer...daughter of Iansã! Drinks whiskey, sleeps around...its folklore, but it is also a lack of respect. If she who thinks that she is paying tribute speaks like this, just think what a layperson would say! (Mãe Stella, in Pretto and Serpa 2002, 39)

Mãe Stella is not the only one to show indignation. In an interview, Antoniel Ataide Bispo, priest of Candomblé, and for 23 years secretary general of the Federação Nacional do Culto Afro-Brasileira stated:

> ... it is a sad fact that neither I nor the Federation have the power to call the
> Balé Folclórico da Bahia to a halt ... I consider them to be one of the main
> exhibitors of Candomblé in the world, they show many of the particularities
> of our religion ... well, this much I must admit: they do not show initiation
> rituals. But the dances of the orixás! The dances of the orixás! Alas, there is
> no way to stop them. Every once in a while, one of their production passes
> on TV. I watch it in horror! The exhibition! I know that in that dance group
> there are numerous people who belong to the African religion. Without
> doubt! And they sing and play the "deep" music and words (*músicas e letras
> de fundamentação*) that they should not be singing and playing. But we can't
> prohibit it, such is the fact. However, I condemn it with all my might...

Both the artistic director of the Balé Folclórico da Bahia, a man called
Vava, and the choreographer, Zebrinha, have been confronted with the
critiques. The latter—tall, black, charismatic, a street kid from Caixa
d'Agua who made it to dance academies in New York and Arnhem (in the
Netherlands), and an adept from Candomblé himself—told me that it
would simply be no option to leave out Candomblé from a program of
Bahian music and dance. Candomblé was the *fundamento* of all the rest.
He stressed that, out of respect, they never entered into the "spiritual part
of Candomblé." They never performed sacrifices or rituals. "We just take
the forms, the specific movements, which we then stylize by exaggeration.
For let's face it, the dancing that goes on in the terreiros is far too boring to
put on stage!" When I pressed him to respond to the critique of Ilê Axé
Opô Afonjá, he got irritated. "Oh, these religious people. We are artists!"
Stretching his muscled legs high up in the air he continued: "... haven't we
seen Maria Magdalena spread her legs? Haven't we seen Jesus fucking?
Jesus as a homosexual? So what's all the fuss about?" Ilê Axé Opô Afonjá,
he insinuated, has been taken over by white people. They're the ones to
make all this fuss. "Have you heard of Cleo Martins, a white attorney from
São Paulo and the long time lover of Mãe Stella? Believe me, she's the one
to make most of the decisions over there!"

Vava too stressed that the Balé Folclórico da Bahia showed nothing that
could not be also seen in the public ceremonies of the terreiros themselves,
where everyone is welcome. "So what are the secrets we're giving away?"
And he too was under the impression that Ilê Axé Opô Afonjá had been
taken over by the ambitions of "that white women from São Paulo" and
suffered from the influence of all the intellectuals who would go there.

> I really do not get their policy. They criticize us, but when they want to pro-
> duce a video about their terreiro they contact us whether we can contract

some dancers. Juanita [Elbein dos Santos, an Argentinian anthropologist who wrote a classic monography on Ilê Axé Opô Afonjá, and married the son of Mãe Stella's predecessor, MvdP] caused a scandal when her documentary film on the secret cult of the Eguns was broadcasted on national TV. But when we were invited to stage some of the dances for an international congress on African Religion, with priests and priestesses from all over the country, as well as representatives from African countries, the people from Ilê Axé Opô Afonjá—including Juanita—made a point of ostentatiously leaving the room. The Africans, on the other hand, were very enthusiastic!

He continued by saying that the national ballets of Cuba and Haiti also put on a section of the dances of the orixás in their programs, and that Casa Branca and Gantois (the other "historic" and prestigious terreiros, and the eternal competitors of Ilê Axé Opô Afonjá) spoke very positive of the Balé, and never created any problems.

> And just look how Ilê Axé Opô Afonjá is accessing the media all the time, seeking publicity, organizing events. If they are so concerned about keeping Candomblé a religion: it is not like they restrict themselves to their religious tasks!

Mãe Stella and her soul mates, however, do not seem to be impressed with such arguments. A priest subscribing to the ideology of Ilê Axé Opô Afonjá asked me: "When do we see people dressed up as nuns, monks, and bishops in a carnival parade? When do we get to see the consecration of the Holy Eucharist in Teatro Miguel de Santana? Huh?"

Undoubtedly, painful histories play up in the condemnation of the Balé. Up until 1976, terreiros intending to have a religious ceremony had to register with the city police at a department called *jogos e costumes*: the very desk where brothels, nightclubs, and gambling houses had to register as well. And yet, there must be more to it. For if films, books, anthropological dissertations, and photographs manage to pass the instruction "don't ask questions, just observe" relatively easy, why then the venomous critiques of the Balé Folclórico da Bahia? What might be at stake became clear to me when Zebrinha took me up to the studio to observe a rehearsal of the dance group. The boys and girls had been stretching and flexing their muscles for over an hour in utmost concentration and dedication. Then the drums were beaten, the sacred songs were sung, and the pupils started to dance. The spectacle was nowhere close to the somewhat obligatory-fatigued dancing of initiates one often sees in the terreiros. The movements were exaggerated, stylized, and highly energetic. There was no adherence to any liturgical sequence. The dancer's beautiful and sweating bodies were only dressed in tights and shorts instead of the baroque costumes of *filhos-de-santo* who incorporate their orixás. Yet for all the obvious differences, the rehearsal produced a genuine effervescence that filled the studio to the brim, transcending the mere rehearsal, producing a spectacle that was as powerful as a religious ceremony of Candomblé.

Dancers told me they would sometimes feel the coming of their orixás during rehearsals, and recalled instances of possession. Yet when I asked Zebrinha about it he flatly denied it, saying "*Orixá é burro*? [The orixá is a jack-ass?] Would not know the difference between a rehearsal and a ceremony? Come on!" For me, however, it was clear that both public ceremonies of Candomblé and the Balé work with the same stuff, the same enchantment, for which in Candomblé terminology there is a word: *axé*, the vital, life-giving force that puts the universe in motion and makes possible growth, progress, and prosperity. In fact, in an interview, this is exactly how Vava, the artistic director of the Balé Folclórico da Bahia, put it: "*o mistério do Candomblé é o encanto do axé*." The mystery of Candomblé is the magic of axé. Given the prevalent boundary politics in Candomblé, the conceptualization of axé as a force that does its work both in and out of religious settings cannot but raise grave concerns. For it is here that the simulacrum has appropriated the "ineffable" and "noetic" qualities of ritual and ceremonial practices, the very stuff through which the Candomblé community had sought to ward off its unsettling effects.

Concluding Remarks

I have argued that the public forms of Candomblé—the reworking of its symbols, myths, rhythms, and aesthetics in other than religious frames— have given a new impetus to the performance of secrecy. Creating zones of silence and obscurity, highlighting the "ineffable" and "noetic" qualities of mystical knowledge, and thus framing the talking and writing of others as "empty chatter" are ever so many attempts to discredit new interpretations of Candomblé and immunize Afro-Brazilian religion for the work of the simulacrum.

In conclusion, however, it is necessary to widen our lens and position these findings in a broader picture. For Candomblé's struggles should not be understood as a heroic fight to "ward off" the evil monster of the simulacrum. However much cult adepts themselves may wish to portray it that way, one cannot fail to notice that there is no such thing as a Candomblé that is situated outside of the simulacrum. There is no community that is still "untouched," and that seeks to maintain its purity and authenticity by keeping the forces of the simulacrum out. To the contrary, following

Baudrillard one could argue that such fights (and the dreams that motivate them) are already an *effect* of the simulacrum. In the broader picture, then, Mãe Stella herself, the public interest in Ilê Axé Opô Afonjá, the "re-Africanizing" and antisyncretistic movements in Candomblé, as well as the anthropologist contemplating the real of silence, or his being impressed by the ineffable qualities of sacred dance: all of this already belongs to that "panic-stricken production of the real and the referential" that follows an awareness of the unsettling effects of the simulacrum. The assignment "don't ask questions, just observe" is an effect of the simulacrum, just as much as it seeks to fight it.

Notes

1. One of the organizations of the *movimento negro* (black movement).
2. Some people may consider the word "cult" and "cultist" pejorative. I wish to stress that I use the word in a neutral sense.
3. In Candomblé, axé is the life-giving force that animates all being, the accumulation of which is central to all activities in the temples. Axé is also used to denote the religious community.
4. Interestingly, Ildásio Tavares identifies himself as "poet and Otun Oba Aré of the Ilê Axé Opô Afonjá," which means that he occupies a honorary post in Mãe Stella's *terreiro*.

Chapter 2

Purity and the Devil: Community, Media, and the Body. Pentecostal Adherents in a Favela in Rio de Janeiro

Martijn Oosterbaan

Now, despite all the techniques for appropriating space, despite the whole network of knowledge that enables us to delimit or to formalize it, contemporary space is perhaps still not entirely desanctified.

—(Foucault [2002]1984, 2)

Defilement is never an isolated event. It cannot occur except in view of a systematic ordering of ideas. Hence any piecemeal interpretation of the pollution rules of another culture is bound to fail. For the only way in which pollution ideas make sense is in reference to a total structure of thought whose keystone, boundaries, margins and internal lines are held in relation by rituals of separation.

—(Douglas 2002 [1966], 51)

Introduction

The small public square in the middle of the favela[1] was crowded when the famous pastor Marcos Pereira da Silva of the *Igreja Assembléia de*

Deus dos Últimos Dias stepped up the stage that was set up especially for the occasion. The church members of his congregation had hung up a huge screen on which were projected images of the service as it was conducted, alternated with images of a service held in an overpopulated prison in the city. The video of the prison showed hundreds of men behind bars, responding to an emotional gospel song performed by a young woman and men praying out loud with the Bible in their hands. The service in the square started with a loudly amplified, live performance of the same woman and was followed by the testimony of a well-dressed man. Clutching a microphone in his hand, he spoke of his life before his conversion. He was dressed in suit and tie and he gave an emotional speech about his life of crime. At a certain point he shouted: "Yes, I was walking around with a gun. I was riding in my convertible. I told everybody I was from the *Comando Vermelho* (drugs gang), but the Comando Vermelho is of the devil. The devil created the Comando Vermelho. He also created the *Terceiro Comando* (another drugs gang). Was I crazy? Was I dumb? No, I was possessed by the devil. But then Jesus came and the devil lost his power and I was liberated by the glory of Jesus Christ." Approximately 300 men and women in the square cheered enthusiastically. Then pastor Marcos introduced a man who was sitting on the stage with him: *deputado estadual* (state deputy) Fábio Silva, son of the owner of the popular evangelical radio station Melodia. He praised Fábio for all the good work that he was doing for the community (*comunidade*), and he asked the audience to welcome him in the name of the Lord. While there were plenty of people present, the pastor complained that there were not as many people as he had expected: "there must be a *baile funk*[2] happening somewhere close by," he cynically added. At the apotheosis of the evening men and women were invited to step close to the stage to be delivered by pastor Marcos and his helpers. The men of the church stepped down from the stage and grabbed people by their heads, praying firmly. Various people fell down to the ground, touched by the Holy Spirit. The conclusion of the night was reserved for the pastor himself. To demonstrate his authority as powerful mediator of the Holy Spirit, he delivered a young man from a distance of several meters. Simply at the gesture of his hand, the young man fell backward as if hit by powerful blow.

While drawing a large crowd, the pastor was highly aware that he was competing with other attractive events during this night. The baile funk parties draw many youngsters and are regularly portrayed as a confirmation of the reign of the drug gangs, who often use them as an occasion to display their power. In the eyes of many converts, the baile funk parties— together with the popular samba and pagode parties—signify the "worldly" domain of pleasure that seduces people and leads them astray. Evangelical preachers criticize these "playgrounds of the devil" and urge their audience to avoid them. During church services pastors repetitively persuade their listeners to separate themselves from the people who live "worldly" lives.

Indeed, during my ten-month stay in the favela, many people who frequented the evangelical churches told me "they were *in* the world, not *of* the world. They were different." Often, when I asked them what it meant to be different from the other inhabitants, people explained they could no longer watch certain television programs, listen to particular music, or be seen in the company of specific neighbors. This insistence on difference kept me puzzled during the course of my stay in Rio de Janeiro. How do people who live in a social environment saturated with mediated popular culture, enmeshed in the politics of daily life decide what is "of the world" and what is not? And how is such a difference, once established as a social category, enacted and legitimized in a complex urban social environment, characterized by constant flux and indeterminate social positions? Many adherents claimed they were not "of the world"; other inhabitants would contest such claims and accuse them of hypocrisy. "Who were they to claim that they were different from the rest, hadn't they danced the samba and courted with them in the past, weren't they still listening pagode or watching *telenovelas* (soaps) when they had the chance?"

Surely, it would not be hard to side with these voices and underscore the fragility of the boundaries between social groups or the superficiality of the conversion to Pentecostal faith of some inhabitants. Nevertheless, plenty of people radically changed their lifestyle, media preference, and mode of conduct after joining an evangelical congregation. Furthermore, as many others have noted in relation to the favelas of Rio de Janeiro, to portray oneself as an *evangélico* (evangelical) is generally regarded as serious and powerful expression of collective identity. How should we understand this collective sense of alterity in such a social environment and what can it tell us of the reproduction of socio-religious boundaries in a very dense life world full of mass mediated images and sounds from a wide variety of sources?

In this chapter I discuss the efforts of two evangelical churches— the *Igreja Universal do Reino de Deus*[3] and the *Assembléia de Deus*[4]—to attract adherents and to instill in them a sense of a community. I will argue that one of the important strategies is to classify, incorporate, and purify the many so-called worldly phenomena that surround people. Evangelical churches attempt to strengthen the sense of the divine order by classifying and incorporating popular cultural practices, symbols, media, and spaces. Such dynamics operate as a double-edged sword, on the one side aiming to attract people through established popular practices and on the other side demonstrating the power of a specific church, pastor, or adherent to confront and overcome the demonic. Crucial for this dynamic is the ability of evangelical churches to link different *scapes* to one another as domains that are eligible for purification through the power of the Holy Spirit. The body, portrayed as a vessel for powers of good and/or evil becomes homologous with both the cityscape and mediascape (Appadurai 1996) of the favela and as such opens up the possibility of purification of all these scapes through deliverance or other ritual practices.

The evangelical churches are able to sustain a homology between the scapes by convincing people that a spiritual battle between God and the devil is taking place in each and every one of them. The remediation of symbols, practices, and sounds from different media forges a strong bond between different scapes. People of the churches continuously attempt to link features of everyday life to the popular media and *vice versa*.[5] One of the main concerns of evangelical churches is the rottenness of the "worldly" media and they continuously discuss other television programs, films, and music in their own media to demonstrate its heretical nature. Through their discussions of these "worldly" media, the churches try to create a sense of alterity and to impose a mode of self-discipline with regard to the consumption of media.

Notwithstanding the fact that the *evangélicos* are indeed often represented as quite a solid community of converts, in practice such a community is under constant threat of erosion. The multireligious popular culture of Brazil offers people a wide variety of spiritual practices and people often choose to stay with a certain church or religious practice as long as it serves their individual needs. To strengthen the unity of evangelicals, churches oppose certain media and certain practices, while at the same time incorporating elements of other popular (religious) practices and popular media styles into their own modes of representation. This tendency to incorporate other styles fractures the distinctiveness of the community of *evangélicos* vis-à-vis the other inhabitants and demonstrates the fluidity of the different cultural practices and subject positions in the favelas of Rio de Janeiro (see also de Abreu in this volume).

Evangelical Politics, Media, and Spiritual Purification

The state and federal elections of the past decade have demonstrated that the evangelical churches in Brazil have shaken off their hesitation to interfere in worldly politics. From the local to the national level, pastors have run as candidates and many politicians have openly demonstrated their evangelical background. One of the recurring explanations of the religious/political transformation in Brazil is the increasing appropriation of mass media by evangelical movements, especially by the Igreja Universal (Freston 1994, 2003; Fonseca 1997; Campos 1997; Conrado 2001; Novaes 2002; Sá Martino 2002; Oro 2003). The Igreja Universal has demonstrated the highest rate of expansion during the past few decades and it has become by far the most visible church in Brazil. According to its own silver jubilee publication in 2003, it has 6,500 churches in Brazil and a total of 8 million members in more than 70 countries worldwide. Over the past 20–30 years, it has built many huge temples throughout the country and it has also bought one of the 6 national public television broadcast networks, *Rede Record,* which consists of 30 broadcast stations. It has a professional Internet site, its own publishing house and record company. It publishes the weekly newspaper the *Folha Universal* and owns several radio stations that broadcast 24 hours a day. The Igreja Universal is one of the few evangelical churches that have undertaken a nationwide political project and it is broadly recognized that their mass media have been pivotal in the constitution of the political support of voters (Birman and Lehman 1999; Conrado 2001; Corten 2001; Novaes 2002).

The messages that are broadcast by the evangelical churches on radio and television are mostly aimed at people living in relative poverty, faced with the insecurities of the urban spaces of the large cities. The churches present utopist visions of a better society, based on Christian values, and they offer concrete practices such as church services, collective prayer, and exorcism of evil spirits, which the churches claim to counter the socioeconomic and personal problems of many people. Charismatic evangelical politicians (men of God) present themselves as trustworthy because they answer to a "Higher Authority" than mankind (Oro 2003; Oosterbaan 2005).

Evangelical movements have launched aggressive media campaigns against other religious and cultural practices (Sanchis 1994; Montes 1998; Birman and Lehmann 1999). Instead of portraying practices such as samba and carnival as the epitome of Brazilianness and of national pride, the evangelical organizations link them to the many social problems of Brazil.[6] Based upon a fundamentalist reading of the Bible, Catholic-, and Afro-Brazilian religious practices are depicted as idolatrous or even as devil worship. Especially the supposed alignment between social misery and Afro-Brazilian spiritual practice has laid the ground for the practice of spiritual purification as counteroffensive to social desolation. Most important in the constitution of the imagination of spiritual purification are the mass mediated expulsions of demons, both on stage during the massive church services and on television, in magazines and in newspapers (Birman 2006; Kramer 2005; see also De Abreu in this volume).

One of the center rituals in the Igreja Universal is the *sessão de descarrego* (deliverance service). This weekly church session consists of highly ritualized mass exorcisms in which people are invited to enact their self-empowerment and to change their social and economic conditions with the help of the Holy Spirit. During the rituals of mass exorcism hitherto invisible forces become visible as well-known Afro-Brazilian deities manifest themselves publicly among the adherents. This demonic possession is recognizable by the bodily postures of the victims, faces that show signs of agony, bodies that show loss of self-control. Often, when interrogated by the pastor in front of the pulpit, the demons confess, through the mouths of their victims, that they are sent by the devil to destroy the lives of the people they posses. After publicly demonstrating the true nature of the Afro-Brazilian spirits the pastor exorcizes them in the name of Jesus and the people peacefully return to their seats. Through this practice of exorcism the church simultaneously identifies and expels the roots of evil and offers direct spiritual interventions in situations of relative poverty and violence in many of the marginalized areas of the Brazilian metropolis (Antoniazzi 1994; Montes 1998; Birman and Lehmann 1999; Birman and Leite 2000).

The mass mediatization of expulsions has thoroughly shifted the relations between religious institutions in Brazil. Rather than dismissing the Afro-Brazilian religious beliefs and practices as superstitions, the Igreja Universal incorporates the spiritual entities worshipped in *Candomblé* and *Umbanda* and represents them as demons. The demons, or *encostos*,[7] are held responsible for physically harming the individuals they posses and hindering them from achieving fortune and happiness in this life and salvation in the Hereafter. While the spiritual warfare of the Igreja Universal is mostly directed against Afro-Brazilian religious practices, the Catholic Church is another prominent adversary. In its services and its media, the Igreja Universal forcefully opposes the presumed idolatry of the Catholic saints. The most famous public incident is known as the *chute na santa*—the kicking of the saint. During a television broadcast, a pastor of the Igreja Universal desecrated a plaster statue of the Catholic Patron Saint of Brazil, *Nossa Senhora de Aparecida*. The assault on the statue was not merely an attack on a Catholic icon, but an attack on the cultural hegemony of Catholicism in Brazil (Kramer 2001; Birman and Lehmann 1999).

Spatial and Bodily Purifications

The practice of mass expulsion of demons is not confined to the temples of the Igreja Universal. Pastor Marcos, for example, takes the practice of spiritual purification to the places where it is supposedly most needed: the favelas of Rio de Janeiro. During the open-air service, sketched in the introduction, members of this congregation linked the presence of the drug gang members (*traficantes*) to the general misery of the favela, while interpreting both as signs of demonic presence. Subsequently, the pastor is able to present a solution for both the individual youngsters involved in the *tráfico* (drug trade) and the favela as a whole. In an emotional sermon he asserted that only the Holy Spirit—mediated through the pastor—can cleanse individual *traficantes* who want to give up their life of crime and thus deliver the favela of its perils.

The rhetoric that should convince the audiences that the Holy Spirit can and will purify the favela, rests on the homology between the individual body and the space of the favela as sites where both good and evil can reside. This strategy is similar to the practices of the charismatic *bispos* (bishops) of the Igreja Universal who also represent the violence in the favelas of Rio de Janeiro as signs of the spiritual battle between God and the devil. Especially in their newspaper, the Folha Universal, bispos proclaim that an ultimate end of city-violence is possible only with the help of the Lord (Oosterbaan 2005). Occasionally, the charismatic bispos of the Igreja Universal also visit favelas in Rio de Janeiro. Shortly before pastor Marcos's visit, bispo Marcelo Crivella, the singing pastor who became a senator in Brasilia, had also visited the favela. He too had exorcized a number of traficantes in the context of a small, though mass mediated prayer meeting with local pastors and youths of the favela. He too linked the possibility of the well-being of the *comunidade* (the favela community) to the spiritual purification of its inhabitants.

These examples indicate that both the pastor and the bispo approach the youngsters involved in the drug trade not merely as perpetrators of violent crimes but also as victims of the demons that haunt them. As such, the lives of the young men can generate popular examples to demonstrate the ferociousness of the spiritual battle and the proof of the power of the Holy Spirit to pacify where all other measures have failed. In small congregations of the Assembléia de Deus in the favela of my research, the presence and testimonies of former *traficantes* who had converted were often regarded as the proof of the powers of the Holy Spirit to purify both the individuals and the space of the congregation, within the favela.

Subsequently, the evangelical churches in the favela were often imagined as permanent safe havens against the dangers of the favela. An example comes from the *missionária* (missionary) Angela, who lived in a house in the favela, close to the site where the drugs were sold. The first time I talked to her she explained that her house used to be of the Comando Vermelho and that the boys of the *tráfico* used it to store their drugs and hide when the police would enter the favela. When I interviewed her, she gave me her long testimony, explaining that she was sent by God to buy that house and preach to those who had not heard the word of God. She outlined her mission as follows:

> I have a team of youngsters, *ex-feticeiras, ex-prostitutas, ex-ladrões, ex-matadores,*[8] who have done horrible things, but today they are cleansed (*limpo*) by the word of God and they are ministers of the gospel (*evangelho*) of the Lord Jesus Christ here on Earth...I have this team of youngsters that are sons in faith, produced by the word of God, recovered not with chemicals but with the power of Jesus Christ who is the liberator.

When I asked her if there had been no complications with the *traficantes* when she bought the house, she explained:

> When I bought it, they came and when I presented myself as the buyer they left the house. I did not encounter problems with them. I am praying for them that God will save them and He will save them in the name of the Lord Jesus. They only charge those that interfere with them, I am here praying... originally it was a hell here, and mind you, I am talking about different periods, it was a hell. Now there is peace in this place, a peace that Jesus Christ granted, before I came here, He had shown me He was going to send me to a place that was a hell and that would be transformed into heaven.

The homology between practices of spiritual purification of individual bodies and of space is enforced by other mechanisms as well.[9] In the Igreja Universal a heavy emphasis is placed on objects (pamphlets, envelops but also stones, salt, and other objects) and fluids (oil and water mostly) as biblical mediators of the Holy Spirit and containers of curative and protective powers. By means of their words and prayers the bispos bless and consecrate these objects and fluids, after which the powers can be transmitted to individuals (see also Kramer 2001). The consecrated salt is meant to be taken home to cleanse and protect the houses of the church attendants against the perceived evil that surrounds them. People are instructed to pour the salt on their doorsteps to safeguard the boundaries between the spiritually purified inside and the threatening outside. Similar practices of spatial demarcation of metaphysical domains of good and evil are also found in other evangelical practices such as in the attachment of evangelical banners, stickers, and nameplates on walls, doors, and entrances. These spatial markers serve to define a house or office as a place of evangelicals and simultaneously to purify and protect a space against demonic invasion.

An example of the popular conviction that one's house in the favela should be protected against demonic presence comes from Leonildo, a man in his forties who had accepted Jesus only a few years before I first met him. Leonildo, a *presbítero* (elder) in one of the congregations of the Assembléia de Deus in the favela, explained to me that, after his conversion, he no longer let certain kinds of people enter his house:

> Before anybody could come in, but nowadays they have to stay on the threshold. They can bring demons in with them, like a dog that carries fleas. As a Christian you should not let all kinds of people inside. My neighbors, for example, do not live like Christians. You should not let people enter who don't have the same faith. The Bible says so.[10]

It is striking that even while straightforward demonic presence and exorcism is less common in the services and doctrines of the Assembléia de Deus, many people of these churches nevertheless envisaged social relations in terms of the fight against demons. This indicates the growing influence of the discourse on demonic presence that the Igreja Universal is spreading. Yet, at the same time, it needs to be noted, the Igreja Universal itself is tapping into a wide range of existing beliefs and practices to put their message across. Many of the techniques of spatial purification encountered in the Igreja Universal and in several other Pentecostal churches demonstrate similarities with purification techniques of Afro-Brazilian religious movements and of the Catholic Church. *Sal grosso* (unrefined salt), for example, is commonly used in Umbanda and Candomblé to purify individuals and to protect them from harmful spirits. It is also striking that in these Afro-Brazilian movements salt is also often used for a *banho de descarrego* (ritual cleansing bath).[11] The Brazilian Catholic tradition also knows many practices, which are meant to protect a place or a person against evil. Some Catholics in the favela, for example, had attached stickers with portraits of Saints on their door to protect their house. One could also think of the popular scapulars (*escapulários*), necklaces that have portraits of Jesus, Mary, or Saints on both the front and back side, thus fully closing of the body (*fechar o corpo*) against any potential threats.

All these and other practices that are used to purify and protect body and/or space strike a chord with the important work of Mary Douglas. As Douglas has taught us, practices of distinction and separation of the pure and the impure are universal ordering mechanisms of societies, which often involve the body as a powerful metaphor for society.

> The body is a model which can stand for any bounded system. Its boundaries can represent any boundaries which are threatened or precarious. The body is a complex structure. The functions of its different parts and their relation afford a source of symbols for other complex structures. We cannot possibly interpret rituals concerning excreta, breast milk, saliva and the rest unless we are prepared to see in the body a symbol of society, and to see the powers and dangers credited to social structure reproduced in small on the human body. (Douglas 2002 [1966], 142)

Taking Douglas' important insight concerning the body and the notions of purity as a starting point, it becomes apparent that evangelical rituals of purification unite religious modes of in and exclusion with other forms of social distinction. As Zygmunt Bauman has also argued, body and community are often perceived as "the last defensive outposts" amidst the uncertainty and insecurity so characteristic of "liquid modernity." According to Bauman, "[t]he body's new primacy is reflected in the tendency to shape the image of community...after the pattern of the ideally protected body" (Bauman 2000, 184). Especially in the favela, the ideas about bodily impurity as a result of spirit possession are related to distinctions between groups of people (communities), which involve strong moral judgments about others. Moreover, the notion of impure bodies enforces the imagination of impure spaces, which subsequently can be purified through collective exorcism. This echoes the proposition of Arjun Appadurai to understand rituals of spatial purification as important "techniques for the production of locality" (1996, 182).

Purification, Social Life, and Media

People who frequented the evangelical churches in the favela often opposed their practices to those of the other inhabitants. In their view, the spiritual battle between God and the devil is visible especially in the domain of popular culture at large. It is in critical dialogue with other practices that evangelical doctrines acquire their meaning. *Musica evangélica* (evangelical music) is opposed to *musica do mundo* (worldly music)—samba, pagode, and funk—because that is the popular music of parties at which people court, drink, and dance without obeying the strict moral prescriptions of the Bible. Most *evangélicos* understand these cultural practices to be the root of all social and individual problems. According to many *evangélicos* in the favela, the immoral behavior was mostly associated with Afro-Brazilian religious practices, even the presence of *traficantes* and the armed confrontations among them (Oosterbaan 2006).

Many converts understand their crossing from a "worldly" to a "godly" lifestyle as a way to protect themselves from the harsh circumstances of life in the favela. Conversion to Pentecostalism is attractive because it offers experiences of empowerment through collective rituals in combination with a newborn identity in the complex power relations of the favela. People can claim a *status aparte*, beyond the *jogo de cintura* (wealing and dealing) and the violence of daily life. The trope of the spiritual battle is crucial to understanding the nature of the conversions and the inherent paradoxes. While their newborn identity is God-given, it is also an identity they must perform[12] on a daily basis. The *status aparte* is generally granted, but other inhabitants only accept it when people do indeed show the signs of God's grace and do not engage in the behavior they condemn of others. This demands extra awareness and a multitude of self-disciplinary performances. *Evangélicos* should no longer practice those diabolical things they did before: no more baile funk, samba, or pagode; no more adultery, drinking, or smoking. Conversion thus restores the feeling of power over their destiny (Mariz 1994) and heightens the responsibility to behave according to the biblical norms (Oro and Seman 1999).

Whereas most studies on evangelical movements and media focus on evangelical programs on radio and television to research its possible influence, the *evangélicos* in the favela of my research watched and listened to an array of popular television and radio programs of many different genres and many of their accounts of their place "in the world" and the meaning of Christian doctrines and practices were based upon information from all kinds of programs, both "worldly" and "godly."[13] When we start from the assumption that religion is a practice of mediation and that religion, media, and culture are co-constitutive (Meyer 2006a), we can leave aside the narrow focus on the relation between media and religion and study their various intersections synchronically and diachronically.

Evangelical leaders try to convince people that the spiritual battle between God and the devil also takes place in the domain of television and radio. The devil works cunningly in various ways and he is always and everywhere busy trying to "steal, kill and destroy," as many of the people told me. Whereas the devil operates through radio and television, by seducing men and women with carnal pleasures that may seem attractive but eventually lead to death and destruction, God can also work through media.

To the evangelicals in the favela, the electro-acoustic amplification of church services strengthens their belief that they are reaching out to the people who surround them. Likewise, radios and CD players that play gospel music are often understood as a positive contribution to the purification of the space of the favela.[14] Take, for example, what the locally famous gospel singer/musician Leandro told me during an interview:

> Music, that is it. *Louvor* is the instrument—in the church we call it *louvor*—sing and everybody sings. *Louvor* is something that flows, so when people *louva* the Lord Jesus, the Holy Spirit comes automatically, you feel that joy and you transmit that to other people. And the people become glorified, become sane, and even people who are ill, physically ill, spiritually ill, feel cured through the *louvor*, people are cured through the *louvor*. For example, those who are on the verge of doing something stupid, who want to commit suicide, who want to leave their family, who want to leave everything behind or do bad things. Normally when those people listen to *louvor* that is dedicated to Lord Jesus, that *louvor* makes them feel different, the opposite to what they felt. Those people open their heart and let it flow, and nothing bad happens.

The unique capacity of *louvor* to reach people through space creates the possibility to experience it as the transmission of the Holy Spirit while simultaneously allowing for the idea of a spiritual occupation of space. Such a link between music, space, and religion was apparent not only in the favela of my research. In her research among *evangélicos* in the favela Acari, Cunha also noticed that the *evangélicos* occupy physical and social space with the aid of speakers, microphones, and musical instruments (Cunha 2002, 92).

As I have argued elsewhere (Oosterbaan 2008), the popularity of evangelical radio should be understood in relation to both the landscape and soundscape of the favela and in relation to the specific affinities between radio and Pentecostalism in Brazil. It is often through sounds that people feel touched by the Holy Spirit and in close contact with God. In the dense social space of the favela, where sound has acquired a privileged position at the crossroads of the public and private, this quality of evangelical radio to touch people is dialectically related to the sounds of other social groups and the perceived moral transgressions that evangelicals are concerned with.

Just as with other cultural practices, the self-disciplining efforts to avoid listening to certain radio programs are strengthened by the dense urban setting and the proximity of people in the favela. Both church members and unconverted neighbors exercise a continuous control over the born-again subjects, eager to expose that they are also "of the world," not just in it. To many *evangélicos* it is of great importance to maintain the boundaries between them and the unconverted (*ímpios*) not only because of their feelings of belonging to those who will be saved, but also because the violent conditions in the dense urban spaces of the favelas put great emphasis on questions of belonging and social identification.

Like radio, television was regarded as an instrument that has to be handled with care. The telescape offers its evangelical spectators a visualization of the spiritual battle between God and the devil, but the medium can also seriously harm one through the programs and images that aim to seduce people to partake in those worldly practices the Bible condemns (Bakker 2007; Oosterbaan 2003, 2005). Consider the following quote of Roberto, a young man who attends the Igreja Universal:

> Like the Bispo said to us: the world is not what it used to be, meaning who is ruling the world God or the devil? It is the devil, you understand, the majority of the news (*as notícias*) is his, the bad news, understand? Lately there has only been death, death, death, understand, in the whole world: the guy who blew up the towers, countries entering into war with each other, here a prisoner killed other prisoners. You think that is coming from God? One feels evil stamped in one's flesh twenty-four hours a day.

Television viewing involves a dynamic of attraction and rejection, which for the *evangélicos* in the favela is related to Pentecostal bodily disciplines and practices. Yet, attraction and rejection cannot be categorized simply into evangelical programs that attract and controversial programs that repel. Some people are attracted to watching immoral programs to identify the work of the devil and to confirm the right or even righteous spectator position (Oosterbaan 2003; Bakker 2007).

Especially with regard to the popular telenovelas and the mass mediated violence the dialectic relation between the telescape and daily life becomes obvious. Telenovelas are part of the popular cultural representations that can be considered common knowledge. They represent features of contemporary Brazilian society, which many Pentecostals perceive as sinful even though they often do watch them. For instance, when the novelas portray adultery and erotic images the novelas are generally perceived as channels of demonic seduction. Furthermore, the attraction and rejection of certain images and narratives in telenovelas are not only related to a symbolic reading of the message, but also to the physical and spiritual experiences of evangelicals while viewing these telenovelas. As Pentecostalism involves a complex interplay between evangelical doctrines and embodied practices[15] that are related to the *charismata*—the gifts of Holy Spirit, such as faith healing and speaking in tongues (*glossolalia*)— the bodily sensations induced or enforced by popular mass media become thoroughly intertwined with religious experience, as Birgit Meyer has forcefully argued throughout her work (Meyer 2005, 2006a, 2006b). To many evangelicals, experiences of watching and hearing are directly related to the presence of the devil and the Holy Spirit. People come to understand certain sensations while watching—for example, arousal, desire, or even anguish—as direct interference of the devil or the Holy Spirit. One informant felt the Holy Spirit "poking" her when she was watching a telenovela she should not. Others explained the erratic behavior of family or friends as clear signs of demonic possession caused by suspicious programs or films (Oosterbaan 2003; Bakker 2007).

In analogy to the fear of contamination of space through sound(waves), there is also a concern for the possible contamination of space through television images. In his work on the significance of television for evangelicals on Ilha Grande, Brazil, André Bakker notes a fascinating account of a woman who explicitly asks her daughters not to watch a specific telenovela in her house because she is certain that it is wrong to have those images in her house (2007, 68). Also, as I have stated above, the images and narratives of violence mediated via the news serve as a powerful link between the occupation of the space of the favela and the occupation of the telescape where there is only "death, death and death," as Roberto exclaimed in the quote above. What becomes obvious is the fact that television functions as the device that offers a view on the spiritual struggle as a confirmation of what is seen around the people in the favela and the city at large and *vice versa*, producing what Schwartz calls a "reality-effect" (1995, 316). As people search for confirmations of biblical truths in television and in their daily surrounding, the multiple scapes become exemplary screens on which to project and confirm biblical truths.[16]

The understanding of television as a scape in need of purification is most straightforwardly noted in reactions of people who would rather watch a different set of programs substituting the place of suspicious television programs. Yet, the technological and stylistic features of television allow for a multitude of time-space experiences and for a differentiation of practices of purification. As telenovelas so clearly show, television and film offer their audiences multiple spectator positions, varying per genre, and format. While the television news is generally considered objective and harmless, telenovelas are considered suspicious, especially those produced by TV Globo. However, even telenovelas and programs such as Big Brother Brasil offer the evangelical spectator the possibility to treat the narrative or the situation as mirrors of real-life experiences and to imagine the right evangelical posture in relation to the situation. Certain programs can thus be perceived as sites that can be purified by adopting the right spectator position. Such a spectator position is generally attainable for those who are *firme* (firm) (Oosterbaan 2006), as the informants in my research called it or which the evangelicals in the research of Bakker described as "structured in the Word" (2007).

Another possibility to experience purification on television is provided through *montage*. In relation to newspaper formats I have demonstrated how images and narratives of urban violence are followed by the voice and image of authoritative bispos, who assert that such violence can only be demonic and thus only fought by the Holy Spirit (Oosterbaan 2005). By means of montage,[17] different images or signs are juxtaposed in order to confirm the power of the Lord to purify the world from malevolent forces. In the television program *Ponto de Luz* broadcast on TV Record, the Igreja Universal also uses such a technique by juxtaposing images and testimonies under the auspices of bispos and pastors. In the program people testify that they have been possessed by demons and therefore lived in misery and pain until they started attending the Igreja Universal. Frequently the hosts—mostly bispos—ask details about the actual practices that people had to perform when they belonged to such a possession cult and the guests explain in vivid detail what they have done. On some occasions, they also show representations of the kind of practices and offerings that people have made. In one broadcast, for example, a pastor ventured out to a cemetery in the city of Rio de Janeiro with an *ex-mãe de Santo* (ex-Candomblé priestess) to show the beheaded body of a goat, used for a "powerful ritual," as the woman explained. In similar vein, the program *Cidade Alerta* (Alert City)—an infotainment program that brings live and recorded news of crime and violence and accidents—images of police interventions and armed encounters in favelas are often followed by a word from a bispo of the Igreja Universal, who responds to these violent images with an *oração* (prayer) in which he asks God to bless the people and protect them from harm. These are two examples of the technique of montage, which, through its mode of address, offers its spectators a position from which to perceive their daily environment as a site of struggle between forces of good and evil. Especially in the last case, the cityscape is quite literally portrayed as a space of malice, waiting for the purifying powers of the Lord.[18]

Conclusion: Incorporations and Transgressions

The last examples of montage reveal an important aspect of current developments. In the attempt to attract an audience and spread the gospel efficiently, many evangelical churches incorporate images, styles, and narratives that can be considered "worldly." The Igreja Universal publishes its own glossy magazines and its own newspapers. It contracts rock-gospel bands under its own record label and play these on its own radio stations. In their weekly newspapers they copy the reports on urban violence in the daily journals and use the genre to factualize the spiritual battle (Oosterbaan 2005). In their glossy magazines they discuss the same issues one would encounter in the *Cosmopolitan* or the *Elle,* illustrated with similar photos of well-groomed women and men.

Other evangelical churches have also stylized their appearance in relation to "worldly" forms. Several fashionable artists and celebrities have publicly defined themselves as *evangélicos* and have thus changed the character of these churches from dull or restrictive to creative and empowering. Gospel singers appear no different from their colleagues on Brazilian MTV, and it is hard to distinguish some evangelical television programs from talk shows we see all around the world. Furthermore, hardly any so-called worldly phenomenon was left untouched in the Folha Universal or the evangelical magazines that people liked to read in the favela. Sex, alcohol, drugs, passion, partying, anything the devil could think of to seduce the men and women, was discussed. The glossy photos in the evangelical magazines *Ester, Plenitude,* and *Enfoque Gospel* are often quite seductive, but framed within the evangelical narrative they are purified and thus supposedly harmless.

While I have demonstrated that the evangelical movement is quite successful in persuading its audiences to experience the acute presence of the spiritual battle in different scapes: cityscape, soundscape, and telescape, one wonders what the effects of these techniques are on the persistence of boundaries of evangelical communities. Is it truly harmless when "the demonic" appears in evangelical media? When pictures are not seen as "mere" representations of evil but as presence of a dark force, as Meyer describes for Ghanaian representation of evil (Meyer 2008a), does it suffice to contain them in a Christian dualist frame of representation in which Jesus interferes to overcome the powers of evil? Does depicting evil not also involve a risk of transgression, when "evil bursts out of the frame" (104)? Some evangelicals criticized the Igreja Universal for this reason, claiming they showed how to do harm to other people when broadcasting the evil of Candomblé. It might seem that all this contradicts the rigid distinctions most *evangélicos* wish to safeguard. The break between past and present, between new self and old self, or between the community of evangelicals and the others is not clear when boundaries are blurred.

Yet, the very fragility of the boundary is what makes this evangelical movement so attractive. The power to differentiate between different domains has largely been delegated from the hands of the church authorities to the people themselves. Since purification is never achieved once and for all, it requires a continuous evaluation and confirmation of one's place vis-à-vis the world and the other. It has become a reflexive project to learn to distinguish between good and evil in all scapes and try to act appropriately. Watching and listening to seductive worldly media can thus be exciting. It provides the religious audience a chance for self-confirmation that would be impossible without the risk of transgression.

Notes

I wish to thank NWO for making this research possible and the members and affiliates of our research program for their stimulating input. Parts of this chapter appear in my dissertation and in several other articles.

1. Favelas can be translated as urban slums, shantytowns, or squatter settlements depending on the various discourses that are related to these mostly "illegally" occupied territories.
2. *Baile* can be translated as dance. Brazilian *funk* consists of electronic dance music that bears some similarities with hip-hop.
3. The Universal Church of the Kingdom of God.
4. Assemblies of God.
5. According to Karla Poewe Charismatic Christianity is postmodern: "it regards the whole universe and the whole of history [be it personal, natural, or cosmic] as consisting of signs. These signs are available to explore the meaning of life in a concretely meaningful way. In other words, these signs are metonymic. They are the current manifestations of the creative activity of the Creator. *In a high tech world not only the television or computer monitor, but also the human being, are manifestations of signs or manifest themselves through signs*" (Poewe 1989, 7, emphasis mine).
6. Such a fierce opposition against cultural practices that are deemed immoral and un-Christian is in some aspects similar to the cultural opposition of the religious right in the United States (Harding 1993, 2000; Schultze 1991; Frankl 1997; Gormly 2003).
7. *Encostar* literally means "to lean on." *Encostos* could be translated as spiritual entities that "lean" on people.
8. *Ex-feticeiras, ex-prostitutas, ex-ladrões, ex-matadores* can be translated as ex-witches, ex-prostitutes, ex-criminals, and ex-killers.
9. For very insightful readings on the relation between spiritual and spatial "occupation" in relation to the workings of the Holy Spirit in contemporary Latin America see the work of Rafael Sánchez and that of Zé de Abreu in this volume.
10. The importance that Leonildo lays on his "threshold" remind us of the work of van Gennep on the ritual significance of the crossing of *limen* (van Gennep 1960[1909]).
11. The purification rituals of the Igreja Universal underscore their seemingly paradoxical projects in which they heavily oppose Catholic and Afro-Brazilian

religious practices, yet incorporate many of their popular beliefs, practices, tokens, and symbols. For example, it uses the term descarrego, originally used in Afro-Brazilian religious movements, for their deliverance services. See also Mariano (2004).

12. I approach the "separation" of evangelical identities according to Judith Butler's work ([1990] 1999) in which she describes gender identity as the *appearance of substance*, which is the result of the performance of certain stylized acts (173–180). For a discussion on the relation between religion, media, style, and embodiment see also Meyer 2006a.

13. Some of the works on the relation between Christianity and media that have inspired me greatly are McDannell 1995, Meyer 2003a, Morgan 1998, Schofield Clark 2003.

14. This type of religious "occupation" of space links up well with the work of Danièle Hervieu-Léger (2002) who argues for new approaches to religious territoriality in modernity: the territorial modalities of the communalization of religion; the geopolitics of the religious; and religious symbolizations of space.

15. See also the work of Marleen de Witte who argues that becoming a born-again Christian involves two modes of knowledge acquirement: a symbolic mode of gaining representational knowledge and a mimetic mode of gaining embodied knowledge (de Witte 2005, 6).

16. As writers such as Nicholas Garnham (1992, 365) or Roger Silverstone (2002, 763) have so eloquently argued, the intricate confirmation of the "reality" of mass media in everyday life and *vice versa* is clearly not reserved for Brazilian evangelicals.

17. Andrew Tolson describes the media technique of montage in the following manner: "...as a type of syntagmatic structure, montage works through juxtaposition. These juxtapositions may be emphasizing conceptual similarities or contrasts...but the crucial point is that the connections between the signs in a montage structure are implicit, not explicit. A montage therefore involves the reader/viewer in an active process of working out the logic (if any) implicit in the interconnections" (1996, 38).

18. Birgit Meyer (2003a) discusses such a form of purification through montage within the domain of the film.

Chapter 3

"More Sexpression Please!" Screening the Female Voice and Body in the Bangladesh Film Industry

Lotte Hoek

> *[T]he female body is made to speak*
> *in place of the female voice . . .*
>
> —*Kaja Silverman (1988, 70)*

Into the Dubbing Theater

Shima sighed into the microphone, breathing heavily.[1] She looked up attentively at the actress Jenny on screen and paced her sighing to coincide with the moving lips of the silent Jenny. "More sexpression, please!" the assistant director hollered at her through the headphones. Jenny's character was about to embark on an erotic encounter and Shima's voice needed to reflect that. The dumb image of Jenny on screen shuddered with antici-pated pleasure. The reel was rewound, and Shima started all over. As the image of Jenny came closer to that of her sleeping lover, Shima's sighs became more pronounced and the small yelps that escaped from her mouth hovered between arousal and endearment.

In the dubbing studio of the national film industry of Bangladesh, Shima gave voice to the image of Jenny's body presented on screen. In his call for more "sexpression," the assistant director encouraged Shima to sigh and yelp, creating a voice "thick with body" (Silverman 1988, 62). Kaja Silverman has suggested in *The Acoustic Mirror: The Female Voice in Psychoanalysis and Cinema* that in the cinema "the female body is made to speak in place of the female voice..." (1988, 70). In contemporary Bangladeshi cinema this collapse of the female voice into the body is paradoxically accompanied with a radical disjoining of female bodies and voices. The female voices that are heard do not often belong to the female bodies that are seen on screen. Female sound artists are used to supply the voices for actresses. This, however, is not the case for actors, who mostly provide their own voices to their characters. For the generation of voice, gender-differentiated divisions of cinematic labor seem to be a requirement in Bangladesh.

In contemporary Bangladeshi popular cinema, all sound, including all dialogue, is recorded after the first rough cut of the film has been made. Not a single sound is recorded during the shooting of the film; not even a general recording of the dialogues, or guide track, is made. The film is shot completely silently. After editing the rushes to a rough cut, the image reels are transferred to recording studios where all dialogues, Foley sounds and background music are recorded. Bangladeshi filmmakers and sound technicians assume that "filmic sound space, like the image space, will be constructed" (Lastra 2000, 133). How this is constructed then becomes a fertile field for social scientific research. Why are certain voices matched to certain bodies? Why is there a gender-differentiated division of sound labor? How are class and religious community implicated in the production of this cinematic enunciation? Why dub a cinema actress with the voice of a dubbing artist?

While these questions may be partially answered from the particular production context of Bangladeshi mainstream cinema in the early twenty-first century, I would like to argue that the practice of dubbing female voices relates crucially to the ways in which female Muslim artists caught up in processes of technological reproduction manage their public availability. As I have argued elsewhere (Hoek 2008), I regard *porda*, commonly understood as practices of female seclusion or concealment within South Asia (Jeffery 1979; Souza 2004), as a range of practices by which the female body can become present in the public realm. Once caught up in processes of technological reproduction, women reconfigure the ways in which they become available to both the technology that records them and the mass audience to which their image and sounds are then transmitted.

In this chapter, I will discuss the composite of sound and image produced for Bangladeshi screen heroines. First, I will argue that this composite constitutes a form of *porda* as the management of the sensory relationship between the female artists, embedded in a Muslim and familial community (*shomaj*), with their mass audience "out there." I will show how collective moral claims on the female body to conform to a particular aesthetics of propriety and piety translate into strategies of comportment to remain out of touch with the mass audience. Second, I will argue that the very aesthetic boundaries placed on the public availability of women also produce the figure of erotic appeal in Bangladeshi cinema. From the material heterogeneity of cinema, producers cut and paste a fantasmatic and desirable heroine on screen, composed of the attributes of various female artists. In the intersection between technology and the female body, fragmentation thus provides the technological possibilities for the availability of the female to their audience as well as sets its limits. Before elaborating these two points, I will first provide an ethnographic account of Jenny and Shima's work in the Bangladesh film industry.

Shima and Jenny: Voice and Body in the Bangladesh Film Industry

"Action!" cried the film director. His cameraman ran the noisy Arriflex 2C camera. The assistant director beside him strained to make himself audible over the violent purring of the dilapidated old Arriflex. "Eh, shut up! *There's nothing you can do to me.* I'll show you what I can do to you!!" he hollered at the two actors in the middle of the crammed set. The assistant director read the dialogue from the pages of the script on his clipboard and screamed the sentences at the actors in flat tones. The actors Sumit Hassan and Jenny repeated the lines with elaborate facial expressions. Their bodies were being recorded, not their voices. The clamor on set, emanating from the actors' lips, the assistant director's screaming, the churning Arriflex, the chatting lightmen, the heavy generator, the assorted enthused onlookers, and the scribbling anthropologist pressed against the plywood walls of the set, none of it being recorded by any device except the human ear. Only the celluloid in the Arriflex recorded the encounter between the two lovers that was being performed by the Bangladeshi film stars Sumit Hussain and Jenny.

Jenny was a Bangladeshi cinema actress of some renown. Unlike Sumit, who had graced the Dhaka stage and who had only recently experienced a decline in his acting career, forcing him to take on side roles in action flicks, Jenny was at home on the sets of Bangladeshi B-quality movies. She had risen to action movie star status on a wave of cheaply made action movies that controversially incorporated short pornographic sequences.

Jenny's first film *Heat*, released in 2001, has been considered to mark a watershed after which films have come to rely on such sequences to sell. Made when she was about 15 years old, *Heat* had included scenes in which Jenny was shown topless. The censorship controversies that came in the wake of the film's release made Jenny instantly famous. She became the unchallenged queen of the so-called "romantic action" genre, producers eagerly casting her as villain-slaying slum queen or sexually hungry college girl. These cheaply produced action movies combined plots detailing urban decay and corruption with elaborate fighting scenes and impossible romances. Jenny had made her name as an actress of this most prominent genre of romantic action movies.

In terms of cinema content, these transformations can be summed up in the move from melodramatic movies dealing with romantic love to action films focusing on sex (see Raju 2002). In the 1970s, family audiences watched family dramas and love stories acted out by celebrated actors and actresses with a past in stage performance. At the beginning of the twenty-first century, young men watched urban action movies with pornographic subplots acted out by actors and actresses who were regularly sued for their impropriety (Hoek 2006). In 2004, for example, 84 feature films were released in Bangladesh. Of these, nine were romantic movies centering on family relations. One was a parallel film (*Durotto Morshedul Islam*), dealing with alienation in an upper middle class family. The remaining 74 films were action movies, 14 of which featured the heroine Jenny.

Jenny's familiar figure could be discerned on film posters pasted to walls throughout the country. Although she had never won a single film award, didn't feature in any discussions of contemporary cinema nor counted among the great heroines of the day, Jenny's image was omnipresent. When after a day of fieldwork on set, I dropped a role of photographs from the day's shoot at the photo lab, the technician who printed the pictures asked me, "this girl, is she really that beautiful?" The picture that his machine released showed a radiant Jenny in close up, the white line across the bridge of her nose only visible to those who were familiar with the optical illusion of straightness that makeup artists tended to apply. Jenny's skin had been smoothed under a thick layer of yellowish concealer, making her skin a couple of shades lighter. Her dark eyes were accentuated with a thick stroke of eyeliner, its color offset by an arch of bright eye shadow. Her lips were crimson red. Along her collar bone, adorned with costume jewelry, the edge of a bright orange and densely embroidered *sari* was just visible. Shiny black hair extensions cascaded onto the dress. Among them sat a plastic floral arrangement, in colors matching the *sari*. "Yes," I said, "She really is that beautiful."

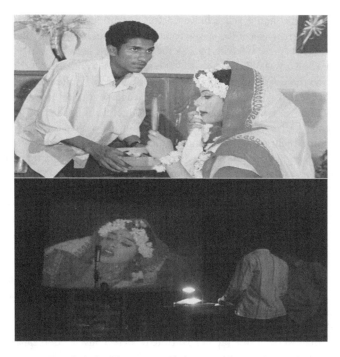

Figure 3.1 Bangladeshi film actress Shahara touches up her makeup on set. Beneath, Shahara's image is shown on the screen behind film director Shahadat Hossain Liton. He waits in the dubbing theater for a dubbing artist to supply a voice to Shahara's image. Photo by Paul James Gomes.

The truth was that if Jenny had walked into the shop at that very moment, the technician would probably not have recognized her. Although she never arrived at the film studios unadorned, on her days off, Jenny would transform. I had met her a couple of times away from the studios and had always had difficulties recognizing her. When out in town, shopping with her husband, a mobile phone salesman, she would wear plain *shalwar kameezes*, made of cheap fabric in earthy colors. Without makeup and carrying her toddler son on her arm, no one would recognize this slightly dowdy middle-class woman as the double of the alluring vixen reaching out from the brightly colored posters all across the city. I had seen her at very busy shopping malls, blending into the crowd. No one paid her any attention. Only her gruff voice was recognizable to me, her thick working-class accent underscoring the *Dhakai* slang that peppered her exuberant speech. Otherwise, she was completely invisible to me.

Jenny's distinctive voice, however, was unfamiliar to the cinema audience. Her gruff voice was never recorded. Although Jenny, in her mid-twenties, was a seasoned actress, she never dubbed her own parts. In the cinema hall it was only the sight of her body that was presented to the audience. To the image of her adorned body, the voice of another woman was added in the dubbing rooms of the Bangladesh Film Development Corporation (FDC).[2] Often, this voice belonged to Shima.

When I first met Shima, she was dubbing Jenny's voice, besides two other prominent parts in the same film, as well as filling in some exclamations and sighs here and there. Echoing the sentiments put forward by many film critics, scholars, and journalists (Khan 2005–2006; Nasreen and Haq 2008), Shima explained to me how the film industry had changed: "New types of people have entered the FDC...because of them, the environment has changed a lot. Nowadays they make commercial films, everything has become commercial." The notion of commerce referred to the practice of including sexually explicit and suggestive footage in action films. The arrival of new people (directors, producers, actors and actresses), from working-class and lower middle-class backgrounds into the industry was often quoted by "old-hands," such as Shima, as the reason for the move toward "obscenity" and "vulgarity." But Shima was aware that this shift was keeping her work schedule filled. The "new" actresses, working in films that were pornographically tinted, were considered incapable of speaking "proper" Bengali, or *shudha bhasha*.

> *Shima*: We have many actresses who don't want to dub, can't dub. Their pronunciation isn't good, the delivery of the dialogues isn't nice. If they had to dub [their own parts], their acting would be spoiled.

By invoking how many actresses would ruin their acting because of their bad pronunciation, Shima confirmed the class difference that spoke through accents of the younger actresses. She felt, with many producers, that this would interfere with a "nice" presentation on screen. What Roland Barthes has called the grain of the voice would disrupt the seamless cinematic fantasy of the woman painted on screen. Barthes defines the grain as "something which is directly the singer's body, brought by one and the same movement to your ear from the depths of the body's cavities, the muscles, the membranes, the cartilage..." (1991[1982], 270), it is "the body in the...voice" (ibid.). Jenny's low-pitched, husky and accented voice would bring her physical self, formed by her social conditions, to the fore and this would "connote masculinity rather than femininity" (Silverman 1988, 61), as Kaja Silverman has suggested about the voices of Mae West, Marlene Dietrich, and Lauren Becall. Instead, middle-class girls such as

Shima, who speak "clear," *spostho*, Bengali were hired to dub over the voices of actresses such as Jenny, thus bringing the aural grain of another body to map onto the image of Jenny's physique.

Shima started her dubbing career as a young girl, dubbing the voices of child actors. With a short break when she first got married and had a child, she had been dubbing ever since. Now in her thirties, she had become an established figure in the film industry and did not lack for work. This didn't translate into fame however. She explained the following to me:

> *Shima*: I like dubbing. No one sees me, no one knows anything about me, won't recognize me. I am dubbing surreptitiously [*bhitor bhitor*], I like that.
>
> *Lotte*: You don't like it if people see you?
>
> *Shima*: My mother doesn't like it. And anyway, in my in-laws' house, the family I got married into, they are a little different. They don't really like me acting. I don't have any desire to act myself and on top of that, they don't like it. And when you dub, no one sees you, recognizes you, or knows you, so there is no problem in doing that.
>
> …
>
> *Lotte*: But you are working here, they don't find it problematic?
>
> *Shima*: No, no, that's no problem. Because no one sees me, knows me. And when a film gets released, then the names of all those who have worked on the film are mentioned in the credits. But the names of the dubbing artists are never mentioned. Because if they gave the names, then the audience would know who dubbed whose voice. The names of dubbing artists are never given.

For Shima, the shift toward "obscene" films has meant she preferred to dub, rather than be publicly associated with the industry, as her own mother had been two decades back. Shima explained that she likes dubbing because it allowed her to be withdrawn, hiding inside the dubbing theater, where the imagined audience couldn't see her. It is the pressure from her family that she quotes as the reason for her preferred invisibility. Interestingly, this invisibility is only required in relation to an imagined "outside" audience. The fact that Shima went to work daily at the FDC, which was popularly imagined to be a space of vice and immorality, seemed not to be an issue with Shima's in-laws.

I would like to suggest that the ways in which Jenny and Shima lend their physical attributes to the film industry and how they negotiated their public availability suggests something about the ways in which community, morality, and mass media come together to produce different sensorial emanations of the female body in Bangladesh. The ethnographic material presented here offers two answers to the question why women's

voices are generally dubbed in the Bangladesh film industry. The first
answer relates to the ability and need for female film personnel to negotiate
their physical availability in relation to the audience "out there." This
answer shows the relationship between moral claims of the community
upon the female body to conform to a particular aesthetics of propriety
and piety, or *porda*, in contemporary Bangladesh. The second answer to
the question of female dubbing relates to the ways in which the aesthetic
expectations of bodily comportment for women also constitute the possibilities for erotic desire. Film producers use these strictures creatively and
to erotic effect in the production of a fantasy female on screen. I will discuss these answers in turn.

Cinema Screens: *Porda* and the Female Film Artist

In this section I would like to argue that the ways in which Shima and
Jenny made different parts of their body available to technologies of
mechanical reproduction relates directly to the nature of that technology
on the one hand, and to the moral community that they are embedded in
on the other. The reason why they effectively made only parts of their
physical selves available to the filmmaking process was because of the
physical proximity it put them into with a mass of unknown others and the
strictures placed on the relationship between women and unfamiliar others within the Muslim majority community of Bangladesh.

To start with the latter, Shima and Jenny's partial availability (aurally
and visually) should be considered a form of *porda* (screen), which is generally understood as practices of female seclusion or veiling. In my opinion
porda is better defined as a set of community based aesthetic demands on
female public presence. Shima's surreptitious dubbing, hiding out in the
"depths" of the dubbing studio, invisible to the audience, not even named
in the credits, as well as Jenny's visual transformations should both be seen
as particular responses to these aesthetic demands. Shima's preference for
dubbing was not only personal. As she suggested herself, it had to do with
her in-laws whom she described as being "a little different." With this
euphemism she gently avoided talking about the religious orthodoxy that
informed the expectations her in-laws had of her. While her own family
had been embedded in the film industry, her in-laws were less comfortable
with their daughter-in-law's labor at the FDC. Shima avoided naming this
sentiment "Islamic," as Islamic orthodoxy was by many considered to be
rather unfashionable in Dhaka, especially among those who thought of

themselves as culturally inclined and modern middle-class Bangladeshis (see Chowdhury 2006). The demands on female bodily comportment, however, were not unique to Shima's in-laws. They are widely shared among Bangladeshi religious communities and have been crucial in the formation of modern Bengali identity in East Bengal (see Rosario 1992).

The imagination of a modern Bengali Muslim identity in East Bengal was crucially centered on gender difference and class. In the colonial context, the rise of a Muslim middle class in early twentieth-century Bengal took shape within a force field of colonial preoccupations with the position of "native" women as well as the interlocking of different communities within the colonial arena (Amin 1995; Sarkar 2001). Rahnuma Ahmed has shown how the debates in early twentieth-century colonial Bengal produced "a consistent modernist position [that] can be identified [among middle-class Bengali Muslims] which was based on the theory of progress as a meta-narrative: simply put, it stood for freedom from ignorance, from religious blindness and superstition, and adherence to what were regarded as 'meaningless' customs. It argued for the rational re-ordering of nation and society, and of the family" (Ahmed 1999, 114). This classic tale of modernity's metanarrative became crucially focused on the position of Muslim women, marked in colonial representations as wretched victims of seclusion and the decadent lifestyles of polygamous Muslim men. "Middle class women writers were near unanimous in singling out *porda* or seclusion as the reason for their 'backwardness,' for their lack of status and power. Seclusion was looked upon as irrational, outmoded and barbaric" (115). In colonial Bengal, the participation of middle-class women in public life became a marker of modernity and civilization.

> This new "publicness" of women was however not without its prescriptions: Among Bengali Muslims the dismantling of seclusion was accompanied by repeated cautioning which urged women not to lose their sense of "shame" or "modesty." Male-female segregation was transformed from a central spatial division of society to an "inner" feeling; a "bodily" feeling which was quintessentially feminine. A redefined sense of shame redrew boundaries around sexual propriety and sexual conduct considered appropriate for a woman belonging to the respectable class. (Ibid., 117)

This translated into a particular comportment and dress in the public life of Bengali Muslim women. Himani Bannerjee has argued for their Hindu counterparts that the Bengali gentle lady, "the moral/aesthetic/erotic configuration of women of propertied classes in Bengal," became projected "as a visual-moral sign" through their "[a]ppearance, in the sense of body-self presentation through clothing" (Bannerjee 1997, 75). Clothing became "a moral signifier of her social role and thus of what [was seen] as the culture

of their *samaj* (society) or class" (73). For Muslim women too, proper comportment was linked to the representation of their society, community, or
class (*shomaj*) in colonial Bengal (Sarkar 2001). The move to public female
propriety among middle-class Muslims also came with a redefinition of
marriage and privacy. "Shongshar means home, husband and children,
these *are a woman's moral possessions, the cornerstone of modern Bengali
Muslim femininity*" (Ahmed 1999, 119, emphasis in original).

In Shima's conceptualization of her own position within the FDC, her
concern about her presence in public, her preference for remaining apparently sheltered within the dubbing studio, and the pressure from her in-
laws, the echoes of the debates set out by Ahmed can be heard. Jenny's
position was constructed in a similar social force field. From a working-
class background, Jenny had used her acting career to acquire a certain
amount of wealth and has climbed the social ladder to her present lower
middle-class position. Married with children, she embodied this middle-
class "modern Bengali Muslim femininity." Her "moral possessions" at
hand, in public with all modesty, her cinematic other was effectively
effaced by her quotidian veneer. She was unrecognizable as the woman
who reached out from the posters on the city walls. Both Shima and Jenny
could extricate themselves from the public by only being available to them
in a very particular form.

Although *porda* has generally been understood to relate to limitations
placed on the visibility of the female body, Jenny's changing visual form
shows that rather than a withdrawing from view, *porda* has to be understood as a becoming visible in a particular form. *Porda*, as a socially, morally and religiously formed aesthetic claim on female comportment, should
be understood as describing the ways in which women's bodies can become
publicly available as "proper" rather than the ways in which they are hidden or withdrawn from view. In my view the veil does not hide or seclude
but makes women visible and available in a particular style. This is not
limited to the visual sense. Sound is similarly bound up with gendered
notions of proper aural presence. Both speech roles as well as vocal pitch
are regimented through gendered notions of permissible public presence.
James Wilce (1998) has elaborately described the possible speech roles
available for women in rural Bangladesh and notes that cultural and social
structures prescribe the ways in which women can become aurally sensible
in public. He suggests that these can be considered a form of "discursive
pardā" (6). In my view, this refers not merely to the limits set for female
speech, but constitutes the forms through which the female voice can
become audible. In the dubbing studio, such discursive *porda* translated
into the use of vocal artists who gave female characters middle-class, or
"clear," accents and made them speak in high pitched voices, marked by

Figure 3.2 Bangladeshi film actress Pinky with a cherished production still of herself acting out a wedding scene. Photo by Paul James Gomes.

repeated sighs, cries, and yelps. Thus an ideal female voice accompanied the visual image. Jenny's guttural and unpolished voice was a sign of improper comportment, the aural equivalent of being without *porda* (*be-porda*), lacking physical propriety.

Once inserted into the technologies of mechanical reproduction, the notion of *porda* becomes reconfigured. If *porda* connotes the management of women's physical availability to unknown others, specifically men, then the mechanical reproduction of the physical attributes of individual women becomes a concern. The forms of bodily comportment displayed by Shima and Jenny have come about at the intersection of cinema technology and the standards of propriety. That the cinema in Bengal, and before it the theater, was considered a space of vice to which women lent their bodies only on threat of being labeled wanton, has been well documented (Bhattacharya 1998; Raju 2000). The stigma attached to cinema actresses relies in part on their explicit flaunting of the norms of female bodily comportment in public, exposed to the gaze of many unknown others. As Walter Benjamin has suggested, the mass audience wants to get hold of things at increasingly closer range (1999[1936], 217). Benjamin sees in the cinema a technology capable of delivering this proximity as in cinema "the distracting element of which is... primarily tactile" (231). The cinema puts the audience literally in touch with what is presented to it on screen. Jenny and Shima were aware that their image was accessible for a rather intimate connection with unknown spectators "out there." This is evinced from their strategies for hiding from this public, which for both involved a withdrawal from that audience. Each had devised a strategy for remaining at a distance from the imagined audience "out there." Although Shima's in-laws would not allow her to act, they had no problem with letting her work within the national studio complex in Dhaka, popularly imagined to be a place of moral depravity. It was from the "public" that Shima needed to remain distant. Similarly, when among her public, in public, Jenny was completely unrecognizable to them, reconfigured by her transformation into a visual-moral sign. Hiding in the studio or dressed unrecognizably, with another's voice to match, Shima and Jenny withdrew from the discomforting visceral confrontation with the mass audience.

Shima and Jenny thus knew what the study of visual culture has of late acknowledged: namely that there is a dense physical relation between an image or object and its beholder (Meyer, this volume). Michael Taussig relies on Benjamin to suggest as much in his *Mimesis and Alterity: A particular History of the Senses* (1993).

> To get hold of something by way of its likeness. Here is what is crucial in the resurgence of the mimetic faculty, namely the two layered notion of mimesis that is involved—a copying or imitation, and a palpable, sensuous, connection between the very body of the perceiver and the perceived.... On this line of reasoning, contact and copy merge to become virtually identical, different moments of the one process of sensing; seeing something and hearing something is to be in contact with that something. (21)

In terms of the cinema, it can be argued that the spectator thus stands in a visceral, "palpable" connection to the figure on screen. Similarly, for Roland Barthes, not only the grain of the voice is visceral, evincing sinew and tissue, but he also remarked on the physical connection between the listener and the person to whom the voice belongs. "I am determined to listen to my relation to the body of someone who is singing or playing and...that relation is an erotic one..." (1991[1982], 276). Both sight and sound therefore establish a visceral relationship or "palpable connection" between the beholder and the object beholden.

Vivian Sobchack (2004) coins the term "cinesthetic subject" to capture the fact that spectators experience cinema through all the senses, not just vision. "[T]he cinesthetic subject both touches and is touched by the screen—able to commute seeing to touching and back again *without a thought* and, through sensual and cross-modal activity, able to experience the movie as both here and there rather than clearly locating the site of cinematic experience as onscreen or offscreen" (71, emphasis in original). Sobchack suggests that a communion takes place between representation on screen and the spectator, which is visceral rather than (merely) visual. This visceral relation is constituted between bodies rather than between gaze and screen. "[T]he cinesthetic subject feels his or her literal body as only one side of *an irreducible and dynamic relational structure of reversibility and reciprocity* that has as its other side the figural objects of bodily provocation on the screen" (ibid., 79, emphasis in original). The body is thus brought into the operation of cinema, where once the disembodied gaze stood unchallenged. When the standards of propriety explicitly encourage the regimentation of the senses to avoid physical impact on an unknown other, the women who lend their bodies to the screen strategize how to withdraw from the sticky claws of an unknown audience.

Jenny and Shima's bodily strategies can be understood as a withdrawal from the visceral relation that is established between the audience and the "bodily provocation on screen" that they combine to become. The palpable relationship between screen and viewers was an immediately tangible reality for women in the film industry, who at every turn were aware of the interlocking of their bodily selves with the audience, which was thought to consist almost exclusively of working-class men. The management of this relationship is also part of *porda*. On the one hand *porda* consists of the visual form that women are encouraged to take up to indicate and signify their social position. This is *porda* as the collective strictures placed on women to be representative of their moral community or *shomaj*. On the other hand, *porda* is also about the management of relations between women and unfamiliar others. While the former element of *porda* relates to the community within which individual women are embedded, the latter form of *porda* relates to the management with what can be called "the public."

It is from this public, in the form of the mass audience of action films, that Jenny and Shima shielded themselves by being available to them only in a particular, abstracted form. By moving between different forms of visibility, Jenny was able to remain "out of touch" with the audience while maintaining herself as a visual-moral sign "in public." If the audience could get hold of her by way of her likeness, disrupting her proper bodily comportment, she salvaged her propriety by producing different visual emanations of herself. Similarly, Shima "hid" from the audience by being surreptitious in the dubbing studio, her voice attached to a different signifier than her own body. Not even her name appeared on screen, her voice properly disembodied, able to attach itself to the image of another woman. And this image would not refer back to the woman who shopped in a shopping mall on busy Friday afternoon, her baby son in her arms. Where sexual propriety and bodily comportment vis-à-vis nonrelated men has become the standard for modern, "civilized" and middle-class female identity, the touch of the mass audience is something that needs to be hidden from.

The first part of the answer to the question why women's voices get dubbed while men's don't in the film industry of Bangladesh thus relates to injunctions that women face in terms of propriety and the community based aesthetic demands on their public availability. Where these standards of bodily comportment meet technologies of mass reproduction, female artists make only certain parts of their body, under particular circumstances, available to a film industry that is generally known as "obscene." However, this is not the entire story. There is second part to the question of the dubbing practices. And this relates to the erotic possibilities of moral norms of bodily comportment and the possibilities offered by a fragmentary technology.

Collating the Fantastic Female

The process of dubbing dialogues for 35mm cinema is a dizzying complex of screens, sounds and images, translations, and repetitions. When Shima dubbed, she stood inside the air-conditioned and soundproof studio where she watched soundless film on a screen before her. Through her headphones, she could hear the assistant director repeat each line of dialogue three or four times. When the image in front of her showed Jenny mouthing the same line, she repeated animatedly what the assistant director had said in a flat voice. Her microphone was connected to the smaller studio, where the assistant director sat behind the sound technicians controlling the mixing panels. Her voice was recorded onto magnetic celluloid. As a dubbing artist, she performed her part in reference to both the image on screen as well as the voice of the assistant director coming to her through the headphones. Watching the screen,

Shima attempted to synch the dialogues with the lip movement of the actors on screen. With inexperienced assistant directors, this task was laborious.

The exclusive use of dubbing, or Automated Dialogue Replacement (ADR), to record dialogues for Bangladeshi popular cinema has technological, financial, and aesthetic reasons. The predominant use within the industry of the noisy Arriflex 2C camera without blimp does not encourage on-set sound recording. The routines of everyday life at the FDC studio floors and the material and human insensitivity to noise reduction are similarly uncongenial to sound recording. For producers and directors, the conventional use of the dubbing theater saves both time and money, as shooting without sound speeds up takes and requires less on-set personnel and equipment. The routinized use of the dubbing studio, with its fixed, FDC employed personnel, similarly encourages dubbing and makes it a relatively efficient alternative to on-set sound recording. The distinctive aural result has become a aesthetic convention within Bangladeshi mainstream cinema, forming an integral part of the aesthetics of popular Bangladeshi cinema. Lack of synch, generic sound, little background sound and a limited numbers of voices within a single film, and across films, mark Bangladeshi popular cinema and make it recognizable. Growing out of the common use of ADR during the 1950s, this representational technology has become normalized and institutionalized at the FDC and has become an aesthetic convention in its own right.

In the case of Bangladeshi popular cinema, then, there exists the peculiar situation that the sound track of the film is in no indexical sense tied to its images. In the complete severance of the image reels from the sound reels, disrupting all connections between the two, the producer of a film can construe female characters on screen who are made up of the elements of two female artists. As predicted by Walter Benjamin, the fragmentary nature of the sound film allows the performance of the actor to be broken up into small pieces and realigned in a contrivance of reality, "the orchid in the land of technology" (1999[1936], 226) where the actor looses against a contrivance of himself that enchants the nonreflecting audience. This contrivance can easily contain the voice of another, as sounds, unlike images, are attributable. As John Belton suggests, "The sound track corresponds not, like the image track, directly to 'objective reality' but rather to a secondary representation of it, that is, to the images that ... guarantee the objectivity of the sounds" (2004, 389). Sounds are attributed to the images and this allows the attachment of Shima's voice to Jenny's image.

In the study of cinema sound, it is more fruitful to think about sound representation than sound reproduction. Rather than thinking about the "mismatch" between Shima's voice and Jenny's body, then, the object of study should be the compound character represented on screen. James Lastra argues that "[c]ontrary to the claims of theory, which locates all the significant ideological work in what the device does to the original event, the primary ideological effect of sound recording might rather be in creating the *effect* that there is a single and fully present 'original' independent of representation" (2000, 134). This effect is the character made up of Shima and Jenny, seemingly referring back to a single, "original," woman.

If sound is then attributed to image and the combination of sound and image produces a secondary representation that seems to refer back to an original, in the case of Bangladeshi filmmaking, this practice does not happen in the same way for men and women. The ways in which Benjamin's orchid is assembled in Bangladeshi popular cinema is differentiated according to gender as the generic use of sound technology is different for male and female actors. There does not seem to be a straightforward financial logic underlying this differentiation. Why would a film producer hire and pay an extra artist like Shima when they could make Jenny dub her own part? Why would a film producer hire Shima at the cost of an extra salary? The answer lies in the symbolic value of the compound figure created by Jenny and Shima.

The way in which sound technology is used in Bangladesh should be understood in a wider social and cultural context as "film sound is in a constant state of interchange with the culture at large" (Altman 1992, 14). After the shooting and the editing of the rushes, the dubbing theater is a crucial location of the construction of the ideological effect of an original preceding its reproduction. This imaginary original is ideological not only in terms of the cinematic technology that hides its own material heterogeneity. The postulated original woman that Jenny and Shima's combined effort refers back to is also ideological in the sense that it urges its viewers to see that representation as a real woman. Mary-Ann Doane notes that the resulting "body constituted by the technology and practices of the cinema is a *phantasmatic* body, which offers a support as well as a point of identification for the subject addressed by the film" (Doane 1980, 33–34, emphasis in original). The resulting body she terms an "enunciation," not just a juxtaposition of elements but a discourse. Kaja Silverman suggests that "what is at stake within cinema's acoustic organization, as within its visual organization, is not the real, but an impression of 'reality'" (1988, 44). Cinema creates this "impression of reality" by participating in the production and maintenance of its culture's "dominant fiction" (ibid.). She relies on Jacques Rancière's idea of a dominant fiction as "the privileged mode of representation by which the image of the social consensus is offered to the members of a social formation and within which they are asked to identify themselves" (Rancière 1977, in Silverman 1988, 44). The woman produced on screen therefore does not refer back to Shima nor to Jenny but rather to a "phantasmatic" woman, an ideological enunciation that fits within social and cultural expectations. In the case of Jenny and Shima, it is the mesmerizing beauty of an orchid made up of the best elements of those available to the producer: Jenny's exposed body and Shima's cultured voice.

The combination of female voices and bodies in Bangladeshi cinema sutures the spectator into the ideological universe of popular cinema. In the case of Shima and Jenny, Shima's voice fits unproblematically onto Jenny's body. Filming Shima's body was an impossibility given the current "obscene" nature of the industry that has driven middle-class actresses to television and away from cinema. But retaining Jenny's own voice would have been jarring, disrupting the cinematic fantasy that is produced in the "fantasmatic body" that is an ideological enunciation. Its "grain" would have revealed both Jenny's working-class origins and her masculine position. To not disrupt the fantasy formation that is purposefully produced on screen by film directors, and implicit in the gendered expectations of female bodily comportment in Bangladesh, Jenny's image had to be safeguarded from her voice. It is Shima's cultured voice that the spectator expects. As Shima said, this fantasy must not be disrupted by displaying her name in the credits. Shima's voice sutures the ideological fantasy, and her voice seems to "fit" onto Jenny's body because "sound 'fidelity' is an *effect* of inscription" (Lastra 2000, 148, emphasis in original). The addition of Shima's voice makes Jenny a legible figure. As Lastra notes, within cinema's aesthetic regimes, it is not about the true origin of a sound, but about "our ability to identify a sound's source" (126). Combined Jenny and Shima produced a well composed and comported female character that fits into the "dominant fiction."

The possibility of separating and rejoining the visual and the aural allows directors to produce an ideological enunciation that they consider most appealing to its imagined audience. This is not a peculiarly Bangladeshi situation. Jeff Smith has discussed the dubbing of the singing voices of Dorothy Dandridge and Harry Belafonte by white opera singers in the case of the movie production of the musical *Carmen Jones* in 1950s America. He highlights how "[t]he technological separation of image and sound . . . enables a white performer to speak through the black body that is seen on screen" (Smith 2003, 39). This was not merely a matter of production logic but the directors:

> were attempting a somewhat peculiar cultural balancing act, one intended to exploit the local "color" and exoticism of rural African-American culture (voodoo, jazz, roadhouses, sexuality) while simultaneously preserving the aesthetic dominance of opera. In this respect *Carmen Jones* could have it

both ways. It could revel in the entertainment values associated with black popular performers like Dandridge, Bailey, and Belafonte while enjoying the cultural pedigree offered both by Bizet and by classically trained opera singers. (38)

Smith thus shows how in the production of Carmen Jones, and specifically in its dubbing choices, the matching of particular bodies and voices followed a cultural logic that valued these bodies and voices in different ways.

I would suggest that the combination made in Carmen Jones, a phantasmatic body produced out of black bodies and Bizet, combined the explicit association of the black body with physicality and immanence (sex and jazz), with a culturally prestigious, and transcendent, form like opera. The phantasmatic body produced is not only one that domesticates the black body for consumption but in its linking to opera makes it desirable. In the combination of Shima and Jenny too, what is most important for producers is not merely that they reproduce the dominant fiction on screen. Rather, it is from the ideal type that they produce an erotic fantasy. From the dominant aesthetic expectations for the public presence of women, as outlined in the previous section, not only the ideal is produced, but also the ideal fantasy object for male heterosexual desire. Jenny and Shima constitute together what cannot be in real life, the fantasy woman of contemporary Bangladeshi cinema: inordinately wealthy, with a middle-class upbringing and education, as well as a tendency toward nudity. It is this fantasy woman that the producers of Bangladeshi cinema tend to recreate again and again, often by means of Jenny and her colleagues. It is exactly the respectable middle-class woman, difficult to approach in real life, which fuels erotic fantasy and desire. It is the notion of perfect composure that suggests the possibility of its very transgression.

The combination of Jenny and Shima produced a cinematic form that film producers consider successful with the imagined working-class audiences in the rural areas. Jenny and Shima were purposefully brought together by film directors. Against the imaginary backdrop of a working-class audience for their films, the scenes sketched in Bangladeshi commercial cinema are marked by images of modern middle-class prosperity. Besides luxurious living rooms, big cars, and television screens, the markers of this wealth and status are imprinted on the women in the films. Wearing georgette *shalwar kameezes* with heavy embroidery, cell phones in hand, these characters are students of city colleges and spend their days drinking Coke in amusement parks. They become the signs of modernity and middle-class prosperity. Aurally, this is represented by Shima's voice. However, this fantasy is not only admirable. A crucial element in the construction of these female characters is their sexual corruption. The mise-en-scène of the city college equates with a breeding ground of lax moral standards. The dense network of associations between the city, modernity, Westernization, immodesty, and lax morals is perpetually invoked in these films. The female characters in the film will eventually be shown to indeed be corrupted thus, often in song sequences and pornographic scenes. The controversies surrounding an actress such as Jenny, bring such associations to an action film from the outset. However, its pleasure can only be fulfilled if Jenny's own voice is edited out. What results from the joining of Jenny's body with Shima's voice plays directly with fantasies about the sexually available and transgressive middle-class woman.

This is the fantasy that film producers attempt to construct in the dubbing studios. They do so by asking the "clear" voiced Shima to give her voice "more sexpression." Her voice marked by a middle-class upbringing and education is underscored by female viscerality through a high pitch and repeated sighs, yelps, cries, and other nondiscursive noises. Kaja Silverman sees in classical Hollywood cinema the tendency to a "subordination of the female voice to the female body" (1988, 68). She shows "the importance of the female mouth...as a generator of gender-differentiated and erotically charged sounds" (67) through which "the female body is made to speak in place of the female voice" (70). What Linda Williams remarks for pornography, that "[a]urally, excess is marked by recourse not to the coded articulations of language but to inarticulate cries of pleasure..." (1991, 4), could be applied to most of Shima's dubbing work. Her cultured voice is shot through with yelps and sighs, her "voice thick with body" (1989, 62), thus constituting with the image of Jenny's body, the phantasmatic female of Bangladeshi popular cinema as an ideologically soothing ideal of real gender difference (the female as flesh) as well as thereby making her available for erotic consumption. Jenny's clearly marked voice would not be able to fulfil this double task. And thus the image of her body is accompanied by the voice of another.

Conclusion

In this chapter I have tried to answer the question why the voices of Bangladeshi cinema actresses are generally dubbed by female dubbing artists. Seeing for men such strictures do not apply, I have suggested that this question went beyond the money-saving logic that dominates film production. Instead, answering this question has provided insight into the ways in which community, morality, and gender combined to make the female body available in processes of technological reproduction.

I have provided two answers to this question. First, the collective claims on the female body to manage its public availability through notions of propriety structure how certain parts of the female body can become available to the filmmaking process. Imagining themselves in an intricate and intimate relationship to the public "out there," female artists in the Bangladesh film industry appear in different forms that are more and less available to this mass audience. Second, I have suggested that film producers make use of the available technology to produce a phantasmatic female on screen that is imagined to appeal to the audience of Bangladeshi action films. This female character can be produced only out of voices and bodies of different women.

I have thus explained the reliance on female dubbing artists in the contemporary Bangladesh film industry as the double effect of moral discourses about female propriety. On the one hand these injunctions make the exposure of certain parts of their bodies possible for cinema artists of different class backgrounds. On the other hand, however, the same injunctions constitute what is considered transgressive and thus titillating, both by film producers and audiences. The peculiarly fragmentary nature of cinema, relying on technologies of fragmentation and recombination, is uniquely positioned to exploit this double-edged sword of notions of morality surrounding women in Bangladesh cinema.

Notes

I am grateful to Birgit Meyer and all other members of our research group, as well as to those who attended the conferences within this project for their comments and suggestions. Eveline Buchheim and Irfan Ahmad have made incisive criticism and offered valuable help. The research on which this chapter is based was made possible by The Netherlands Organisation for Scientific Research (NWO).

1. All names and film titles have been given pseudonyms to protect the identity of those involved in the production of the controversial "romantic action" movies.
2. The FDC is the national film studio that dominates filmmaking in Bangladesh. It is a public enterprise under the Ministry of Information and is governed by state-appointed directors. The compound in the middle of the city contains all equipment for filmmaking, from floors and makeup rooms, to a lab and sound studios. Production companies rent this equipment from the FDC, as well as basic staff, such as light men or sound technicians, who are permanently employed by the FDC. Creative labor, from editors to dubbing artists, work freelance. All popular film production in Bangladesh takes place within the FDC structure.

Part 2

Religion in the Public Realm

Chapter 4

Tamil Mythological Cinema and the Politics of Secular Modernism

Stephen Putnam Hughes

Since the 1990s the relationship among religion, media, and politics in South Asia has attracted considerable attention from a wide range of scholars. This is to a large extent due to convergence of the highly successful Indian television serialization of Hindu epic stories and the rise of Hindu nationalism during the late 1980s and early 1990s. At the time the only TV available in India was offered by the state-run television broadcaster, known as *Doordarshan*. They broadcast 78 weekly episodes of the *Ramayana* between 1987 and 1989 and then followed it up with a serialization of the other great Hindu epic story, *Mahabharatha*, during the early 1990s. The popular success of these Hindu epic TV serials coincided with the first large-scale expansion of television and the watching of their weekly telecasts became something like a collective national ritual, which marked the moment when television first became a mass medium in India. Suddenly, the newly emergent medium of television appeared to be the privileged means for constituting a national Hindu community, which would also be invoked politically as part of the mass mobilization that led to the demolition of the Babri Masjid (mosque), widespread communal violence, and the eventual electoral victories of the Hindu nationalist Bharatiya Janata Party.

Many have argued that this new articulation of media and religion was part of a profound reconfiguration of nation, community, and culture in relation to the politics of Hindu nationalism (Mankekar 1999; Rajagopal 2001). At the time it seemed that television had created a sudden and spectacular resurgence of religion in a public media domain that had previously been monopolized in the service of a state-sponsored secularism. This new public presence was even more striking because the Indian film industry had for the most part stopped making Hindu mythological films and had long presumed that they were no longer a viable commercial investment. But when the surprising success of religious materials on television was followed by electoral success of a Hindu nationalist political party, it seemed to many critics to be a profound failure of Indian liberal democracy to live up to the teleology of secular modernity. Thus the success of Hindu television serials was caught up in a complicated causal chain that seemed to unleash religion into the public sphere and push secularism into crisis.

While this unique historical conjuncture during the late 1980s and 1990s has undoubtedly served to help underscore the importance of the relationships between religion, media, and politics in South Asia, most critics have overlooked the fact that this moment was also implicated within much longer and complex historical relationships. I contend that if we want to appreciate the contemporary reconfigurations between religion, mass media, and politics, we also need to be more attentive to how they have been part of the ongoing, shifting, and mutually constitutive relationships throughout the twentieth century. As part of an ongoing effort to rethink historically the recent scholarship on religion, media, and politics in India, this chapter examines how the emergence of an earlier "new" mass mediation of Hindu epic stories in the 1930s produced its own cultural politics of secular modernism. To do this I am, in part, following up on the work of the anthropologist Milton Singer, who writing about research undertook in the south Indian city of Madras (now known as Chennai) during the 1950s, claimed that the development of the mass media of print, radio, and film had not eliminated the older cultural media of traditional religious themes but transformed and incorporated them. Writing during the heyday of modernization theory, one of Singer's main arguments was that the development of mass media had not led to a secular culture, which was distinct in values and organization from traditional religious culture in south India (Singer 1972, 148–149 and 161). Indeed more recent scholarship has shown that contrary to the expectations of modernization theory, the introduction of new media technologies in India over the course of the twentieth century has very often led to the emergence of new and spectacularly successful forms of religious expression (Babb and Wadley 1995; Pinney 2004; Dwyer 2006). Rather than conforming to an orderly and linear teleology, the religious and secular have been mutually interrelated as part of the emergence of modern mass media in India in ways that have produced a complicated and unstable cultural politics.

In this chapter I consider the beginnings of commercial Tamil cinema in south India during the 1930s as a key site for examining the articulation of media, religion, and politics. Following on from previous work concerning silent film mythologicals during the 1920s (Hughes 2005), this chapter continues the story into the 1930s when the introduction of the new sound film technology posed a new set of problems and possibilities, which shifted the articulation of religion and modern mass politics in colonial south India toward new regional agendas. The transformation of silent cinema through synchronized sound inflected film with a new Tamil linguistic identity and defined a new regionally based cinematic tradition in south India. As with my earlier work I have been primarily working with extra cinematic sources, mainly contemporary journalism and government documents in order to examine how contemporary filmmakers helped to craft Tamil cinema as a religious mode of address and how critics understood the various political stakes of mythological films.

Early Tamil Cinema and
Its Religious Modes of Address

At no other period and in no other language anywhere in India has there ever been such a convergence between religion and film as early Tamil cinema. The degree to which those in Tamil cinema reworked what were already familiar Hindu stories, songs, and characters during the 1930s is unprecedented in the history of cinema in India. The numbers of Tamil films produced reveal a broad outline of this dominance. Over the decade from 1931 through 1940 there were approximately 242 Tamil films produced. Of this total, films based on Hindu stories outnumbered all other kinds of films by roughly three to one. However, during the first five years of this period the dominance of Hindu religious films was almost total. All but a handful of the first 60 Tamil films produced from 1931 through 1935 were based on either Hindu epics or the lives of famous devotees or other Hindu folk stories. From 1936 other kinds of films, not based on traditional Hindu materials, were increasingly introduced. Even so during the second half of this first decade of Tamil cinema between 1936 and 1940 Hindu religious films outnumbered other kinds of films by two to one. Indian mythological silent films had been especially dominant in the earliest years of Indian film production, but the enthusiasm for them faded markedly throughout the silent period so that they only accounted for about 15 percent of overall silent film productions by the late 1920s. So in comparison to the trends in Indian silent film, the first decade of Tamil cinema represented a return to mythological sources. But it was a return that coincided with a period of unprecedented growth and consolidation for the new Tamil film industry. It has become commonplace to dismiss this early period of Tamil cinema as being a primitive and backward early phase in its development. This has prevented scholars from taking the religious content of this early period seriously.[1] However, this kind of dismissal will never help understand how and why religion and early Tamil cinema were so closely related.

Before addressing early Tamil cinema's religious mode of address, this section starts by posing this question: What exactly was Tamil cinema in the 1930s? After almost 80 years and 5000 films, it is all too easy to take the "Tamil-ness" of Tamil cinema for granted. It now seems obvious that by definition the primary qualification for a film to be categorized as being Tamil is the language spoken within the film. But because this primary linguistic identification seems an unambiguous differentiation of the Tamil-ness of a film, no one now bothers to pose the question: What is Tamil about Tamil cinema? However, during the early history of Tamil cinema this "Tamil-ness" was not so easily taken for granted. It was, in fact, a matter of experimentation, confusion, debate, and contestation during the 1930s. Early Tamil film producers had to figure out what a Tamil film was—how it might be different from other kinds of Indian films and how it might address its linguistically bounded audiences in south India. When sound media technology reinvented cinema as "talkies" Tamil cinema producers and directors were confronted new and as yet untested linguistic and geographic parameters for imagining their audiences.

From 1931 sound technology immediately began to reorganize the Indian film industry through a proliferation of regional language–based cinemas.[2] Already in 1931 the new problems and limitations facing Indian market for talkie films were apparent (Anonymous 1931). Before sound the Indian silent film market had been relatively well integrated. Indian silent films had an all-India market and, even though they often reflected regional specificity and used intertitles in regional languages, they routinely circulated to all corners of British India—from Karachi to Rangoon, from Lahore to Madras. However, with the introduction of sound Indian cinema had to address new, more restricted and still uncertain linguistic and cultural constituencies. As Lakshmana Raju (1933), a south Indian editor of the cinema journal, *Screenland*, observed in 1933, the "people in the south do not seem to be interested in talkies in north Indian languages which always fail to draw crowds. The majority of south Indians were not patronizing north Indian talkies because of what he identified as 'the language problem' in Indian cinema." Especially for the purposes of film exhibition and circulation, sound helped create a new set of linguistic restrictions and regional preferences that radically redefined film markets throughout India.

At first there was still a tremendous amount of interaction and exchange across languages and regions within the contexts of production because the early sound film studios in India were concentrated around Calcutta and Bombay. For most of the 1930s the majority of Tamil films were very cosmopolitan affairs made outside of south India in Bombay and Calcutta by producers and directors from all over India who were not necessarily Tamil speakers themselves. In fact the film that is now conventionally recognized as the first Tamil film was not entirely Tamil. The film, *Kalidas*, produced in Bombay by Imperial Films in 1931 was in fact multilingual—the heroine spoke in Tamil and the hero in Telugu. A contemporary newspaper review, which described the film as a well-known mythological story dealing with the legendary life of ancient Sanskrit poet and dramatist, hailed the film as the first talkie film to be screened with Tamil and Telugu songs (*The Hindu*, 30 October 1931). Even in advertisements that accompanied the film's debut in Madras promoted it as "100% Talking, Singing and Dancing" without any primary linguistic identification (*The Hindu*, 31 October 1931). In retrospect the film was dismissed as a unique conglomerate medley of both Tamil and Telugu dialogues (Muthu 1936), but this linguistic confusion speaks to the initial difficulties Indian film producers had in using sound technology to address and identify a new public in south India.

Confronted with the uncertainties of the new sound medium, the selection of religious themes was one of the ways that early Tamil film producers sought to reach out to south Indian audiences. Broadly speaking there were two main and closely related kinds of Tamil Hindu religious film genres during the 1930s, which at the time were referred to as mythological (*purana*) and devotional (*bakthi*) films. These two genres were closely related and are impossible to separate as completely distinct ways of constructing film narratives. My use of these terms is based on how the Tamil film industry and critics in the 1930s explicitly categorized films with Hindu religious origins. In general mythological films were moral tales based upon the Hindu epic story traditions (*puranas*) and legends about exploits of the gods, most often relating to either the *Ramayana* or *Mahabharatha*. These stories have their roots in ancient India and were certainly composed orally through continuous retellings over many generations before they became written texts. The oldest of the *puranas* are in Sanskrit, though there are also numerous relevant Tamil *puranas* as well. They have conventionally been attributed to single authors, but it is important to note that there is no original text, nor any single, correct version of these epics.[3] Several early Tamil films continued this living tradition in

producing their own versions of these epic stories in their entirety
(*Ramayanam*, 1932 and *Srimath Mahabharatham* 1936).

However, it was more common for early Tamil mythological films to
focus on particular episodes from the epics around which to base their

Figure 4.1   Tamil film songbook cover for *Srimath Mahabharatham* (1936).

films—for example, the story of Sita's wedding in *Sita Kalyanam* (1933) or a series of events from Krishna's youth in *Krishnaleela* (1934).

During the first years of Tamil cinema all Hindu religious films were referred to as mythologicals, but from about 1935 the term devotional started to be widely used to designate films, which, instead of having gods as the main characters, followed the biographical life narratives of great saints and devotees (*sants* and *bhaktas*). In south India these saints were singing poets considered to be historical figures associated with specific places, temples, divine miracles, and devotional musical traditions (Zvelebil 1973). For example, the song book for the Tamil film, *Bhaktha Purandardas* (1937), introduced the story synopsis with the claim that "India has for a long time been the abode of many a great devotional bard who illuminated the hearts of people by preaching morals and devotion, through a natural flood of beautiful melodious songs so keenly appealing to everyone from prince to peasant." The commercial intent behind this promotional claim was to link the film to the tradition of devotion that *bhakti* saints had used to overcome differences of caste and class and fashion popular religious movements through the medium of music.

Many of these devotional films followed a similar plot development. They started with the saint's early life, which frequently involved various forms of immorality such as a miserly attachment to wealth, consumption of alcohol, and illicit sexual relationships. Greedy and/or debauched behavior was eventually punished by some hardship or misfortune that would lead to a religious awakening, penance, and supreme devotion resulting in miracles and a manifestation of the divine. The promotional headline synopsis on the film song book for the Tamil film *Baktha Tulasidas* (1937) succinctly summarized this typical plot: "Can you believe this! First he was victim to a Prostitute. He had no other thought than women. But lo! Miraculous is the change now. He has become a great *Baktha*! Now he has no other thought than God! So he stands supreme, devoted by all." These films shared a simple egalitarian message of salvation through self-less acts of devotion, such as worship, singing, praying, and pilgrimage open to all (Vasudevan 2005).

The introduction of sound not only posed a new set of problems and constraints, but also created new opportunities to reinvent cinema according to south Indian performance genres. Even though Indian silent film conventions were an obvious precedent, sound technology allowed early Tamil filmmakers to draw upon and adapt from the already familiar musical stage drama materials. In ways that had been beyond the reach of Indian silent cinema, but similar to the south Indian gramophone companies before them, Tamil cinema immediately tapped into what was then a thriving commercial business in live stage performances with a well-known musical drama repertoire and an established field of star singing perform-ers (Hughes 2007). For the purposes of my argument here, the key feature that the example of south India musical drama contributed to the making of Tamil cinema was the overwhelming importance of the Hindu mytho-logical sources. During the first years of Tamil cinema, the industry competitively reproduced the entire mythological repertoire of the Tamil professional drama companies turning out films that were little more than filmed versions of the mythological musical stage dramas.

The influence of drama on the early development of Tamil cinema was a favorite and oft repeated topic for early film critics. Just months after the first Indian talkie films were released they came in for heavy and repeated criticism on account of their dramatic origins (e.g., Sesha Ayyah 1932). Tamil cinema was widely considered to be "a child of the Tamil stage" so that all the problems, defects, and criticisms of the latter were immediately applicable to the new medium. Tamil theater provided an inescapable model for what Tamil talkies should and should not be. It was also the critical angle that allowed many critics to define both the mistakes and essential qualities of the new medium. Or in the words of one early film critic, "When ones sees a Tamil film, one gets the feeling that one is seeing a play. We see the same obscenities on screen that we see on stage. This is because our film producers and actors have not realized the special nature of cinema" (B.N.R. 1935). However, we must be careful not to confuse this critical discourse relating the Tamil stage and screen for a historiographic first principle that overdetermined a teleological relationship between the stage and cinema. All too often standard accounts of the beginnings of Tamil cinema tend to presume a seamless, linear, and determinant conti-nuity with popular theater as if one monolithic cultural form turned itself into another.

Even though a wealth of drama experience, stories, artists, and songs from the south Indian stage obviously contributed significantly to making of Tamil cinema a religious medium, there was not a simple transfer from one cultural form to another. The highly fluid relationships between the-ater and cinema should be understood as part of more general ongoing processes of remediation within a wider field of cultural performance, media, and politics in south India. Instead of a simple stage to screen equa-tion we must consider a broader historical convergence and collaboration around mythological subjects. During the 1930s an emerging set of over-lapping, mutually constituted and parallel media practices involving drama, gramophone, cinema, and print converged upon mythological materials through ongoing processes of remediation (Hughes 2003). As Singer (1972, 149 and 161) noted in the 1950s the stories from the Hindu *puranas* were endlessly told and retold in a wide range of media ranging from temple sculpture, oral recitation, song, microphones, gramophones, loudspeakers, drama, painting, film, and dance. His informants commonly explained the continuing popularity of these Hindu stories in new media formats as their being "eternally new," which Singer glossed as the modernity of traditional religious practices in south India (152). In this respect the religious origins of Tamil cinema was part of a broader encounter between Hindu religious practices and a set of new media technologies during the twentieth century. The practice of Hinduism in south India easily embraced and adapted the introduction of modern media technology in ways that enlarged their scope by including more people over a larger territory and within a shorter time span.[4] In this context we can see the emergence of sound cinema during the 1930s as another and particularly privileged new form of religious involvement, which produced new ways of participating in Hindu practices in south India.

In choosing Hindu mythological stories early Tamil film producers redeployed the familiar as a way of dealing with the uncertainties of the new mass media. But mythological subjects offered an easy and safe way to ensure a return on the considerable investment of making a film. It is clear from early advertisements that religious themes were considered to be one of Tamil cinema's main attractions. Early Tamil producers explicitly constructed the new cinematic appeal of their sound films in religious terms with film exhibitors also readily following their lead. Take the example of *Prahalada*, a well-known Vaishnava Hindu story produced as a Tamil talkie in 1933. The management at the Crown Theatre in Madras triumphantly announced the film's premiere, "*Puranas* now transferred to the Talkie Screen" and claimed that the film featured "Songs and Tunes that will lift you to emotional heights and fill you with religious fervour" (*The Hindu*, 18 November 1933). After the first successful week they raised the religious stakes further by advertising that "No Hindu should miss this sensational mythological picture that offers you something unique and transcendental" (*The Hindu*, 25 November 1933).

This promotional practice singling out music as a vehicle of transcendence was not about religious conversion or proselytization of nonbelievers, but was making a direct appeal to what south Indian exhibitors considered to be the main selling point of the cinematic experience to Hindu audiences. Like the earliest silent mythological films, early Tamil mythologicals held out the promise of appealing to the widest possible audiences and drawing new comers that might not otherwise have gone to the cinema, such as orthodox Hindus, women, and families (Hughes 2006, 54). But unlike silent cinema, music added another important path toward spiritual realization. There are many different Hindu practices oriented toward turning one's emotions toward god and salvation from

Simultaneous Release on 22-11-35 at the following stations —

MADRAS   SALEM
MADURA   TINNEVELLY
TRICHINOPOLY   TUTICORIN
COIMBATORE   OORGAUM

Figure 4.2 Advertisement for the Tamil mythological film, *Ratnavali* (1935), depicting two Brahmin priests/pundits pointing to their "audience." *The Hindu*, 14 November 1935.

suffering—such as worship of images, reading, and listening to writings on divine glory, singing, yoga, congregational devotion, and chanting the many auspicious names of god (V. Raghavan 1959). Of these practices music in south India has long been a privileged aid to devotion and contemplation of the divine through the subtle powers of sacred vibration (Cousins 1935). The importance of music as a mode of Hindu worship added a powerful new dimension to the ways that Tamil cinema articulated film spectatorship as a form of religious discipline. Yet, Hindu religious themes were simultaneously a commercial practice for promoting cinema attendance, which provided a widely shared rubric for imagining Tamil audiences based on the presumption that the majority of south Indians shared common religious attachments.

Shifting Politics of Mythological Films

Silent mythological films contributed significantly to discursive framework within which Tamil cinema was produced, especially in the manner it had foregrounded a nationalist mytho-politics. However, with the beginnings of Tamil cinema this nationalist framework was rearticulated through the new medium of sound with a new influx of singing drama artistes giving voice to a new musical medium in response to changing political scene in south India.

Throughout the 1920s silent mythological films had provided a position from which to critique Western modernity and uphold the moral and religious superiority of Indian tradition. Mythological films were explicitly and favorably compared to the usual fare of imported cinema, which was portrayed variously as chaotic, immoral, materialistic, and forever tainted by colonialism. In contrast the *puranas* and epics provided a kind of eternal and endless font of feeling, sentiment, and moral guidance, which were upheld as being "pure and free of moral objections from the Indian standpoint" (Aiyar 1928). In this sense mythological films allowed Indians to remediate the cinema as part of a religious discourse on India's spiritual superiority over the West and an affirmation of a distinctive Indian national culture. A particularly good example of this is Dr. Mrs. A. R. Lakshmi Pathi's (1928) written statement submitted to the Indian Cinematograph Committee in 1927. She argued in favor of cinema as a form of Hindu religious expression, which underpinned Indian national identity.

> Films depicting Indian themes, Indian traditions and culture, particularly the religious ones and which are in accordance with the Indian temperament,

extremely appeal to the religious instinct of the average cinemagoer in India. On important religious festival occasions when films of the kind of *Krishna Janam*, *Krishna Lila* and *Keechaka Vadha*, people throng to these shows because they feel they are stories of Indian origin with which they are very familiar and which they appreciate better. Such films with a highly moral purpose behind them cannot but help raising the moral standard of the public.

Lakshmi Pathi concisely made the case for mythological films as appealing to what she assumed were the essentially religious instincts of average Indian cinema audiences. On this account film-going was equated with public Hindu devotion, festivity, and higher moral purpose. This quote also attests to how Hindu devotional practices offered a powerful model for understanding the early success of mythological films. Mythological themes infused cinema with religion as a form of worship, as a sensuous and emotional engagement with the divine, and as a form of moral uplift and improvement. This formulation effortlessly embedded modern cinema technology within the terms and priorities of traditional Hindu practice, which in turn were equated with and enabled a certain kind of nationalist politics.[5]

The beginnings of talkie cinema precisely coincided with a period of intense nationalist political agitation in south India sparked off by events in other parts of India. Under Gandhi's leadership the Indian National Congress launched a movement of Civil Disobedience (*satyagraha*) in 1930 as a means of defying colonial civil authority and forcing Britain to grant complete independence (Brown 1977). In sympathy with Gandhi's well-publicized protest march in Gujarat, western India, against the salt tax, the Tamil Congress organized a wave of deliberately provocative protests throughout south India in order to invite a predictable heavy-handed response from local authorities and thereby gain support for their cause. Following on from the initial salt march, local activists aggressively picketed liquor shops and foreign cloth shops purposely courting arrest. In addition to Congress organizers and volunteers, large numbers of unemployed port laborers, textile mill workers, and weavers, laid off by Depression era cuts, joined in numerous Civil Disobedience agitations, which resulted in many thousands being arrested and almost 3,000 convictions over several years (Sarkar 1983). By the time Congress called off the protests in 1934, the British colonial government had already effectively and often brutally crushed the movement. But in south India, the nationalists had emerged stronger than ever having mobilized new recruits, organized local committees, and gained widespread support from new sympathizers.[6]

All the political energy of the Civil Disobedience movement poured into the Tamil drama with song writers taking the lead in composing new material that was not only performed on stage, but on political plat-forms and during picketing as well as being printed in songs books, leaf-lets, and even recorded on gramophone plates (Hughes 2003). Thus, while the nationalist mytho-politics of silent mythological films clearly informed early sound film productions, the strong political engagement of Tamil musical drama was the greater influence on how Tamil cinema incorporated political content. Theodore Baskaran (1981) has docu-mented how almost all of the important political activist song writers and actor/singers and from the Tamil stage brought their nationalist agenda as they moved into Tamil cinema. With the emergence of talkie films, songs became a privileged medium of conveying covert nationalist political messages, which might not otherwise get past the regional film censor board. The musical format of Tamil cinema provided the frame-work for embedding nationalist political songs within mythological nar-ratives. They worked like detachable set pieces that could be inserted in any kind of mythological film regardless of the story. For example, in the first Tamil film, *Kalidas*, the well-known stage artist T. P. Rajalakshmi sang two nationalist songs not directly related to the story, urging the need for unity among Indians and the other praising the *charka* (spin-ning wheel), a nationalist symbol popularized by Gandhi.[7] Both songs had been originally written for the stage by the nationalist song-writer/poet Madurai Baskara Das and were already widely circulated and pop-ular (Baskaran 1996).

The nationalist themes interwoven into these songs were also always motivated by more than politics. There was also a financial calculation involved. For example, an anonymous (1931) author writing in a Madras newspaper article about how best to market Indian talkie films during the first year their production suggested that the cinema should follow the example of the stage in exploiting nationalist themes.

> He [the Indian film producer] should take a cue from the present condi-tions of the stage such as it is. Whenever there is a vernacular play put on the boards with a national theme, interspersed with national songs and dia-logues, the theatre is fully packed. So if any film story whether silent or sound is screened with a "national" setting without giving away the show by high sounding titles, with popular songs there is no reason why such a film may not bring a good return for the producer.

The widespread involvement and publicity surrounding Civil Disobedience movement had mobilized an extremely popular constituency for national-ist themed entertainment, which both Tamil drama and cinema were able to call upon.

Devotional Films and
the Emergence of Regional Politics

Over the course of the 1930s the religious themes in Tamil cinema shifted
from a predominance of mythological stories toward devotional narratives
about poet saints. This coincided with a general move in Tamil films
toward a new political engagement with regional, linguistic, and cultural
issues that had not featured in the nationalist mytho-politics of Indian
silent cinema or early Tamil cinema. Over the course of the 1930s the
representational burden of Tamil religious films generally shifted away
from an anticolonial nationalist critique toward the construction of a
regional Tamil identity politics.

The rising importance of Tamil devotional films over the decade
reflected a series of shifts as film production increased and moved south.
For the purposes of this chapter we can separate the first decade of Tamil
cinema into two distinct phases before and after 1935. This was not an
absolute break, but the year represented a kind of tipping point for Tamil
cinema where it reached a critical mass. Up to that point Tamil talkie production was insufficient to provide a steady supply of films and their exhibition at most cinema halls in south India was only sporadic until 1935.
This was the year when contemporary sources began talking about "the
craze for vernacular talkies."[8] It was widely recognized that Indian cinema
was for the first time coming into its own: "The first phase of the great
Indian talkie boom is now in. Hindi, Urdu, Tamil, and Telugu talking
pictures are now sweeping the country like an avalanche. We are now
reaching the adolescent stage."[9] Between 1934 and 1935 Tamil cinema
production jumped from 14 to 34 films a year marking the first regular
supply of Tamil films for exhibitors. From that point through the rest of
the decade the number of Tamil films produced remained more or less
constant until the Second World War reaching a peak of 39 films in 1940.
The increases in the Tamil film production totals were matched by greater
numbers of devotional films, which reached a peak in 1939. With devotionals accounting for about 14 out of the annual total of 30 films, 1939
was dubbed the year of the *bhaktas* in Tamil cinema in an editorial review
in one of the leading south Indian film journals.[10]

Another important change that coincided with the rise of devotionals during the 1930s was the gradual shift of Tamil film production
from the studios in Calcutta and Bombay to south India. Early Tamil
film producers had been forced to travel long distances with a large
troupe of actors, artists and musicians and hire a studio and accommo-
dation for the duration of the shoot. One Tamil film producer explained

these difficulties: "The cost of traveling, the prolonged enforced stay in distant places, vastly different in mode and clime, the absence of familiar settings for South Indian themes and tunes, the step-motherly treatment accorded in the studio, have been serious factors against the successful growth of the Talking films."[11] The fact that during the early years all Tamil films were produced outside of south India had been a matter of considerable concern and complaint. Throughout the 1930s it was common for critics to accuse the Indian film industry of exploiting the south Indian film market for the sole purpose of commercial gain:

> The lack of a producing unit in Madras afforded enterprising producers of Bengal and Bombay fresh field for exploitation with some tens of thousands of Rupees, these Bengal and Bombay producers issued pictures in South Indian vernacular and their returns were always in lakhs [100,000s]. (Anonymous 1933)

The problem main was not just that north Indian film producers were exploiting a wide open market for talkies in the south, but that they were doing so without the same care about the quality of Tamil and Telugu talkies as they did for Hindi or Bengali films. A south Indian cinema journal complained that "some of the leading Bombay and Calcutta producers, in their attempt to produce talkies for South Indian market, committed the greatest blunders, resulting in a product inferior to that of a decade old." He felt, as did many other south Indians that the north Indian film producers lacked the interest and responsibility necessary to produce films, which were best suited for south Indian conditions (Raju 1933). These complaints against the north Indian production of south Indian films represented the beginnings of a significant regionalist reorientation from the 1920s nationalist concern over the dominance of imported foreign films (Arora 1995).

These concerns over where, who, and how Tamil films were being produced continued through the 1930s, but the situation began to change from 1934 when the first south Indian film sound film studio, Srinivas Cinetone, was established in Madras with the production of the Tamil mythological film, *Srinivasa Kalyanam* (1934). This first effort was then quickly followed by the opening of Vel Picture Studios, National Movietone Studios, and Meenakshi Cinetone in 1935 and then Madras United Artists in 1936. Outside of Madras several other important studios also opened in provincial centers during 1935 with Modern Theatres in Salem and Central Studios in Coimbatore. Within a remarkably short period of several years new film studios were for the first time offering an alternative to production facilities elsewhere. These early south Indian

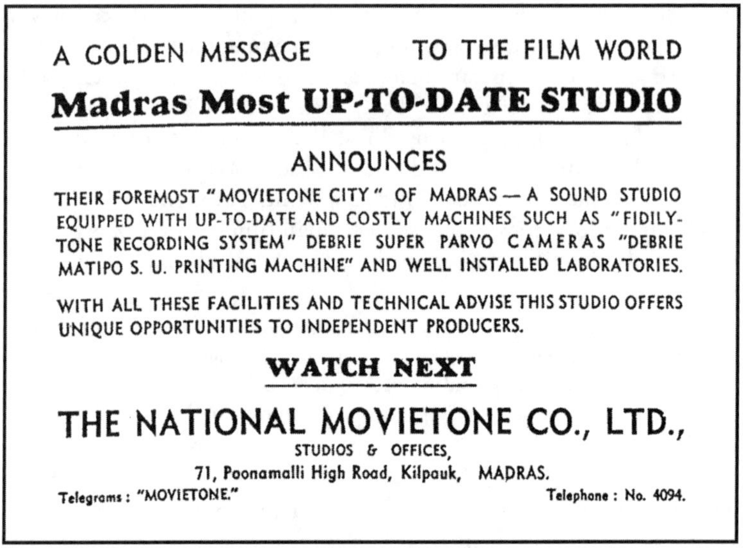

A GOLDEN MESSAGE   TO THE FILM WORLD

Madras Most UP-TO-DATE STUDIO

ANNOUNCES

THEIR FOREMOST "MOVIETONE CITY" OF MADRAS — A SOUND STUDIO
EQUIPPED WITH UP-TO-DATE AND COSTLY MACHINES SUCH AS "FIDILY-
TONE RECORDING SYSTEM" DEBRIE SUPER PARVO C A M E R A S "DEBRIE
MATIPO S. U. PRINTING MACHINE" AND WELL INSTALLED LABORATORIES.

WITH ALL THESE FACILITIES AND TECHNICAL ADVISE THIS STUDIO OFFERS
UNIQUE OPPORTUNITIES TO INDEPENDENT PRODUCERS.

WATCH NEXT

THE NATIONAL MOVIETONE CO., LTD.,

STUDIOS & OFFICES,
71, Poonamalli High Road, Kilpauk, MADRAS.

Telegrams: "MOVIETONE."   Telephone : No. 4094.

Figure 4.3   *The Hindu*, 5 April 1935.

studios were so successful that by 1940 all but a small number of Tamil
films were being made in south India. For south Indian film critics this
was a matter of regional pride, but for producers this shift meant that it
was easier for them to address their audiences with familiar settings and
local flavor. Or as one Tamil film producer explained, "A natural and correct background can be given to the films, thus ensuring the maximum
amount of direct appeal to the illiterate."[12]

As film production increased and became more rooted in south India,
there were increasing efforts to make Tamil films more Tamil, that is, to
address the linguistic and cultural specificity of a uniquely Tamil audience. This was the beginnings of a regional cultural politics that began to
complicate the nationalist mytho-politics of Tamil cinema during the
period of Civil Disobedience. On one hand the life stories of religious
heroes carried didactic messages of spiritual equality and social justice for
all classes and castes, which could easily be mapped out on to nationalist
political and social reform projects. Clear parallels were made between
Gandhi's campaign against untouchability and harijan uplift and the
medieval wandering poet saints who used the transformational aspirations
of devotion to preach against caste hierarchy and for the emancipation of
social oppression (Kaul 1998; Kapur 2000).

Figure 4.4   *The Hindu*, 2 October 1935.

For example, the popular story of Nandanar, the "Untouchable Saint" (Dalit) was advertised as "a story of self-help and self-realisation which is not without topical value at the present day; how a man, low born and uncultured can rise superior to his surrounding influences through sheer force of his unconquerable faith is the moral of the story."[13] While devotional films could be plotted as part of a nationalist mainstream, they were also read as a regionalist celebration of Tamil language and culture.

In this regard the increasing prominence of devotional films in the latter half of the 1930s offered important referents for articulating claims about Tamil identity. Devotional films were used to construct a shared imagination in a Tamil religious past. For example, one of the first hugely successful Tamil devotional films was *Pattinathar* (Lotus Pictures 1935), which was advertised as "The soul stirring life of the miracle working saint of the 10th century known to every Tamilian. It depicts the riches and life of Tamil Nad a thousand years ago." The producers hoped to evoke a glorious Tamil past that had survived intact as a continuous living tradition over one thousand years. And in order to distinguish this film from other mythological subjects, they prominently advertised it as being based on the "True historical background designed by University Professors of Research" (*The Hindu*, 19 April 1935).

Figure 4.5   *The Hindu*, 17 September 1935.

The promotional discourse clearly aligned the film with the scholarly rediscovery of Tamil literary classics during late nineteenth century and early twentieth century, which has been called the Tamil Renaissance and considered a key part of the emergence of Dravidian nationalism in the twentieth century (Nambi Arooran 1980; Ryerson 1988). The fact that the Tamil *bhakti* singing poets were an important part of a Tamil literary tradition that began in the sixth century was used to support the idea that Tamil-speaking people had a distinct national identity (Irshick 1986).

Tamil cinema was able to materialize and give voice to this imagined heritage in ways that allowed audiences to constitute themselves as part of a specifically Tamil religious past. Critics praised devotional films as apt vehicles for highlighting the greatness of Tamil: "As a Tamilian I would request these people to bear in mind that we should immortalize our glorious and enviable heritage and the talkie screen is a good medium for doing this. The soul-stirring ditties of our ancient composers and poets introduced in appropriate occasions would enhance the effect of the situations." The author singled out another and even more successful film version of *Pattinathar* (Vel Pictures 1936) as being exemplary in this regard: "Its sole cause for success is the songs. Those songs are pure Tamil tunes, which every Tamilian is conversant with. These songs make their direct appeal to our minds and we long to hear the sweet melodies again and again" (Thangam 1937).

The Secular Critique

As Tamil film producers imaginatively reached out to a new linguistically and culturally defined religious public with mythological and devotional themes, these very films also became a conspicuous site for the articulation of a strident secular modernist politics. The nationalist mytho-politics and the regionalist celebration of Tamil religious heroes were both challenged and refigured as part of new discourses on secular modernism that were emerging over the 1930s.

Of course, not all secularisms are the same, but are always uniquely embedded within historically contingent and shifting practices (Asad 2003; see also Larkin in this volume). This discourse of secular modernism that I am referring to here needs to be distinguished from what later emerges after Independence as a political discourse of the Indian state and its characteristic mode of governmentality. Instead, the discourse of secular modernism, which took Tamil mythological films of the 1930s as their key negative referent, was an elite discourse of cultural criticism and social reform. In contrast to the late 1980s when televised mythological serials seemed to raise new questions about the place of religion within a modern secular national politics, the key issue raised during the 1930s in south India was how to reconcile modern secular within an overwhelmingly religious cinema. Secularism in this case was in a different register and not yet explicitly linked with any state-sponsored project of liberal democracy, but was more a matter of cinematic representation. Cultural elites used a secular modernist discourse as a mode of film criticism to demarcate high from mass culture.

The critique of religious films was often presented as a matter of urgent reform. There were repeated demands that instead of "fossilized *puranic* themes," films should reflect contemporary Indian reality and social problems more "suited to modern life and conditions" (Chettiar 1936). For example, A. Ranganathan (1936) wrote: "The first reform that should be made is to put a full-stop to the idea of *ad nauseam* Puranic plays. Films with social and historical background must come in" (*The Hindu*, 30 October 1936). This was discursive framework within which the new Tamil social film genre was promoted as the modern answer to the mythological. Starting in 1935 the first few Tamil films not based on mythological sources were released. There were a number of films that simultaneously and competitively claimed to be "the first social Tamil Talkie" around August 1935. The producers of *Dharma Pathni* claimed the title "The first social hit of the Tamil Talkies world" with a story of a London returned gentleman who married a high class, educated girl, but then drove her out into destitution only to be saved by her in the end when he falls victim to his modern vices (*The Hindu*, 9 August 1935). But when an earlier released film, *Dumbachari*—about a wealthy young man who was brought to ruin by frequenting the brothels of Madras—returned to Madras for a second run it was also advertised as the first social film. These films were followed in the same year by *Menaka*, which was based upon a popular novel of Vaduvoor K. Doraiswamy Iyengar, which had previously been adapted for the stage. Advertised as being "modern and realistic", the story was about a young wife who was victimized by her husband's two widowed sisters, who abducted her and tried to sell her to a pimp. This exposed social evils and domestic problems in a Brahmin family and notably contained nationalist songs, which made direct political reference to the social reform agenda of the India National Congress. From this point onward throughout the rest of the 1930s the relatively small but stable number of Tamil social films produced every year offered the first alternative to religious subjects.

A film was deemed "social" in so far as they featured contemporary stories, settings, and costumes. Usually adapted from popular novels and dramas, the stories in social films usually revolved around crime, romance, comedy, satire, and sometimes stunts. They tended to focus on lifestyles of wealth and luxury enjoyed by urban social elite, either as a parody of Indians who had adopted Western habits, clothes, and attitudes or as advocating social reform of contemporary problems such as child marriage, dowry, alcohol, Hindu-Muslim unity, caste inequality, or the treatment of widows. Though the Indian cinema industry produced silent social films as early as 1921 and social dramas had been extremely popular on the Tamil stage from the mid-1920s, this genre was slower to develop than the other film genres in the south (Hughes 2006). The film censor boards of British India were more aggressive, especially during the period of Civil Disobedience, in policing the political implications of social films.

As a mode of a social critique, secular modernist film criticism in the 1930s and early 1940s was based upon a developmental discourse of progress that was supposed to leave religion to the past. In so far as the secular modernist critique argued that mythological films were old-fashioned, traditional, and out of date, it constructed a teleology that relegated religion to an earlier stage in history. Especially for a younger generation of educated, self-consciously modern oriented south Indians the popularity of mythological films was something of an embarrassment. These films were dismissed as a reflection of an essentially spiritual mind of Indians and attributed to the general ignorance, lack of education, illiteracy, poverty, and superstition of the Indian masses. Much of the criticism of mythologicals crystallized around the notion that they were inconsistent with and could not be accommodated within a progressive modern cultural politics. For example, one of the most persistent criticisms of mythologicals throughout the period was that they were an anachronistic confusion of modern elements inappropriately mixed with *puranic* stories (Samy 1935). For these critics, mythologicals could only signify India's past, needed to be more carefully delineated from the present and should strive toward more "realistic" representation of this mythic history. This was a variant that would widely be recognized as a secular vision of modernity, but in this case one that measured its own progress by its distance from mythological and devotional films.

The Tamil social film genre carried the representational burden of secular modernism, yet did not always live up to the high minded social reform agenda that film critics had been advocating:

> The social aspect of a story does not merely consist in the heroine smoking a cigarette, drinking a glass of wine or playing tennis. Nor can you call a story social simply because there is a race course or an aeroplane scene. Social stories must be reformatory in character. Unfortunately [for] some social stories of our province too much emphasis is laid on the darker side of the social customs. Defects in our present day social order should be

gently and lightly touched in a manner that will set them off against the dangers of ultramodern notions but never over-emphasised so as to lose their real purpose. (Ranganathan 1936)

This reflects a widespread anxiety and mistrust that too much modernity would lead to a dystopic loss of moral direction. In fact, the argument above was less an endorsement of modernity than a prescriptive call for social films to serve as a moral critique of modernity. In this regard most social films carried remarkably similar message as the devotional films of the same period. Both genres served as cautionary tales about the dangers of immoral lifestyles and how humility can lead to salvation and set one on the path of advancement and social justice.

In many ways the mythological and the secular were linked in a kind of mutual dependency, each enabling, informing, constraining, and justifying the other. In the 1930s debates as to the comparative merits of the various Tamil film genres the sacred/secular distinction was still not fixed, everything was in play in an unstable and experimental mix. Just as the stories of the medieval poet saints were justified in terms of making modern political arguments about social justice and reform, some defended the religious proclivities of early Tamil cinema against their critics in remarkably secular terms. When the mythological film, *Rukmani Kalyanam*, was released at Broadway Talkies in Madras, a prominent Indian judge on the Madras High Court, V. V. Srinivasa Aiyangar spoke during the interval. He alluded to the growing secular criticism of mythological films and claimed that he was not one of those who were against representation of *puranic* episodes on the screen. But his defense of the genre amounted to a secular reading of the film in that he denied that there was anything really *puranic* about it. He explained that the film should be regarded as a modern story of a girl falling in love, resolving to marry the man of her choice and then how she goes about successfully doing so (*The Hindu*, 19 October 1936). Tamil cinema of the 1930s was open to secular readings of religious stories and religious understandings of modern situations in ways that suggest that the mythological and the modern, the religious and the secular were mutually constitutive categories. Social films did not simply replace the religious themes in Tamil cinema as might have been assumed as an inevitable outcome of the secular modernity. But instead they helped to produce a new cultural politics of religious cinema, which articulated them anew as a key part of the contemporary nationalist and Dravidian movements.

By way of conclusion, I will return to where I began by asking what this brief tour through 1930s Tamil cinema tells us about the contemporary relationships among media, religion, and politics in India. In focusing on how the introduction of the "new" medium of sound cinema changed the complex and productive relationships between film, religion, and politics in the 1930s, I want to suggest that the emergence of another "new" mass medium in the 1980s and 1990s was not as new as it seemed to commentators at the time. The articulation of media and religion in contemporary India are part of a long history of political representation and contestation. If we understand and study media as "unique and complicated historical subjects" (Gitelman 2006, 7), we will be in a much better position to critically evaluate what is new about "new" media configurations of religion and politics. To paraphrase Bolter and Grusin (1999, 15), what is new about new media are the specific ways people refashion older media as well as the ways people refashion older media to answer the challenges of new media. The new relationships among religion and media must be read against the grain of the past.

Notes

1. Recently the work of Philip Lutgendorf (2003) and Rachel Dwyer (2006) are important exceptions that have done much to change this perception and open Indian film scholarship in important directions.
2. This proliferation of numerous linguistically specific cinemas within the category of Indian cinema is unique among world cinemas. As a "national cinema" there is no other that can match the range and volume of linguistic and regional diversity, which constitutes Indian cinema.
3. Paula Richman (1991) convincingly makes the case for the multiplicity of these epic traditions. Also see Rachel Dwyer (2006, 18) for a useful discussion of how these mythological materials relate to the history of cinema in India.
4. This was not limited to just media technology; it included transportation and electricity. The development of transportation—automobiles, buses, trains, airplanes—all contributed to major changes for pilgrimage. And electric lighting was immediately extensively used within temples and at religious festivals to visually enhance the ritual practices of worship. See Milton Singer (1972, 140) and Babb and Wadley (1995).
5. For a more extensive discussion of this position see Hughes (2005).
6. For a detailed account of this period see Arnold (1977).
7. The translated songs title/first lines are roughly as follows: "Why are we Indians fighting among ourselves?" and "The charka is a weapon in Gandhi's hand."
8. This is from a film review of *Dhruva* at Kinema Central in *The Hindu*, 24 May 1935.
9. In the weekly film column, "Stardust" in *Merry Magazine*, 27 April 1935, 16.

10. *Talk-a-Tone* 3, no. 12, January, 1940, 17.
11. This quote is from the business prospectus for the launch of Modern Theatres film studio as a joint stock company as advertised in *The Hindu*, 9 March 1935.
12. Ibid.
13. From an advertisement for the record set released by the south Indian music recording company, Saraswathi Stores, as a tie-in with two Tamil film versions of the same story, which appeared in 1933 and 1935. *The Hindu*, 1 October 1934, 13.

Chapter 5

Islamic Renewal, Radio, and the Surface of Things

Brian Larkin

In 1992 when the Nigerian cleric Sheikh Abubakar Gumi died he left behind him the Salafi inspired group, *Izala*,[1] one of the most dynamic and influential religious movements in West Africa. Scholarly analyses of Gumi, Izala's intellectual leader, have portrayed him as a quintessentially modern religious figure.[2] Colonially educated, cosmopolitan, the first major Muslim cleric to use new media technologies, Gumi redefined religious practice in Nigeria, not just for his own adherents but for his Sufi and Christian opponents. The modernity of religious renewal movements often refers to a sense of rupture from previous traditions a rupture that is asserted by those movements to define their difference and distinction. In this chapter I wish to inquire into what exactly it is that is modern about Gumi and why this is claimed by both his adherents and detractors. How might we understand the causes of this phenomenon and the forces that drive it? What does this tell us about religious movements more generally?

There are theoretical lineages one could draw on to answer this question. One derives from media theory and explores how it is that the materiality of technology organizes human experience. This point of view is less interested in how humans use media to achieve certain ends, and more in how communication machines create the technological a priori for human experience and sociality. "[I]t is the medium that shapes and controls the scale and form of human association and action," Marshall McLuhan argued (1994[1964], 20), standing in a line of technicist thinking that moves from Martin Heidegger (1982) and Lewis Mumford (1963) through

Norbert Weiner (1961) and cybernetic theory through to Friedrich Kittler (1990). Following this logic, as media systems change so too does the sensorial, psychological, and social fabric of individual and society. When public recitation became privatized reading, for instance, the change in the medium of religious communication entailed changes in sociability, in ideas of presence and reference, in experiences of exteriority and interiority. Kittler refers to this as a shift from the signifier to the signified, the "medium of print [making] it possible to bypass signs for sense" (1990, 230) helping language "become precise and thoroughly transparent" (Funkenstein 1989, 10). When the Bible, Qur'an, or Torah are electrified, no longer trapped inside the borders of a book but exploded over space by loudspeakers, radio transmitters, and televisions, the ways in which religious communities gather, how they experience their own collectivity and their engagement with the divine changes too. In this epistemic history of media, society, community, or religion are second order realities that emerge out of the technics of media.[3] Media are not "used" by religion; they are the conditions of existence that make the expression of religion possible. Heidegger (1982) referred to this as technology calling forth the human. To be transmitted to subjects, religious ideas and philosophies must be encoded in material signs and when they do so they become hostage to materiality of those signs. For, as Kittler has it, "once the soul speaks it is no longer the soul that speaks" (1990, 238) as its voice is suffused with the noise of its transmission.

Following this argument, to understand the modernity of a figure like Gumi we should look not at his theological beliefs, but at the shift in communications systems that took place during his life—a shift of which he is less the author than the expression. It means to understand the vernacular press, the rise of radio networks, and the building of television systems as much as his biography and theology. Gumi wrote a regular religious column for the secular Hausa language paper *Gasikya Ta Fi Kwabo*. He was most famously identified (by both supporters and detractors) with his radio and television broadcasts and the cassette reproductions of them that form a unique part of his and Izala's organizational structure. But as he used these media he subjected his teachings to their centrifugal dispersal, the refiguring of their content as they are swept up in the logic of communications media with their particular conditions of storage, transmission, and retrieval. The possibility of his critique of Sufi Islam, of his rejection of the magical power of Sufi saints, of their claim to a mastery of the hidden meanings underlying everyday life, is tied to these media. Gumi and Izala advocated for a religion based on surfaces, not depths, where each Muslim had access to religious knowledge through reading and comprehension of the holy texts of Islam, the Qur'an, and Hadith rather than through access to a sheikh and his *baraka* (charisma). And the extension of those texts over space and time, drawing followers into a religious community based around access to mediated texts as well as communal practice is part of what defines his movement as different, and modern.

A contrasting way of analyzing the distinction of religious movements is also concerned with the operation of media but places their value differently. Michael Warner (2002) and Charles Taylor (2007) have argued that the distinction of contemporary religious movements is that they are organized using forms and epistemological structures taken from the secular public sphere. Media are central to this process, but Warner emphasizes the articulation of technology with the wider political ideologies and cultural structures of a public rather than the autonomy of technology itself. To address or inhabit a public, Warner argues, is to be constituted in a certain sort of way, to imagine a particular type of collectivity. Unlike say, clan membership, or inherited religious identities (such as Judaism) a public is expansive, potentially open to anyone, whose ability to join depends on individual choice. This voluntaristic association is a powerful part of contemporary religious movements (certainly different from the closed initiation of Sufi orders) and reveals how far they have moved away from exclusivist ideas of religious belonging. Similarly, these movements depend upon the distanced, reflexive understanding of religion as a system, with each religious tradition seen as one of a range of similar such traditions. Religion is not automatically internalized as an unquestioned truth but is reflexively questioned, as the availability of differing possibilities of belief and practice places a burden on the adherent to choose her way from a range of other competing possibilities. This is where Habermas's (1989) model of a public as a realm of open debate and choice that fragments existing sacral authority comes into play. Secularism provides what Taylor (2007) calls the "background" or "context of understanding" that reorders the place of religion and restructures the way individuals imagine religious belonging. Conceived of in this sense, the modernity of Gumi and Izala can be found again, not in terms of religious beliefs per se, but in the form of organization in which those beliefs are imagined. It is a form whose organizational and epistemological structure is shaped by secularism as much by religion itself.

Warner argues that because a public is constituted as a relation between strangers the circulation of cultural forms—from pamphlets and cassettes to radio shows and television programs—is central to providing a unified cultural experience. Media are as central to this analysis as they are for more technicist scholars, but their role is conceived differently. Like McLuhan (1994[1964]) and Benedict Anderson (1991) who see the standardization of print and particularly the circulation of newspapers as a key element in creating the preconditions for nationalism, Warner sees the circulation of cultural forms as important in bringing strangers together into a relationship whereby they interact through the consumption of those forms. Moreover, Warner argues strongly for the "cultural mediation" of technologies and how they are shaped by metalanguages of political and religious ideology that frame their use. In distinction from McLuhan, Walter Ong (1967), and Kittler, he argues against the idea of a medium such as print having an inherent technological logic unmoored from cultural and political philosophies—a "mere technology, a medium itself unmediated" (1990, 5). The history of printing for Warner is not just one of machines but of the public within which printing took place. Ideas of democracy and rationalization, theologies of divine inspiration and mystical presence are thus seen to be as constitutive of "print" as the technological features of mass-produced text. Following this theoretical paradigm, the modernity of Gumi and the movement he spawned lies in their articulation of religious renewal through the forms of a public. It involves analyzing changes in education and taking seriously the lineage of thought and practice within Christian or Muslim tradition that produce new religious subjects and govern their interaction with technologies. This is something Charles Hirschkind (2006) explores in his study of the use of cassettes within Egyptian piety movements (see also De Abreu and De Witte in this volume) and indeed is a central problematic governing the volume as a whole.

In this chapter I wish to draw these traditions together by using the figure of Gumi as an exemplar of both a new religious public in Nigeria but also to interrogate how the shape of that public is formed by the materiality of the communications technologies he used. Like McLuhan and Kittler I want to insist on the organizing power of media, that they are not simply "used" by people for certain purposes but have an intransitive nature that organizes and uses people as much as vice versa. But like Warner and Hirschkind I think that this can only be appreciated by comprehending the wider cultural and religious logics that are also determinative in producing religious subjects. To do this the chapter tacks between examining media technologies and the wider educational and religious shifts of which they were part.

Mediated *Tafsir*

In Kano, Nigeria, during Ramadan, radio and television switch from a broad program of entertainment and news to a wholly religious one offering instructions on how to pray and fast, commentaries on religious matters and most importantly, the broadcast of the exegesis or *tafsir* of the Qur'an. Conducted from the house of a prominent cleric, a *mai bita* recites a section of the Qur'an and the tafsir *mallam* (teacher) then explains its meaning to the surrounding audience, drawing on his knowledge of the commentaries about that section and sometimes making referential asides to contemporary issues. Each night during Ramadan a certain portion of the Qur'an will be covered in varying degrees of detail according to the particular mallam and, over the course of a few years, the entirety of the Holy Book will be explained to adherents. Tafsir is and has been for centuries a privileged religious activity for Muslims and a powerful and necessary way of securing an authoritative reputation as a cleric. Prominent mallams will attract hundreds of people to their teachings so that their mosque fills up and people spill out to occupy surrounding streets. Attending the tafsir of a particular mallam is a declaration of allegiance and for particularly prominent clerics only wealthy and important individuals will get to be inside the mosque itself. Because of its importance, who is allowed to offer tafsir has historically been tightly controlled by the Emir and his council, though in recent years the ability to assert that control has weakened considerably.

Gumi was one of the first clerics to have his tafsir broadcast over the radio in 1967 and his success led to demands that a Sufi preacher be allowed to air a Sufi interpretation of Islam. Since that time, radio and television stations in northern Nigeria air a range of tafsir from differing mallams who represent contending Muslim traditions. In the 1990s when I first began my research, for instance, it was possible on alternating days to hear Gumi's tafsir on the radio, to watch the prominent Qadiri Sufi cleric, Sheikh Nasir Kabara broadcast on NTA (Nigerian Television Authority), and to hear Gumi's rival the Tijani cleric Dahiru Bauci on Radio Kaduna.

On one level this broadcast of tafsir seems to present an established religious event, one familiar to generations of Hausa Muslims and performed in much the same style as a tafsir from decades before television was even invented. There is, seemingly, very little change brought about by the television or radio: the broadcasters go to a house or a mosque, the sheikhs do not go to a studio; the camerawork on television is geared toward replicating the spatial configuration of a single viewer's experience of the event, preserving the idea that one views as a congregant. The vast majority of Hausa Muslims see these broadcasts as an age-old ritual activity made available to people who, because of social hierarchies and physical distance, could never have gained access to these events before. Muslim clerics realize the importance of being broadcast on the media, but this rests on a concept of media as extension, making it available to more adherents than can attend the mosque. Audio and video cassettes intensify that broadening, preserving the event over time as well as moving it across space. But for most Hausa Muslims, what is being moved is conceived of as essentially the same thing whether in person, on television, or on video. This was expressed to me by Sanusi Gumbi, a founder of Izala and one of Gumi's most prominent disciples, when he pointed out that Gumi had "been teaching...since the sixties" and that when the new invention emerged they simply went to "record what he has been saying for a long time just to go and spread it more."[4] Gumbi focuses on media's ability to disseminate, seemingly understanding that what is being transmitted remains essentially the same.

In circulating image and sound from one setting in another, however, the act of mediation transforms that which it circulates. It is a process of entextualization, freezing the live event as a cultural artifact, objectifying it, moving it around as a disembodied chunk of discourse where it enters into new relations with the different objects that surround it. The work of mediation splits the event into two—the face-to-face performance and its televised recreation—initiating a connection between the two. Tafsir broadcasts display a religious event as if it were an ongoing phenomenon outside of the mediation of microphone or camera. But when these are framed within the space of a broadcast, before the tafsir of another mallam, or in distinction to the tafsir taking place at the same time on a different channel, this shift in context provides a radical change in religious practice reconfiguring the deeply religious event of Qur'anic exegesis within the secular space of the public sphere. For instance, in Muslim Nigeria the traditional Sufi transmission of religious knowledge occurred through the personal encounter of a disciple (murid) with his Sheikh (muqqadam). This allegiance was expected to be total and a person's sheikh was to be their source of knowledge and practice. As one Tijani cleric described, to be a disciple is to be "like a corpse at the hands of the one who washes it"; such is the totality of that devotion.[5] Students were privileged to be able to receive the transmission of knowledge from their sheikh—seen as a gift—and expected to internalize it without comment or question. By placing series of tafsir commentaries on television and radio, offering competing interpretations of various Qur'anic passages, the norms of balance that regulate public service broadcast create a wholly new context for religious information. In presenting a range of opinions from which viewers can judge, television enacts Taylor (2007) and Warner's (2002) argument that the distinction of a secular public is based on the idea of a collective potentially open to anyone. It is a movement in which adherents' belonging is premised not on unthinking loyalty but on the voluntary selection of superior argument from a range of competing points of view. Broadcasting tafsir on the television is not just an act of extension then, but one of transformation as well, reordering what the nature of the tafsir is, transforming ideas of publicness, of religious affiliation and authority as the recitation and commentary move from the face-to-face to the mediated event. Standing behind the technology of television, built into its institutional histories are deeply held epistemologies concerning ideas of publicness, equal access, and relativism.

Public Islam

Gumi's religious renewal took the form of what is defined now as a public Islam, emphasizing debate, egalitarianism, open-access, and critiquing ideas of inherited charisma and the use of secret knowledge for which Sufi clerics are famed. Sufism is organized around a core of mysticism whereby, at its highest levels, Sufi saints receive special revelations and access to powerful prayers that become an immense resource for their orders. These revelations are kept within the order, revealed to disciples when they progress in knowledge and training. Sufi orders are thus typically organized around a founding saint who exhibited exceptional learning and mystical abilities. Believed to possess *baraka* (magical charisma) and *fayda* (an overflowing of spiritual energy) and skilled in the arts of magic and healing, elite Sufi Sheikhs are understood to be masters of the "underneath of things" (*batin*) the hidden world of meanings that underlies the phenomenal daily reality (*zahir*) we observe.

Gumi, by contrast, represented an entirely different philosophy of learning and practice, one that he traced to his training at the School for Arabic Studies (SAS). SAS was established to teach Islamic subjects using Western pedagogical methods. Training in Arabic was excellent and the consequence of this mix of Arabic and Western learning was students were able to engage more fully with broader currents of thought and reform in the Muslim world. The historian Auwalu Anwar (1989) argues that this shift in educational style was the key to defining modern Islam in Nigeria by instituting a split between "liberal" and "traditional" clerics based on their mode of education. SAS was at the center of this split, training a whole new administrative and religious class whose power derived from the bureaucracy and military rather than traditional trading and royal elites. This is the class of scholars Muhammad Sani Umar (2001) refers to as "Islamic modernists" derided by established ulama as *malamin gwamnati* (government mallams) or *malamin zamani* (modern mallams)[6] and who later became known simply as 'yan boko[7] (the elites). Gumi became perhaps their most prominent early leader and the first major cleric to emerge from this new configuration of knowledge and power.

Gumi praised the style of learning at SAS which encouraged debate between master and student and introduced students to different philosophies in Islam. "[T]he Law school had an intellectual tradition that made it unique... Very often we were encouraged to assert our own independence and initiative rather than the blind obedience to the views of our teachers. We challenged them frequently... [and] I never saw them get angry" (1992, 33). This is a dialogic statement implicitly referring to the protocols of Sufi learning and the hierarchies it entails. "The whole experience left a deep impression on my mind and today there is nothing I love better than to be challenged about my views" (ibid.). Two things are at play in this statement. First, he foregrounds the shift in educational style as an integral part not only of his biography but of his philosophy and practice. Second, he publicly stages his commitment to an epistemology of openness and debate that marks enlightenment secularism. This public staging of openness to debate and welcoming of egalitarian challenge became part of Gumi's public persona woven into his religious practice but also his personal style. His tafsir sessions, for instance, ended in question and answer sessions where he would take inquiries from any speaker in the mosque regardless of rank.[8] Gumi was most often referred to by his supporters as *Mallam*, the word for teacher in Hausa but also for any adult male (and thus a title everyone can lay claim to), even though he was entitled to the more rarified title of *Sheikh*. He was known for wearing plain white gowns rather than the ornately brocaded robes of his Sufi counterparts and famous for speaking in simple, comprehensible Hausa rather than an esoteric religious vocabulary. In their attack on Sufi orders and traditional royal elites Gumi and Izala criticized the elaborate forms of salute and greeting in Hausa society whereby social inferiors greet superiors by crouching down and saluting. They argued this was against Islam, that it was a residue of pre-Islamic Hausa practice and it was unnecessary to constantly demonstrate the hierarchies of social status. Each of these decisions represents a stark contrast to the performative hierarchies that surround Sufi Sheikhs and royal elites. Implicit in the wearing of white, or being called mallam, for instance, is a critique of status as derived from inherited rank rather than from knowledge and learning. In a typical comment, one Izala member said to me, "Anyone, *anyone* could ask mallam a question, even a child so long as they based their question on the Qur'an and Hadith," emphasizing Gumi's deeply egalitarian style.[9] This statement rests on a concept of a world organized by differing modes of legitimacy where, as Habermas has written of a different context, "the authority of status is reduced to the authority of debating skill" (1994, 36–37) and influence emerges from the "public clash of arguments" (97). It stages that mode of learning as an aspect of religious legitimacy and it was a mode of presentation that had enormous affective power.

In broadcasting his tafsir over the radio a centuries-old religious practice was encoded within the radically different form of electronic waves reorganizing that practice and subjecting it to the spatial and temporal disfiguration brought about by the medium. It also placed the tafsir within the institutional and professional guidelines of a public service broadcaster, one that emphasized balance between competing ideas rather than a single truth; comprehensibility to a mass audience, rather than a display of theological erudition; and familiarity with the professional and cultural codes associated with the civil service bureaucracy within which both Gumi and broadcasters were trained. It is the link between the technological capacities of the medium, combined with wider educational and social shifts brought about in Hausa society at that time that created the affinity between aspects of radio as a material and professional practice and an ideology of religious reform emerging from within a modernizing Muslim revival. We can see how this articulation works by exploring in closer detail the link between Gumi and radio and the bitter controversy it provoked.

Gumi and the Rise of Izala

Gumi's role in religious revitalization in northern Nigeria has been widely discussed.[10] Because he was trained at the SAS Gumi learned Arabic fluently and was one of the first students to be sent outside of Nigeria for study to the Sudan, initiating his connection with the wider Muslim world. Returning to Nigeria, Gumi became part of the colonial civil service first as a teacher, and later an Islamic judge, finally reaching the position of Grand Khadi of Northern Nigeria. Grand Khadi was one of the most important bureaucratic posts in the region and gave him access to Ahmadu Bello, the Sardauna of Sokoto and Premier of the Northern Region of Nigeria at independence. Because of his fluent Arabic and connections in the Middle East Gumi came to act as the Sardauna's translator and religious advisor at a time when Bello was becoming a prominent player in international Muslim politics (Paden 1986), opening up new networks of support and influence for Gumi. Indeed it was from the Gulf states that Gumi and later Izala received much of the funds to build mosques, translate and publish books, train and fund teachers, and distribute cassettes. Gumi became the most important figure in the intensified relations between Hausa Muslims and the rest of the Islamic world that took place during the 1970s and 1980s.

It was a result of these bureaucratic and religious connections that in the late 1960s Gumi was chosen to broadcast his Ramadan tafsir over Radio Kaduna, the largest radio station in West Africa. Gumi was already known for his regular religious columns written in the Hausa language newspaper *Gaskiya Ta Fi Kwabo* (Truth Is Worth More Than a Penny) and his regular radio, and, later, television appearances gave his teachings tremendous exposure. From these fora Gumi developed his Salafi inspired attack, arguing Sufism was an innovation in Islamic practice that went against the basic teachings of Islam and that those who followed it were not even Muslims. Given the largely Sufi character of Nigerian Islam, his teachings had a volatile effect, drawing intense criticism from Sufi leaders and sharply dividing Nigerian Muslims. In 1979 the rise of a dynamic new anti-Sufi movement was formalized with the creation of Izala whose fierce attacks on Sufism resulted in sustained, often violent, religious conflict that dominated Nigerian Islam for decades.

The Surface of Things

Gumi forcefully articulated the ideological basis of his anti-Sufism in a variety of different media: articles, books, audio and video cassettes, radio, and, later, television programs. Up until this time religious conflict in Nigeria had largely been *between* differing Sufi orders, especially the Tijaniyya and Qadiriyya and sometimes within those orders themselves (Anwar 1989; Paden 1973). This conflict came to a head in the 1950s and 1960s as both of these orders underwent their own revival at the hands of two charismatic Sufi sheikhs, the Senegalese Ibrahim Niass of the Tijaniyya and the Qadiri cleric Sheikh Nasiru Kabara. In 1972, however, the dynamics of this conflict were upended when Gumi published his main theological assault on Sufism, *Al Aqidah Al-Sahihah Bi Muwafiqah Al-Sharia'* (The Right Belief Is Based on the Shari'a, 1972), plunging him into immediate controversy. This was a summation of ideas he had broached in public and in newspaper articles over the years and now collated in a sustained attack.

In the *Aqidah*, Gumi attacked Sufism for innovating new rituals and prayers and for claims by Sufi Sheikhs that they had secret knowledge hidden from ordinary Muslims. In response, Gumi claimed Sufis used magic "to fill the hearts of the weak ones with fear" and to fool the unwary who do not question their leaders because "they follow them blindly in their inordinate greed for earthly desires" (1972, 25). Later he continued his attack referring to Sufi sheikhs as "vicious learned men" who "deceive people and chop [steal] their money" (34). Gumi's main tactic was to take rituals central to the practice of the different orders and cite from the Qur'an to demonstrate their illicitness,[11] especially those involved with awakening ecstasy (*sama*) through trance. His aim was to undermine the Sufi claim that sheikhs, at the highest level, could use trance to enter into states of ecstasy through which they could gain special and extraordinary knowledge hidden from ordinary Muslims. He ridiculed claims to revelation by quoting from the Qur'an to prove that Mohammed was the seal of all Prophets, and that with him all revelations closed. "The Prophet did not conceal anything in his lifetime," Gumi wrote (1972, 22), and Mohammed was the final vehicle used by God to reveal his teachings to humanity. Gumi targeted the concept of the "sheikh." He argued that "one of the blameworthy innovations which lead to disbelief" is to believe there are special beings with special posts such as Qutb or Gawth with special powers (44) and who "possess an esoteric knowledge" (45). "All these claims are void and false; the whole of them are the handiworks of impositors [*sic*] in Islam" (ibid.). Gumi argued that no one possesses hidden knowledge: Allah says, "Say none of the inhabitants of the heavens and earth except Allah knows of the hidden things" (Qur'an 27:65, cited in Gumi 1972, 45).

Gumi's use of media should be seen as part of his critique of systems of religious learning that were organized around the restriction of knowledge and the inculcation of esoteric practice. But it also should be seen as a theory of knowledge. His aim was to bring more Muslims into a system where knowledge was transparent and that focuses on the surface of things rather than their depths. Gumi was the first cleric in Nigeria to translate the Qur'an into Hausa and to arrange for the translation of collections of Hadith and his own religious writings into the vernacular. While he was an advocate of Arabic learning, these acts of translation and the recording of these texts onto cassettes inaugurated a huge shift in the language of religious debate from Arabic to Hausa (Brenner and Last 1985). In 1964 he helped found the *Jama'at Nasrul Islam* (JNI, Society for the Victory of Islam) whose aim was to support religious renewal by distributing Qur'ans, funding public preaching, and reforming religious education to improve the religious learning of ordinary Muslims (see Gumi 1992; Kane 2003; Loimeier 1997; Paden 1986). Gumi's Salafi inspired argument was based on the concept that the source of Muslim knowledge is rooted in the Qur'an and the Hadith and that these texts alone should be the basis for Islamic law. Sufi saints, who claim specialized knowledge denied to other Muslims through their mystical abilities, are introducing innovations (*bid'a*) that are illegal, he argued. Gumi's Salafism is thus rationalist and legalistic: "There is no mysticism in Islam," he wrote, "Everything has been laid out clearly and the individual Muslim never stands in need of anyone else's intercession between him and God" (Gumi 1992, 135). Gumi was advancing a religious renewal based on the promotion of individual understanding, rather than one rooted in ritual participation. It was a theology animated by surfaces rather than depths, part of a wider systemic shift in Nigerian society under colonial rule that fed on the dispersive qualities of a media system anchored around the Enlightenment norms of transparency, balance, and education.

The choice of Gumi to preach on the radio reflects the rise to power and intellectual maturation of a new cadré of colonially educated government elites. This class of Hausa Muslims were likely to be fluent in English, educated and often contemptuous of the backward nature of traditional Hausa education. While staunchly Muslim, they looked to modernist Islamic ideas coming from the Middle East and contrasted this cosmopolitanism with what they saw as the parochialism of "local" mallams. Gumi effectively became the de facto religious leader for this new political class. Where nearly all Sufi Sheikhs were based in traditional religious centers of learning, such as Zaria, Kano, Katsina, or Sokoto, Gumi's home base was the government center of Kaduna. It was this close connection to the new political class that facilitated his appearance in the media. Sheikh Sanusi Gumbi, one of Gumi's most famous disciples, ridiculed the *turuq* (Sufi orders) for their isolation from these centers of power and saw these connections as decisive in separating the two sides in the conflict. "Mallam knew about tradition, he knew about modern education," Gumbi told me in an interview. He was "part of government. Those ulama working in their houses they don't know government... That is the difference between him and those people."[12] Dahiru Bauci also argued that Gumi's position in government and his connections with radio professionals was decisive.[13] The professionals working for Radio Kaduna at that time argued that the choice of Gumi was neither religious nor political but purely technical, based on the professional norms of radio broadcast rather than any religious orientation.[14] Broadcasts had to be from Kaduna and, unlike most clerics, Gumi lived there. His fluency in Hausa, Arabic, and English allowed him to move between the different worlds of Islamic clerics and colonial and postcolonial bureaucrats with facility and his explication of the Qur'an was easy to follow and understand in marked contrast to most of his colleagues. According to Aminu Ahmed who worked at Radio Kaduna at the time, the choice of Gumi was "neither an act of commission or omission." Rather, Gumi was "available, disposed and keen."[15]

Nearly all radio professionals commented on the difficulty of following the tafsir of the dominant mallams of the time and the problems this posed for the norms of radio broadcast dedicated to intelligibility and communication. Louis Brenner and Murray Last have referred to this style of discourse as *malamanci* or, "the vocabulary, grammar and spelling common to mallams (scholars) when being at their most scholarly" (1985, 443). In my discussions with radio professionals the name of the learned Qadiri cleric Nasiru Kabara was often mentioned in this regard. As Aminu Ahmed described it to me, Kabara "speaks to a selected audience who have a very deep knowledge. He is too philosophical, too deep for the ordinary person. His interpretation is more difficult than the original texts itself. He is a mallam's mallam." Gumi, by contrast, was "down to earth and simplistic" (ibid.) and fit well with the technocratic norms of radio broadcast. In Kano, where Kabara was based, media professionals referred to the fact his tafsir was "incomprehensible," as one official at CTV Kano put it, and that this was a problem with many Sufi mallams who assumed listeners had "read as much or knew as much as" them.[16] Dahiru Bauci, the Tijani preacher selected by the Sufi orders as the main counterweight to Gumi on Radio Kaduna was chosen because of his more comprehensible style yet even he presented difficulties because of the "depth of his learning." (ibid.) This suggests the possibility of a different philosophy at work behind the tafsir event. Tafsir exegesis is always an occasion where scholars demonstrate their depth of learning before an audience. It may be that for Sufis, for whom weight is placed on following the guidance of a sheikh as well as on individual understanding, that the ritual function of tafsir may be as important or take precedence over whether the audience understands and internalizes the overall message. For Gumi, of course, communication and understanding was the bedrock of his religious reform. It indicates the fit between his practice of *da'wa* (renewal) and the norms of a public sphere integrated into the architecture of radio as a public broadcast medium.

Up until the rise of Gumi, radio was seen by Hausa Muslims as a new, colonial, medium at best irrelevant to the securing or maintenance of religious authority and at worst part of a secular colonial project that was hostile to Islam.[17] Gumi's success, however, changed that as both supporters and opponents realized the enormous power his broadcasts were having in attracting followers to his wider program of renewal. By the mid-1970s leaders of the Sufi orders Tijaniyya and Qadiriyya, who had long been fierce enemies, came together in a series of alliances to combat Gumi. They began efforts to drive out pro-Gumi supporters from mainstream organizations such as the JNI and expanded Sufi preaching programs to actively resist Gumi's spreading influence (Anwar 1989). Sufi leaders also turned their attention to the base for Gumi's proselytizing, the media.

In 1977 leaders of Tijaniyya and Qadiriyya in all northern states signed a joint letter to the Managing Director of Radio Kaduna, Dahiru Modibbo, attacking their patronage of Gumi. "We, the undermentioned leaders of the Tijaniyya and Kadiriyya sects of the northern States have enough patient [sic] for the last five (5) weary years in the way and manner you are playing or putting tafsir recorded from Alhaji Abubakar Gumi which is abusive, deformative [sic] to us and making all of us pagans (KAFIRAI)."[18] The letter goes on to chastise the radio station for their complicity in Gumi's attacks. "We have 27 recorded cassettes made by Alhaji Abubakar Gumi which was played through your media all abusive and deformed [sic] to us and the sects." The letter was written "in the name of peace and stability" that was a veiled reference to the fact that violent confrontations had been breaking out regularly between Sufis and followers of Gumi even leading to several assassination attempts of Gumi's life (Gumi 1992; Kane 2003; Umar 1993).

In the context of Northern Nigerian Islam this letter is almost unprecedented. For much of the twentieth century the Tijaniyya and Qadiriyya had been bitter opponents but in Gumi they were faced by a frontal assault on Sufism as a whole. Modibbo responded assuring the leaders that the radio station had no intention of promoting one branch of Islam over another. He recommended the orders choose one mallam who would alternate with Gumi during Ramadan (forcing them to decide which mallam that would be). After debate the orders chose a powerful Tijani orator, Dahiru Bauci, and arranged for him to move to Kaduna in order to counter the influence of Gumi.

The intensity of the controversy over tafsir broadcasts meant that the Director of Radio Kaduna, Dahiru Modibbo, had to initiate a policy designed to maintain the peace. He instructed mallams to use a neutral mode of exegesis in which they would stick to explaining the Qur'an and refrain from attacking other Muslims. This proved to be difficult to institute for two reasons. First, Sufi followers viewed the radio station as a Gumi stronghold biased in his favor that had attacked them and they wanted space to attack Gumi back. Second, they were largely right in that Gumi had massive support within the radio station and was seen by most Hausa media professionals as simply correct in his interpretation of Islam. Halilu Getso who worked at Radio Kaduna at the time said many of the top people were followers of Gumi long before he even came onto the radio.[19] This partiality was recognized by Modibbo who wrote to the head of programs in charge of the tafsir broadcast after violent confrontations between Izala and Sufi followers broke out in Jos and Kaduna in 1977: "Some two weeks ago I gave definite instructions that our Tafsir transmissions must not contain references to any sects that could reasonably be construed as condemnatory. The Tafsir transmission of last night did contain such a reference. I am taking a very serious view of this...You are perfectly aware of the delicate nature of this issue...*I warn that personal emotions must not be allowed* to override the undertakings we have given to the...sects" (my emphasis).[20]

The difficulty arose from the strong identification between the new professional media class and Gumi. Years later this attitude surfaced constantly in my interviews. "What Gumi was saying wasn't controversial," one said to me, "it was just the truth." Another said, "He [Gumi] had no point of view. What you must understand is that all he did was read the Qur'an and interpret it. He gave no opinions."[21] Another referred scathingly to pressure by politicians to give the tariqa the "semblance of equal time" that was clearly seen by him as undue pressure. He continued, "I believe his [Gumi's] interpretations of Islamic jurisprudence" are completely innocent and harmless "except for those who want to take offence." All of these were people working in Radio Kaduna at the height of the controversy over tafsir and echo the general sensibility of the time. For these professionals Gumi was shaping a more modern Islam, one tightly connected to currents in international Islamic thought. They believed this would move away from the parochialism of Nigerian Islam and lighten the restrictive dead weight of aristocracy, poorly educated traders, and their Sufi clients who were doing little except hold Nigeria back.[22] Because of the intensifying nature of the controversy, including attacks on the radio stations and serious bomb threats and because of the attitude of his workforce, Modibbo had to forcibly institute a new policy for tafsir that remains today. Each tafsir is recorded a day ahead of time. The Manager of Programs is then personally responsible for listening to the tape and editing out any controversial comments. Any reference to any group that might reasonably be deemed derogatory was to be eliminated. "Members of staff involved must *never ever* attempt to judge the correctness or otherwise of the interpretations; whatever personal religious convictions may be we must avoid taking sides on doctrinal issues" (emphasis in original). Modibbo had to request extra security and raised the possibility of stopping broadcasts altogether "should the situation deteriorate to a point where I or you consider that the continuation of these programmes would pose a real threat to public peace."[23]

After the rise of Gumi, to broadcast over the radio went from being an irrelevant part of securing religious authority to a bitterly contested and key aspect of religious legitimacy. Gumi himself was well aware of the central place of radio Kaduna in his rise to prominence. In his autobiography he remarked how one friend confided in him, "You know...the last six years during which your readings were broadcast over the air, have been far more effective [in spreading your message] than all the years in which you previously spent preaching" (Gumi 1992, 149). To this day, radio and television stations are careful to keep a balance between different religious movements in their programming. Some, like CTV Kano explicitly chose "independent" mallams (such as the noted cleric Sheikh Isa Waziri) in order to avoid this conflict altogether. Following the example of Pentecostal movements, clerics not selected by the stations often pay to air their programs realizing that access to media is key to securing a religious reputation. And political pressure over the choice of tafsir mallam is exerted particularly after the change of government regimes.

The clerics involved in giving tafsir perceive the use of radio and television as a means of extending religion—of reaching new audiences unable to attend the mosque. But the inherent logic of this transmission is based on the ideas of balance inherent in a public broadcast medium with its roots in a deep tradition of secular enlightenment thought. As Sanusi Gumbi put it, with Dahiru Bauci on the radio giving his tafsir on alternate days to Gumi, now "the people listen to understand [and] choose." If the tariqa are correct then "Dahiru Bauci will represent their ideas. If Izala are true then Abubakar Gumi will represent their ideas"[24] What Gumbi reveals is that the radio operates in much the same way as the pedagogy Gumi was trained in at SAS. There, religions and religious movements were presented as systems and students were taught the basic ideas of those systems and encouraged to choose between them. Broadcasting tafsir on radio and television is not just an act of extension but one of transformation as well, reordering what the nature of the tafsir is, transforming ideas of publicness, of religious affiliation and authority as the recitation and commentary move from the face-to-face to the mediated event. Standing behind the technology of radio, built into its institutional histories are deeply held epistemologies concerning ideas of publicness, equal access, and relativism, ideas that at times can seem commensurate with religious beliefs, while at others they become sites of bitter controversy.

Conclusion

Charles Taylor (2007) argues that secular modernity forms the "context of understanding" or, borrowing from Wittgenstein, the "background" that forms the preconditions by which modern thought about society and even religion is organized. Secularism, for him, is not the absence of religion or its relegation to the private sphere; it is a process that reorders the place of religion in society and restructures our consciousness to conceive of religion as one option among others. Talal Asad (2003), similarly, sees secularism not just as a negative process of disenchantment, or of the separation of religion and politics, but as productive of the laws, modes of sociability, and forms of life in contemporary societies. One way to think of Gumi and Izala is to see them as exemplars of a modern religious movement shaped by secularism. In this sense Gumi is as secular as anyone, not because he is not religious, but because he articulates religion within a context of understanding shaped by secularism. Gumi's renewal took the form of what we see now as a public emphasizing debate and egalitarianism, and by critiquing inherited charisma and obedience. Media are central to the articulation of this public by disseminating knowledge to social strangers rather than passing down secret teachings to initiates, and also, of course, because their institutional structures in colonial and postcolonial Nigeria were themselves shaped by the norms of a public broadcast medium. What makes Gumi and Izala "modern" to Nigerians is their use of technologies, their connections to the wider Islamic world, their introduction of Salafi ideas of renewal, their revolution in education, in modes of sociability, and in religious practice. Gumi explicitly stages this public as a key aspect of his legitimacy, and a main source of his distinction from traditional Nigerian sheikhs.

What is important to recognize is that the claim to open debate and equal access is as much a part of the presentation of a religious movement used by its adherents as it is an evaluation of a state of affairs. In actuality the split between Sufis and Salafis while fiercely constitutive of Nigerian Islam over the past few decades is something that needs to be interrogated and not just assumed. Because my focus in this chapter is to throw into relief the role media play in shaping religious movements I have concentrated on those elements of distinction and difference. But Sufis were very quick to adopt many elements of Salafi revivalism just as many Izala leaders are insistent on hierarchy and reflexive loyalty. This rupture between the two movements should be seen as a *claim* staged by participants in a polemic while reflective of significant divisions can sometimes hide the way these movements overlap.

I began this chapter by stating that many, if not most, people in Nigeria view Gumi as a "modern" mallam and Izala as a "modern" religious movement. This chapter has been an exploration into the role media played in producing this sense of difference—the rupture that separates Gumi from "local" mallams—and how the use of media signals a transformation in Nigerian Islam. One theoretical lineage sees the distinction of media lying in their ability to shape the contours of a new religious public, the operations of the medium shaped by theologies and political philosophies that dictate how media are to be used and for what purposes.[25] In contrast to this lineage are those who insist on the materiality of the technology itself and how the technics of media create the infrastructural conditions that set limits on our experiences and social orders. Print, radio, and television reorder the information they transmit. They impose conditions on the recording and storage of that media and on the bodies and senses of those that retrieve it. We need to pay attention to how the technics of media institute that ordering precisely to understand how those wider philosophies are caught up and transmitted in networks that they do not completely determine. Modern religious publics are creatures that emerge from the interweaving of these two theoretical lineages: those that stress the materiality of media technics and those that insist on cultural mediation of technology. In the case of Gumi this assemblage draws together the dispersive qualities of broadcast media with the professional codes that define the use of those technologies and the theologies and practices of Salafi revivalism within the Muslim world. My aim in this chapter has been to try to tease out some of the complexity of this assemblage, the layering between competing systems of ideas and organization that constitute the dynamism and force of new religious movements.

Notes

Research for this chapter was funded by the Wenner-Gren Foundation for Anthropological Research and the research program on which this volume is based. I am grateful for feedback during seminars at Emory University, Wesleyan University, the University of Jos, and the University of Amsterdam. And I am particularly grateful to Birgit Meyer for a close reading of the chapter and to the Pionier Project fellows for discussion and debate from which I benefited greatly.

1. Their full name is *Jama'atu Izalat al-Bid`a wa Iqamat al-Sunna*, or, The Movement Against Innovation in Favour of a Return to the Sunna.
2. There have been a number of excellent studies of Gumi and Izala's rise and influence. See, for instance, Barkindo 1993, Gumi 1992, Kane 2003, Loimeier 1997, Umar 1988, 1993.
3. Benedict Anderson's (1991) imagined community of nationalism is a powerful case in point. For Anderson, nationalism is a new mode of belonging tied to a transformation in the experience of time, space and human association brought about by a media technology (print) and an economic system (capitalism).
4. Interview, Sheikh Sanusi Gumbi, Kaduna, June 7, 1995.
5. Interview, Sheikh Yusuf Ali, Kano City, July 31, 1995
6. Yusuf Ali, a prominent Tijani Sheikh in Kano who attended SAS said opposition against the institution by traditional ulama was so intense that as late as the 1960s students had to enroll without them knowing. When his teachers

found out he had joined, he said they accused him of becoming a pagan and a Jew and some refused to speak with him. But for his generation this was also the modern education they aspired to. Interview, op. cit.

7. *Boko* refers to Hausa written in Roman script (before the coming of the British Hausa was written in Arabic [*ajami*]). *'Yan boko* refers to those educated in Western schools and has come to have a more general meaning of "the elite."

8. It was in question and answer sessions that Gumi was asked the most direct questions about Sufism and so often gave his most inflammatory answers. These were edited out from Radio Kaduna because of their propensity to provoke religious conflict but included on cassette often leading to the cassette's popularity. For a discussion of these sessions and Gumi's tafsir see Brigaglia 2007.

9. One can get a sense of this affective power in a description of meeting Gumi by the scholar Ousmane Kane, himself a grandson of a major Sufi sheikh and well versed in the social norms of Sufi orders: "I was quite struck by his egalitarian tendencies. In his living room all the visitors were sitting in armchairs, including young people and people from apparently modest origin. Everybody shook hands with him as a way of greeting. It would never occur to any member of a Sufi order to shake hands with a Sufi *Shaykh* or to sit in an armchair in the same room as a Shaykh" (2003, 138).

10. See note 3.

11. In the case of the Tijaniyya Gumi attacked claims that the salat al-Fatih prayer, the recitation of which is a key part of Tijani practice, was equal in merit to reciting the Qur'an 6,000 times. This merit was believed to have been revealed to Ahmad al-Tijani through mystical communication with the Prophet. Gumi pointed out that the Qur'an states the Prophet Mohammed was the seal of all prophets and that there would be no new revelations after his death. As none of the Hadith mention the salat al-Fatih then any recitation is an illegal innovation (*bid'a*) in religious practice. In the case of the Qadiriyya Gumi rejected the use of the drums in the mosque as a means of aiding possession. He cited from the Qur'an to argue that "those who combine drumming with religion or the recitation of the Qur'an and the praises of Allah in the mosque, such people are considered as those who reduce their religion to a plaything and make thereby a mockery of it. They therefore fall within the group of those the Qur'an refers to when it says 'And their prayers in the house of God is nothing but whistling and clapping of hands. They would taste the punishment which they disbelieve'" (Q 8:35. Cited in Gumi 1972, 43).

12. This is a dismissive reference to the traditional mode of Islamic education in the north. Traditionally students pursuing higher studies in Islam would not attend a school or learn from a set syllabus but travel to the house of a respected Sheikh to learn about a particular text that Sheikh had mastered. Students came to sit in the *zaure*, the room at the front of the house dedicated to receiving visitors and where instruction would take place. This is a practice that continues today among Sufi circles. *Mallamin zaure* became a derogatory reference by more Salafi inclined followers to stereotype this mode of education as backward. Interview, Sheikh Sanusi Gumbi, Kaduna. 18 May 1995.

13. Interview, Sheikh Dahiru Bauci, Kaduna, Nigeria, 14 May 1995.
14. Interviews: Halilu Getso, Director, Radio Kaduna 24 April 1995; Usman Shettima 24 April 1995, and Ibrahim Bak'o, 26 April 1995, all in Kaduna Nigeria. Aminu Ahmed Director Kano State Ministry of Information, 27 May 1995 and 3 July 1995, Aminu Isa, Head of Programs, City Television Kano, 20 May 1995; Hassan Suleiman, Kano State Ministry of Information 2 July 1995—all in Kano, Nigeria.
15. Interview, Aminu Ahmed, Kano, 3 July 1995.
16. Interview, Aminu Isa, Kano, 27 May 1995.
17. See Larkin 2008, Chapter 2.
18. Federal Radio Corporation of Nigeria (FRCN)/File D60/Islamic Religious Affairs. Letter, Leaders of Tijaniyya and Kadiriyya Sects of the Northern States to Managing Director, Radio Kaduna. 14 August 1977. The awkward English of the letter, sent to executives whose English was likely to be flawless, indicates the extent of the cultural gap separating the social make-up of Sufis from the 'yan boko who made up the professional echelons of the civil service.
19. Interview, Halilu Getso, Director, Radio Kaduna, Kaduna,.24 April 1995.
20. FRCN/D60/Islamic Religious Affairs. Memo from Managing Director to Head of Programmes. 31 August 1977.
21. Interview, Ibrahim Bak'o, Radio Kaduna, Kaduna,24 April 1995.
22. For an analysis of the rise of this class of bureaucrat and thinker see Yakubu 1996.
23. FRCN/D60/Islamic Religious Affairs. Letter, from Managing Director to Commissioner of Police, Kaduna. 11 August 1978.
24. Interview, Sanusi Gumbi, op cit.
25. One can see this lineage in work as diverse as Eickelman and Anderson 1999, Hirschkind 2006, Meyer 2004a, Meyer and Moors 2006a, Warner 1990, 2002.

Chapter 6

The Sonic Architects of a New Babel: The Politics of Belonging of DJ Shadow and Fernando Clarke

Francio Guadeloupe

Let me tell you a story about an island inhabited by people who knew they were slaves of capital, but who were nonetheless happy to remain so. I was at a Calypso extravaganza on the binational Caribbean island of Saint Martin and Sint Maarten (French and Dutch West Indies), where with a broad smile on their faces, young and old were shouting "they fool we again." They were singing and dancing to commemorate the fact that the political elites and big business had managed to fool them again. The latter had banked all the Benjamins, and left them with pennies, but they were happy to be fooled again. To be fooled required that they fool themselves time and again. A truth they knew well.

The chorus was being led by the Shadow, a handsome Rasta radio disc jockey and accomplished music artist, who was elated that the crowd was in ecstasy. He reminded me of his colleague DJ Fernando Clarke, a Richard Pryor look-a-like, who enticed Saint Martinoise and Sint Maarteners to see the inescapability of sin as a blessing that God consented to. There was no revolutionary subject on this island, no effective organic intellectuals striking against the system, just men and women of all classes who for different reasons kept the capitalist machine running. A community of the "perfectly emancipated, perfectly servile" (Baudrillard 2001, 28).

It is the high noon of Carnival on this 37 square mile rock, inhabited by 70,000 souls, entirely designated a Freeport, which receives over 1.5 million tourists annually. Saint Martin is an overseas department of France, while Sint Maarten constitutes an integral part of the Dutch Kingdom (see Daniel 2006 and Oostindie and Klinkers 2003 on the political constitutions of the nonindependent French and Dutch Caribbean). This is the only place in the European Union where France and the Netherlands border each other, and as a sign of goodwill border patrols are nonexistent. There is no need for such measures since tourism and European subsidies guarantee that these islanders are spared the endemic poverty that characterises much of the politically independent Caribbean. They are not vying for political cessation or engaging in anti-colonial politics.

Though the island is divided between France and the Netherlands, there also exists the supranational imagined community of SXM (read St. Maarten) that encompasses both sides of the island. This imagined community ideally includes the 80 different nationalities—whereby newcomers outnumber the "natives" four to one—that reside on the island. The wealthy North American and European hoteliers, East Indian businessmen, native political elites, Chinese grocers, native civil servants and professionals, West Indian, Asian, and metropolitan working classes—an enumeration emulating the economic hierarchy on the island—must be embraced by this SXM.

If the tourist industry is to be unperturbed by the exclusivist fantasies of ethnic difference, which is a catastrophe for islands that sell themselves as hedonistic heavens, operations of all-inclusive community building must be promoted. In other words, orchestrated imaginations of community must surpass the nativist nineteenth-century New World political nationalisms—the United States, Haiti, and Spanish America—that Benedict Anderson (1991) and C. L. R. James (1963[1938]) have written about. These collectives were imagined in relation to external and internal outsiders: European colonial powers and discriminated "minorities" and "majorities." As a mode of imagining community, these New World inventions continue to form the template of First and Third World nationalisms.

On SXM, however, the self-other dichotomy of political nationalism is transposed to the economic realm, since political independence is not sought after. The Other is reconfigured as those who are accused of jeopardizing the livelihoods of the islanders by promoting exclusivist notions of community. As the island's prosperity is based upon being open to the outside world, the entire population is enticed to behave as actual stakeholders in the capitalist enterprise of promoting the island as a place of fun and sun. This enticement is forwarded through the media.

Like elsewhere in the affluent West, media play a vital role in people's understanding of belonging and the capitalist dynamics operative in their societies. Unlike other parts of the West, however, TV and newspapers are not the main conveyers of local public moods. SXMers grow up on CNN, BBC, ABC, CBS, NBC, Canal +, BET, Tempo, BVN, Deutsche Welle, and other such channels broadcasting from the mainland West. For just 45 U.S. dollars a month they get to choose between 55 international TV channels. Local TV is virtually nonexistent, as competing against these big budget production companies is financially suicidal. The same can be said for local newspapers. These have had to package themselves as regional papers catering to other islands such as Saba, Saint Eustatius, Anguilla, Saint Barthelemy, and Saint Kitts and Nevis, to remain lucrative. An additional factor is that few SXMers take the time to truly read through the newspapers. Newspaper reading is primarily a middle-class practice. The working classes will swiftly browse through the paper to read the sports columns or a newsflash that captures the eye.

Radio is thus the main local media on the island. And as all media, radio is privately owned on SXM, the owners are usually wealthy businessmen and women. To protect their interests, which is the tourist industry's image of a bounty island inhabited by bountiful people hailing from the four corners of the globe, SXM as a modern day Babel that works, a de facto censorship exists. Religious or ethnic fundamentalism is strictly prohibited. Those who wish to go against this prohibition are either not hired or fired. Radio disc jockeys may be critical of the establishment, but must always promote a Christian-based ecumenical politics of tolerance for ethnic and religious diversity. The way of the Lord must be the way of the tourist industry.

In choosing a Christian-based ecumenical politics of tolerance, these disc jockeys imitate and therewith enhance the role of public Christianity, which is the role of *the* privileged metalanguage in the public sphere to speak about and promote an all-inclusive politics of human belonging. As a metalanguage, which one encounters in school curricula, campaign speeches of politicians, advertising ploys of businesses, manifestoes of civil societies, and everyday speech, public Christianity mediates and simultaneously alleviates existing tensions between groups and individuals. It is a politics that also seeks to go beyond ethno-religious and class distinctions promoting a theological notion of elemental humanity that binds all SXMers. The devout Ganesha worshipper easily adopts a Christian tongue when she feels the need to assert her right to be rich. "In God's kingdom there is also room for the wealthy." Similarly prostitutes speak Christian to countercritiques of middle-class Catholics. "Didn't Jesus accept Mary Magdalena by his side?"

Its panoptic presence notwithstanding, all over and everywhere, the most widely disseminated articulation of this public Christianity is to be found in Caribbean popular music (Guadeloupe 2006b; Cooper 2004; Mahabir 2002).[1] Born of the creolizing of the Judeo-Christian Word with African and Asian religious and rhythmic motifs, Caribbean popular music at its best legitimates pleas for social and economic equality and above all human dignity. From the late Bob Marley and Celia Cruz, to contemporary artists, such as Juan Luis Guerra and Richie Spice, an all-inclusive Christian-based politics of human belonging is promoted. Every bounded community must seek to be open to the community of all men and women.

However, in its most circulated form this radical West Indian politics *sui generis* cannot be divorced from the market—from the capitalist logic. More concretely how the message of these Caribbean artists and organic intellectuals is heard, after the music executives have had their say, is largely determined by radio disc jockeys. These make the public aware of new releases, how one should judge these releases, and what the main message of the artist is. Caribbean music and the everyday metalanguage of Christianity are enlisted by DJ Shadow and DJ Clarke who as sonic architects entice SXMers to create and maintain a tower of Babel that works. This chapter treats the way these two popular disc jockeys create all-inclusive architectures of Babel within the teeth of Capitalism and with the willing consent of the slaves of capital.

A Diatribe against Politicians Who Forget Conscience

And the anthem goes:

> Promises is only promises: when they get in office, they going fix we busi-ness/Promises is only promises: once they get in power they say we could go for the future/But when I take a stock of the truth what I really see it both-ering me/One race controlling the currency [white Western capitalists]/The next corrupting democracy [dark skinned political elites]/They fool we again, They fool we again, They fool we again: waving up the banner, one Love joint together/They fool we again, they fool we again: things looking so bad who will guard the guard. (DJ Shadow)

DJ Shadow summons the band to play slower and softer. His background singers antiphonally whisper, "stop fooling, stop fooling," as the Shadow begins to speak and tell us, his interpellated crowd of the fooled, that the Almighty is the ultimate guard. This guard does not live in the sky, but in our hearts. It is called Conscience.

> Conscience people. Conscience must be your guide. Them politrickians and false prophets [his term for political and religious leaders], and many of them money man [affluent businessmen and women] don't listen to their Conscience. So you don't listen to Them. Tell them a *Me*, the Shadowman say so. Politrickian the Shadow exposing you tonight.

Though of a darker hue—owning several businesses and prime lands on SXM and the surrounding islands—his millionaire family is part of *the money men* who he so condemns. The SXMers who are cheering him on know this, but they don't seem to care. Wisely he doesn't direct his vehement critique on the business classes or members of the political establishment to which he is related. His criticism is mostly directed toward fringe native politicians. To be more precise the Baines brothers, Carlton and Clayton, who forward a politics of belonging that solely privileges the locals—the term employed for the natives on the island who can trace back their ancestry to at least three generations. The Baines are middle-class businessmen who own considerable real estate. They also own a construction company that builds many of the mansions and hotels of the wealthy newcomers.

Having returned from the Netherlands in the early 1980s with an MA degree in education, and a radical politics based upon autochthony and Black Power, the youngest of Baines, Clayton, decided to enter politics. He presented himself as the political leader of the true SXMers. The island was black and the descendants of the whites had to take a second seat. It was time for the grandchild of a slave, which had undone himself of "Uncle Tomism," to rule. I was told that he would stand on a podium talking Black Power accompanied by his pink skinned wife from the Netherlands. Many wondered that if whites were so bad, why did he marry and have children with one of them.

Except for a few scattered votes, undoubtedly cast by family and friends, neither black nor white locals endorsed him. Let alone the newcomers. Disillusioned and feeling discontented that the dominant political and economic establishment did not hail him as an expert on how to manage society and guide black redemption, Clayton and his older brother became radicals. Financially stable they proclaimed that SXM culture and the true SXMers were being socially exterminated by the newcomers. They had a Marshall plan (their term) to save the country: all government tenders, all licences, and all vacancies must first go to locals and thereafter the rest.

They wanted to control and direct the movement of Capital. They also wanted to establish hard boundaries between insiders and outsiders.

Theirs is an impossible politics on an island consisting of newcomers and where most locals practice exogamy. And to add to the impossibilities, an island state, officially run by Paris and The Hague, with little resources, dependent on wealthy newcomers bent on keeping the island open. The Baines know it. For all their rhetoric they willingly do business with the wealthy newcomers, exploit the working-class migrants, and walk around with mistresses from Jamaica and the Dominican Republic. Most SXMers I spoke to interpret the Baines' politics as one of greed. They wanted to climb the economic ladder and earn as much as the wealthy Americans did, and if that meant promoting a politics of differential privileges then so be it.

Tonight the Shadow goes out of his way to remind us that the brothers B (he doesn't mention their full names), are the worst kind of politicians. They want to share the wealth with a privileged few: their friends and family. Other politicians who thief seek to hide from God, but Carlton and Clayton have forgotten that Conscience exists. The Shadow ended his diatribe against the Baines by reminding his audience that God loves all colors and has never put a fence dividing the earth. No state officials should seek to do so. As far as the other politicians were concerned, because they at least knew Conscience, they could and continued to fool us time and again.

The Shadow turns to his band, raises his hand and they let loose raising the volume and the tempo. "Stop Fooling, stop fooling" is being sung louder and louder and we are summoned to join in. Blacks, whites, and browns of various nationalities and faiths have lost their inhibitions. The wealthy tourists and SXMers of all classes are in frenzy. They are gyrating, screaming, waving, and the most fanatical even wetting themselves down with beer and rum. Everyone can relate to the Shadow, for critique of and being fooled by politicians is a universal. One of the most eloquent renditions of this truth was offered by Nestor, a Texaco worker from Providencia:

> A little boy come from school ask his father what is politics. His father say boy you're too young to know. But let me explain it to you this way. Politics is like our household. I is your father, I am the prime minister. You is the country, your mother is the cabinet, and your brother the people. Oh yeah and the maid the working class. The Boy say daddy I don't understand. Then the father said I know you wouldn't understand. That night his little brother shit all over him. So the boy went to the maid room to let her clean him. He saw his father screwing the maid. He went to his mother but she wouldn't wake up. So disillusioned he went back to his bed full of shit. The next morning he told his father, daddy, now I understand politics. So the father said tell me what you understand son. The boy said daddy while

the people shitting on the country, and the prime minister screwing the working-class, the cabinet lays fast asleep, so the country has nowhere to turn to. That, Francio, is politics on this island.

The Shadow feeds upon these sentiments on and off the air. Five days a week on the popular PJD2 radio station he informs SXMers that they should understand themselves as Rastafari individuals, meaning persons containing a relatively independent Self and a personal God and Devil. These two opposed forces—a brilliant illustration of the *panhuman* tendency of articulating personal identity to transcendental cosmologies—are reconfigured as our inner guides that we can't control and who we should listen to in order to be successful in life. Sometimes our personal God is right, but at other times we should heed the advice of our Devil and employ cunning against our fellow human beings. If everyone were to pay attention to these inner guides, political and religious leaders who cause us to misrecognize our common human identity would not dupe us. The Shadow believes in universality, and reminiscent of Bernard de Mandeville's (1924[1732]) grumbling beehive metaphor, he avers that if everyone lives his or her individuality to the fullest SXM would be a sound society. Private vices, public virtues.

Revolution against Babylon, the Rastafari term for global capitalism, was an internal one. It did not entail dismantling the capitalist system or redistributing wealth. Neither did it entail having a strong state regulate the movement of capital. All it entailed was recognizing one's personal God and Devil, what tonight the Shadow synthesizes as Conscience. All the rest are abstractions that "the One Love People" who reside on the island have no time for.

How Christ and Capital Met and Together Created Babel

This is the image of SXM the tourists came looking for, and also the way SXMers like to see themselves. CNN events—men and women killing men and women in the name of a Holy Nation and a Holy Book, or fighting against the injustices brought on by big business—takes place elsewhere. Not here. Not on SXM. Here tourists come face to face with, and aurally encounter a symbolic tower of Babel.

Now according to Jewish-Christian lore, as creolized in the Caribbean setting, the world became multilingual and multicultural after Babel. Babel signaled the wars and misrecognitions of common humanity recorded in the Old Testament *and* experienced in colonial times. Let me explain this transposition of Jewish history to *panhuman* history. In the Caribbean setting the Old Testament trials of the Jews are also read as metaphors for the bondage of the enslaved and indentured that landed on these shores. Bob Marley's classic *Exodus* is a telling example hereof. In this song the Middle Passage is likened to exile in Egypt and mental emancipation to the Jewish sojourn to the Promised Land. The hyphen between Judaism and Christianity, between the Old and New Testament, which in many Western societies has led to the persecution of Jews as the murderers of Christ, is interpreted as a continuation of the age old battle of Man against Man.²

Similarly Babel is conceived as being connected to the day of Pentecost; the day when Jesus' apostles received the Holy Spirit and learnt the metalanguage of Christianity; God's tongue. Since then the enlightened went around the world spreading the Gospel; spreading the message of human dignity. Paradoxically, however, the spreading of this message was deeply implicated in the nightmarish birth of the Caribbean. In the name of Christ and the capital many were massacred. Many were enslaved. Many were discriminated. Yet in the name of Christ and equal access to the market, the downtrodden in the Caribbean also spoke and fought for human dignity. A new episode in Pentecost was inaugurated when the enslaved and the indentured reconciled Christ and the capital to African and Asian religious and rhythmic motifs. Pentecost, in its Caribbean form, is the event that accepts the tower of Babel as a shifting whole of constantly deferred religious and cultural differences under a capitalist-Christian banner. A banner that proclaims that human dignity should be indestructible and commensurable with the market. How does such a thing work?

Though not sufficiently recognized, the genesis of capital in the Caribbean is Amer-Indian encomienda, African slavery, and Asian and European indenture (Quijano 2000; Mintz 1996; Beckford 2000).³ Amer-Indians, Africans, Asians, and poor Europeans were forced to move and through movement had to reconstitute themselves in order to survive. Those who did not learn to move, or weren't able to move, in *their own way* to the shifting rhythms of capital, that awesome machine for shredding incommensurables, perished. The deep structure of Caribbean imaginations of community is movement: securing the right of community members to move to the dance of capital.

As a general rule, Cuba's Soviet backed exemplar exception notwithstanding, island states in the region have always lacked the power to effectively control the movement of capital or construct anticapitalist national identities or policies categorically excluding outsiders. Engaging in these types of politics meant destroying the crop based plantations and the tourist industry. The Caribbean's logic of survival and imaginations of community is thus intimately connected to, and born of, the power of the logic of capital. Its national identities usually whither when seduced by the dance of capital. And the dance of capital is mild in the nonindependent Caribbean (Guadeloupe 2006b; Oostindie 2006).

One could go further and suggest that especially in the Caribbean microstates where the governing apparatus could not tame the movement of capital, poorer West Indians constructed a highly creolized public Christianity outside the strictures of the Africanized and Europeanized churches. They discerned that the success of Christ's radical gospel was based upon being able to move around and spread the message of our common Adamic and Edenesque roots. In Christ all the hierarchies based on color and status *ought* to be demolished. Whether Christian or not, one can posit that West Indians embrace and balance Christ and capital's logic of movement.

They employ the creolized universality of public Christianity to counter the partial universality of the latter. This is their most effective way of staying alive; a way of moving and benefiting; a way of imagining community that remains open to the outside world.

The balancing of capital and Christ is what I am experiencing. The tourists, the money people, as the islanders call them, those who still have the financial and technological power though the notion of their cultural superiority has diminished considerably, are being encouraged to participate in building this new Tower of Babel and engage with one of its main sonic architects, DJ Shadow. They have heard about him from the hotel personnel, they had heard him through the airwaves, now they can put a voice to a face. They love him.

Figure 6.1   Capital and Christ under the same roof: SXM's famous Bethel Shop where church is held on Sundays and rum is served from Monday to Saturday. Photo by Pedro de Weever.

"They fool we again" is being sung by so many enthusiastic voices and its accompaniment by such an intoxicating beat induce my lips to sing along and my hips to gyrate even before I am aware that I am doing so. The lyrical content is Manichaean—us against the politicians—while the rhythms are nonopinionated; festive. Even the politicians can participate and sing about their wrongdoings. Like public Christianity and capitalism, text and music in Caribbean music forms are agonistic opposites that commune.

And like capital nowadays, the music too seems to be winning out. Not only in me but also in most if not all the people I am surrounded by. I look to my right and my eyes and ears zoom into my companion, an old school friend who now resides in the United States. With a roasted chicken leg in one hand and a daiquiri in the other, she is brazing "that's right, the boy right; you give them hell, Addie [Addie is the Shadow's Christian name]." But there is a telling difference between her bodily movement and her words encouraging DJ Shadow to criticize the political establishment. As she moves her hips to "They Fool We Again," there is not a trace of anger or urgency on her face. Her mouth is saying one thing, the rest of her body another. It is a mix that I can only describe as socially critical with a heavy dose of hedonism and a party mood.

She reminds me of my conversations with DJ Fernando Clarke, the other popular sonic architect and pop star on the island. Clarke held the position of a bank manager at the Royal Bank of Trinidad and Tobago (RBBTT), but his hobbies were disc jockeying and stand up comedy. During one of the many conversations we had, Clarke had told me that through Calypso and other forms of Caribbean music many West Indians learn from an early age to be critical of societal injustices without losing themselves to a quixotic form of social activism. In other words music educates them in recognizing the ambivalence of life.

Life Is Neither Black Nor White

Like DJ Shadow, Clarke too had a recurring message. His was that the two vitamins C toward successful living and a sound society were Calypso and Christianity. Calypso stood for the art of artifice and Christianity for the techniques of virtue. For an island like SXM to run smoothly one needed more Calypso, with Christianity acting as a corrective of the excesses generated by the money tie system: the indigenous ideology that all SXMers were connected because of their common desires for more money and power. All the islanders were equal, and all belonged, according to Clarke, for none stood outside the irresolvable dialectic of Calypso and Christianity.

I had sat in last week during Clarke's radio programs where like the Shadow he, too, employed Calypso to critique the political order and school his public in the ambivalence of life. In that program he stated that reincarnation is a farce. Death is the ultimate limit. But he quickly then stated that Hindus were partially right, for there was a breed of people who did reincarnate, namely, the politicians. All religions had some truth to them. He then called the name of three unsuccessful but verbally strong fringe politicians, known for their autochthony politics, which he claimed were reincarnated souls. God had asked them what they would like to come back as. The first two answered as a dog and a butterfly. God complied, for in these incarnations no one would vote for them. SXM people might pet them, and even considerer them cute, but would never put their future in their hands: "A dog is man's best friend, never he master." The third politician, the most avidly antinewcomer of the three, asked an almost impossible the request. He asked to return as a jackass. Clarke said that God laughed and said: "but you can't take on the same identity twice."

He continued by stating that though the more successful politicians on SXM caused all kinds of confusion, people should not criticize them too harshly for God was ultimately in charge. And He had a weak spot for these politicians as they reminded him so much of our common grandfather Adam. Clarke then greeted the lieutenant governor and said that he was an honest man, only to add that he was still waiting for the governor to process the residence permit of his *mira,* his Columbian mistress.

After this lesson in the inseparableness of morality and immorality, with the latter having the upper hand, he played a Calypso classic called *Politicians Prayer* by Ellie Matt and the GI Brass where politicians accompanied by an intoxicating beat were asking God to forgive their former corruptions and help them rig the coming elections. As the song ended he stated that the politician's prayer resembles the prayer of all SXMers: "Forgive us our trespasses Lord, so that we can have it better than we neighbor."

Raised in the Dutch Caribbean, Clarke's lesson on the inseparableness of morality and immorality, and using this knowledge to get ahead in a largely immoral world, was not new for me. It was experiential knowledge that lay dormant since I was living in the mainland West where morality *seemed* divorced from the immoral. It took my conversations with him, and sitting in during his programs, to consciously remind me of how I had been socialized to see and live life.

The contrapuntal relationship between the text and music played a vital role in this socialization of embracing moral ambivalence as the basis of

life. The polyrhythmic harmonies and melodies of Caribbean music, especially those sanctioned by the culture industries, temper the lyrics
(Guadeloupe 2006b). The political within the lyrics, which need to be
black and white to be effective, are interrupted by the improvisational
dynamics of the music that reminds one of the messiness of life (ibid.).

I realize that I cannot divorce the politics of Peter Tosh's *Equal Rights*
and Willie Colon's *Che Che Cole* from the many childhood parties where I
danced to these songs while enjoying Planters cheese balls and the Fisher
Price toys. America, the Western world, the trinkets of capitalism, the virtues of Christian love, and the struggle against class oppression and racism
met and shook hands at these parties. Revolution was in the dance, in the
party, in the assertion and pursuit of happiness, not in concrete actions
that asked Caribbean people for unforeseeable sacrifices to dismantle capitalism. We had to keep moving to capitalism's drum, as most of our ancestors had done in order to loosen their joints and survive the Middle Passage.
The dialectics of resistance within not without capital's logic is what
birthed us. This is what we had in common; what allowed us to imagine
ourselves as a community.

My friend and I stand observing at the Calypso extravaganza as DJ
Shadow performs "they fool we again" exemplifies this, as do the majority
of the audience. Do they recognize the dialectic I discern in Caribbean
music and Caribbean culture? And if so, can they clearly articulate it? DJ
Shadow can. After his performance he simmers down and undoes himself
of his "Bigger Thomas," working-class image. While drinking Guinness
Stout he greets his fans and exchanges pleasantries with acquaintances and
friends. When I question him about his relaxed posture he replies,

> I am Caribbean man when I done speak my mind, I want party. Take a
> whine, free up myself. The Bible say a man can't live by bread alone, I
> say a man can't live by warring alone, Seen [Rasta speak for have you
> understood].

Man can't live by warring alone; man can't live by the political within the
lyrics alone. This is just a moment within the flow of music, of the logic of
capital. The other songs DJ Shadow performed that memorable night were
primarily party songs, which had little to do with denouncing the rich and
the powerful. Yes the Shadow knows, implicitly and explicitly, that Caribbean
culture is not an either or culture, a culture that seeks the Apocalyptic, as
Benitez-Rojo (1996) would put it. It is a culture born of capital that seeks to
Christianize capital's logic in order to limit its violence. If movement is the
essence of capital, then for Christ's sake let all move freely.

Figure 6.2   A reveler celebrating multinational conviviality on a 37 square mile rock. Photo by Pedro de Weever.

As I speak to my friend and others at the venue about DJ Shadow's performance, I am told that the reason they like him so much was that even during his most damning critique of the political establishment, he is positively seeking to promote unity among all SXMers. The words one of these persons uses is "he know bout life," meaning he knows life is a give and take. Life in this Caribbean world that is structured by capital is about being able to detect and accept difference, to critique inequalities, and yet construct commonalities. Constructing provisional commonalities is what allows one to move in a way that secures and opens up tomorrow.

If the logic of life in a world where Capital seems inescapable is movement—movement of the world moving in a nonsynchronous synchronicity, then this leads to a recognition of the tower of Babel that is SXM society.

To engage with one another in this Babelesque society, every SXMer is compelled to perform various social selves in order to build temporary bridges of commonality. The constant construction, privileging, and canceling out of these performances to fit the occasion leads many SXMers to conceive of themselves as containing multiple identities and conflicting forces.

The Tower of Babel as a Metaphor
of Multiple Identities

The politics of belonging of DJ Fernando Clarke and DJ Shadow is about promoting a positive recognition of Babelesque SXM, and the multiplicities of selves SXMers entertain each other too. Herein contradiction is the name of the game. As Caribbean pop stars, usually saints and sinners at one and the same time, Clarke and the Shadow specialize in being many things to many different people. In this they actually mirror the way Caribbean people engage each other on a daily basis, and therefore are a mirror for all Caribbean people to see themselves and the Babelesque societies they are constantly building.

SXM is an extreme form of this Caribbean trait of taking on and putting on identities. The 80 nationalities officially registered in the census offices on both sides of the island were an inaccurate indication of the many national identities SXMers performed in their daily interactions. The fact that SXMers hail from the four corners of the globe, and their livelihood depended exclusively on tourism, created a social environment in which all the inhabitants of the island had to continuously perform a series of national and transnational identities to create common worlds. These performances depended on their routes—the places they had lived— the socially ascribed roots of their ancestors, and the passports they wielded.

For the islanders this was a normal state of affairs. When I asked Miss Maria, an ex-school teacher in her late sixties to whom I had gotten close on the island, which of her national identities she considered to be closest to her, she replied in her usual temperamental style, "all of them are important to me; they have a reason. Now stop minding my business." I had questioned her on the fact that while she considered herself a *local*, she also displayed national allegiance to Anguilla and Curaçao. There was no contradiction according to her, since she was born in Anguilla and had lived practically all her life in Curaçao. Furthermore as a *local* she claimed both Saint Martin and Sint Maarten (SXM) as her own, the national boundary notwithstanding. Besides her Anguillan, Curaçaoan, and SXM sense of national belonging, Miss Maria had several other national and transnational allegiances. As an Anguillan, part of the British Overseas Territories (BOTs), she identified with the United Kingdom (see Clegg 2006 on the political constitution of the BOTs). Since she also carried a Dutch passport she likewise identified herself as being a member of the Dutch nation. Finally, Miss Maria also identified with the West Indies and the Black Diaspora in "the West."

Depending on the person with whom she was interacting Miss Maria would perform one of her national or transnational identities, canceling out others. Herein she was not exceptional as most SXMers did the same. Even the fringe local politicians who were as autochthonous as can be, and the Christian fundamentalists who supposedly lived as Jesus did, also forgot their localness and righteousness when it suited them. Many SXMers informed me that when it came to matters of business with American newcomers, there was not a trace of their otherwise anti-imperialist or antihedonistic rhetoric. Devout priests did not refuse checks from Hindu merchants or Atheist hoteliers, like the Baines did not refuse newcomers who wished to rent their apartments. It is simply impossible on an island such as SXM to remain performing one national identity or to be pious 168 hours a week.

DJ Shadow and Fernando Clarke made a sport out of the performance of multiple identities, national and otherwise, and therewith reminded SXMers of what they all necessarily do to survive and enhance their power and wealth. Clarke presents himself as the devout Christian when he shares the podium with priests at Christian charities, at other occasions he plays the Calypsonian displaying his virtuosity in misogynistic and sexist lyrics, yet in other public events he champions the rights of women, and he is also the well-known comedian who often plays the role of the poor old man from Antigua critical of upper echelons of society yet longing to be there; the proletariat with the soul of a capitalist. The latter, his theatrical self, has such an impact that offstage people refer to him in this way.

In one of the bars that we stopped to have a drink, a fan came in and said "what going on old man, how the family in Antigua." Clarke responded, "things a dread me a tell you. Sonny [referring to the man behind the counter], that woman a go pay for we drinks, so me can send more money home." This Antiguan Clarke who lived in the body of the Clarke born in Aruba wasn't joking as he let his fan pay for our drinks. All these aforementioned "Clarkes" have to share their space with his job persona, Clarke as a scrupulous manager at RBTT bank, who knows no God or unconditional friendship when it comes to financial matters.

DJ Shadow is as multiple as Clarke. During another live gig, a couple of weeks after I saw him perform *They Fool We Again*, DJ Shadow metamorphosed. I could not detect a trace of the Calypsonian in him. The party man was gone. He was all pious and radical Rasta that night. He was performing the role of the Master of Ceremony at Junior Gong's concert, one of the heirs of Bob Marley's legacy of immanent social critique. At this concert DJ Shadow was the righteous Rasta criticizing Babylon and promoting livity (messages of radical egalitarianism). The

audience, teenage "wannabee Bob Marleys" were elated with his performance. He touched a nerve every time he said "we a going Chant Down
Babylon tonight," [we are going to revolt against the Western dominated
capitalist order tonight] and, "a inity we want" [inity means an explicit
wish for unity and equality], and, of course "politrickians run, judgment
soon come."

The teenagers and young adults I spoke to after the concert felt that DJ
Shadow was a genuine "rebel man." Many tell me that they are loyal fans
who follow his program on a daily basis. He was as genuine as they were.
But if they tuned into his daily program, which aired Mondays to Fridays
from 1 pm to 5 pm on PJD2 radio, they must know that he is many things
to many different people. One can guess that he reminds them of the many
compromises they too must make despite their love for Rasta. They
couldn't be Rasta 24/7.

On the radio there is Shadow the romantic balladeer who always blames
men for love relationships gone sour, there is Shadow the Calypsonian who
specializes in double entendre, there is the Shadow of the *mucho fuego* who
knows his Salsa and Bachata, there is Shadow the Rastafari rebel who is
angry with Babylon, and then there is the capitalist Shadow comfortable
with Babylon. The latter Shadow is the one *the money people* know they can
trust and do business with.

Fascinating was the way the various "Clarkes" and "Shadows" shared
the same bodies and smoothly alternated one another. One of the things
that the Shadow and Fernando Clarke did, no matter how raunchy a show
they were performing at, was to end with the words "God bless y'all."
Furthermore their whole discourse was always saturated with biblical terms
and references to God being the ultimate power. Their public was always
delighted when they did this, and believed it to be genuine expressions of
their religious reverence. They did not seem suspicious, and I took their
response seriously.

Taking the public's response seriously means understanding the issue of
a person's authenticity and the truthfulness of his or her discourse differently. It means forgetting the view that presupposes another man, a more
authentic one lurking in the background. Instead I prefer to understand
these gestures as temporarily authentic. This requires us to take seriously
the conceptualization of the person as being able to inhabit various positions requiring specific performances, as well as the person coming into
being at every performance.[4]

With Clarke and the Shadow this became even more evident, as these
DJs were also performers in the artistic sense of the word. Their main stage
to entice SXMers to see society as a sin-ridden-yet-sanctimonious place
that they all should embrace was through the airwaves.

SXM Society as a Tower of Babel of
Sin and Sanctity

Clarke's specialty was the on-air presentation of SXM society as a sinful sanctimonious place. He was as vulgar and rambunctious as he could be during his radio programs. Nothing was sacred for this provocateur that in a joking manner reminded SXMers that their honest hospitality was always accompanied by the "what in it for me" ethic. No one stood outside of the money tie system: the indigenous ideology that presents SXMers as united by their individual quests for more money and power. This according to him was a universal that transcended class, ethnic, gender, and religious lines. It was what made SXMers the same despite their manifold differences.

Those who wished to distance themselves most from this conception of society and themselves—the highfaluting fringe ethno-political and religious leaders, the ethnic and religious fundamentalists—were made an example of, and cunningly presented as the slyest of all SXMers. I witnessed this most explicitly in a radio program where he countered arguments of a local Christian of the pious type, someone with a leadership position in the Methodist church, who called in stating that the vulgar style of dancing of newcomers from the British islands during carnival was most unbecoming. It was not part of SXM culture.

Clarke agreed and then went on to tell one of his characteristic tales dismantling his prior assertion. He said that when he had just finished high school he had ambition. He wanted a job where he could earn lots of money, did not have to think, and did not have to work in the hot sun. Two professions came to mind, becoming a politician or a priest. He chose the latter for he said that most people knew you had to be full of tricks to be in politics. He wasn't that good. So there was nothing left than to become a priest. He was a Methodist, but didn't want to be a Methodist preacher. The reasons were obvious: according to him, since most SXMers were Catholics, it was in that church that he would make a killing. The Catholics had mass many times a day and the collection plate went around regularly. The priest would then raise the collection plates on top of his head letting God take whatever he wanted. The rest went into the priest's pocket. This was the profession he was looking for: not too much work and earning a good buck.

There was, however, a problem, which was celibacy. He felt that he should enjoy himself as much as possible before entering a seminary, so he became a frequent customer of a whorehouse. One night he saw a man sneaking out of the brothel acting all conspicuous. He thought he was a politician who didn't want anyone to see him, so he decided to blackmail the man. Taken aback and frightened, the man offered him US$50 dollars so he would keep his mouth shut.

Happy as can be he went home and told his mother that just as she got the tourists to give her nice tips, he got this man to pay him for his silence. She was not too happy with what he had done and told him that if he wanted to become a priest he had to go and confess this sin. The following day while sitting in the confession box he recognized the voice of the man who had given him the 50 bucks. As it turned out, he was the new Catholic priest on the island.

Necessarily with such a story the phones began to ring as his fans called in to engage the matter, and speak about Christianity and carnival. As usual Clarke took all sides and at the end of the program he went back into his story telling mode and claimed this time around that he used to be a Catholic priest. He said that he got fed up with the job because SXMers did not understand that they had to confess their sins and not their achievements. The straw that broke the camel back for him was a man whose supposed sin was sleeping with his neighbor's wife. Clarke said that if every man and woman who slept around would take confession there would be endless cues in front of the Catholic Church. Since he got tired of hearing about everyone's achievements, he left the preaching profession and became

Figure 6.3 DJ Clarke's ideal church: who would not want to preach the Word of God in this street temple! Photo by Pedro de Weever.

a Calypsonian. He ended the discussion by stating that he now preached the message of the Lord while whining with the revelers behind the big trucks on carnival day.

That was for him the only type of honest Christianity on the island. Becoming such an honest Christian entailed recognizing the contesting forces of sin and sanctity within. The Shadow was the most philosophical therein.

Connecting the External Babel to the Internal Dynamics

Father God I am just learning how to pray/First I thank you for the life of everyone that's here with me/Then I thank you for the love you gave me/ Why?/I don't know/I don't deserve it, and it hurts inside/Many a nights I have cried, and called your name out loud/But didn't call you when I was doing good, I was too proud/ And still you gave me love, I wasn't used to that/Most people that gave me love ended up taking it back/That's something new to me, so I'm asking you for time to adjust/Let me make it there, I will be one you can trust/ What I stand for, I put my life on it, I do/I guess what I asking is, show me how to stand for you/And I will rap for you, sing for you, teach for you, reach for you/I will love you like you love me, unconditionally/And I will always be prepared, for whatever the mission will be/ Give the nutrition to me, and I will properly digest it/And when I give it back, I'll show you word well invested/And whenever I go, before I go, let me give thanks to you my Lord, for my birth, for everyday that I've lived/ You gave me love most of my life, I didn't know was there/In the name of Jesus, I give you my life cause I care.

This a cappella prayer, by the American rapper extraordinaire DMX, accompanied by a thumping dub rhythm, opens and closes the five-hour radio program of DJ Shadow. His role, in the first hour of his show, which was dedicated to social commentary, was of course that of the angry and righteous Rasta. After that hour his other personas take over. However, the distinctions were not that clearcut as there were always traces of his other more hedonistic personas discernible when his Rasta Self took front stage. Shadow endorsed Mammon's products during every commercial break.

That Mammon and God, capital and Christianity, are compatible is lent extra credence in his choice of DMX whose pop theology resembles that of the Shadow. Each of DMX's albums contains tracks where he converses with God and the Devil. DMX chooses God's path, but leaves room for the Devil to continue asserting his influence in his life. His "nigga Damion," a corruption of the Damion character in the Hollywood cult classic the Omen, cannot be exorcised.

The general format of radio programming on SXM, which DJ Shadow imitates in his five-hour program, also endorses the idea of having to live with Damion. There is no strictly religious based radio station on SXM. All radio stations are Christian oriented, emulating the dominant form of doing religion on the island. Monday to Saturday from 5 am to 7 am all one hears on the radio is devotional programs where Gospel music or Conscious Reggae is broadcast. This is followed from 7 am until 8 am by serious news casting. The rest of the day is dominated by worldly music and upbeat shout outs and request lines. It is only after 12 midnight that most radio stations switch to easy listening prerecording to begin the official broadcasting at 5 am with religious music.

Saturday and Friday midnights are, however, exceptions since on these days lots of party songs are played. This has to do with the fact that these are the days most youngsters and adults visit clubs. By playing music that gets SXMers in the mood, radio offers itself as a companion for those who are going clubbing.

Sundays work somewhat differently since, on the Lord's day as they say on the island, devotional radio begins at 5 in the morning and usually lasts until around 12 in the afternoon. This is followed by easy listening, which is alternated with more up tempo party music in the late afternoons. The switch in the afternoons has to do with the fact that many persons who work six days a week, mostly the working class, will go clubbing on Sunday evenings to dance the stress away.

What this sequencing of radio tells us is that most SXMers are socialized to see human living as starting with the Lord, as theological, which is transfigured into the political of worldly matters of concern, which quickly gives way to the hedonism that reigns supreme. This hedonism, however, cannot resist the higher ethics of the theological from which it was born and to which it returns. There is thus a circular logic of an eternal return in this mode of Christianity.

The Shadow works exactly in this way. He starts out with a prayer, after the prayer one gets an hour of Conscious Reggae where he will tackle a major societal issue or international affair, giving his political point of view on the matter. It is during this hour that he exalts the Lord and blazes politicians and religious leaders. Thereafter he goes on to play Calypso, Jamband, Salsa, Meringue, RandB, and Soul. He ends his program with DMX's prayer wishing his audience God's blessing.

The switch was most discernible in one of his shows on Haitian boat refugees that were being refused in the United States. He sang a brief a cappella version of Bob Marley's *One Drop*. The words he chose to high-light were "they made the world so hard everyday the people dying. Give us the teachings of his majesty cause we no want to Devil philosophy." He then began the Bob Marley song, welcomed his audience for tuning in—a diverse group, ranging from youngsters, civil servants, bank tellers, store managers and personnel, and visiting tourists—and then added that this song was dedicated to those Haitians on rafts that political leaders would have us forget. How could the U.S. authorities refuse mothers and young children risking their life? In that hour he continuously criticized the polit-ical establishment in the United States, but also those in Haiti who he felt were to blame for this human disaster. He played songs that added truth value to his claims and let his audience speak out on the matter.

What was also interesting is how he tied the local to the extra-local and made sure not to ostracize the visiting tourists. He made it clear that the policies of the U.S. government bore some resemblance to the comments of some fringe local politicians who wanted to make distinctions between SXMers. The logical outcome of such distinction making was the disaster that was taking place off the coasts of Florida. Like the majority of the SXMers who did not follow these political radicals, he saluted the American citizens who also showed great solidarity for speaking out against this atrocity. The United States like SXM was an immigrant country and therefore according to him should always be hospitable to strangers.

The only way of doing so was remembering what made us common, which was our humanity and the supernatural forces of good and evil that we all contained. This is our moral compass. When we recognized those forces within ourselves and in other human beings, we would cease follow-ing crooked political and religious leaders. Only then would the Haitian boat refugees stop being refugees and become fellow human beings in our eyes. Persons with the right to move.

This moral lesson was directly followed by an hour of double entendre Calypsos. The first song he played was a tune about the delight of sucking Julie mangos, which are mangos with hairs that do not prick or stick in one's teeth. This, of course, can also be interpreted, as it often is, as the sucking of a woman's vagina. The mischievous Shadow of that hour seemed oblivious to the plight of the boat refugees. Even when he ended his pro-gram with DMX, the political was nowhere to be heard.

This was a man, and his colleague Fernando Clarke too, who "know bout life": living life in accordance with the capitalist-Christian order of movement and demolishing of incommensurables—the only life worth living according to islanders. I often wondered if there was another life, a better life, and would SXMers embrace such a search? It was wishful think-ing. "[T]hey know very well what they are doing, but still, they are doing it" (Žižek quoted in Beasley-Murray 2003, 119). They were fine with the Marriage of Christ and capital. They were willing to be fooled time and again by big business and the political elites as long as they remained part of capitalism's privileged few. As long as they too could move. The sonic architects just legitimized and gave legitimacy to the Babel that they willingly construct.

Notes

1. The transformation of Christianity in popular culture thereby creating a characteristically Christianized public sphere is not a unique Caribbean phenomenon. See the work of Birgit Meyer (2004a) on the *Pentecostalization* of the public sphere in Ghana, and also the work of David Chidester (2005) on the prominent role of Christianity in the North American Culture Industry.
2. In Europe we are also witnessing the recognition and the acceptance of the hyphen between Judaism and Christianity—Judeo-Christian—as a bridge. This, however, is still a point of contention and was born after the Holocaust. For an interesting discussion on the matter see Jean-Francois Lyotard and Eberhard Gruber (1999) in discussion on the hyphen.
3. Dialectically we must remark that however ridden with power differences, processes in the Caribbean also affected Western history. See Sidney Mintz's *Sweetness and Power* (1985) on the importance of sugar for the dietary needs of British industrial workers and elites. Here we see an account of how production and consumption are related and affect Western lifestyles and conceptions of taste. See also C. L. R. James' *The Black Jacobins* (1963 [1938]) on the importance of Haitian revolution in the evolution of the notion of human dignity and inalienable rights of every individual.
4. This way of looking does not omit the idea of a particular spark of life, or, less substantial, a possibly more enduring trace. However, as David Hume long ago put it, we can say nothing sensible about this (1975[1758]). The moment we do we are actually prioritizing a prior performance as being more real and enduringly authentic. All we have to go by are performances, as we too are busy performing.

Part 3

Mediating Immediacy

Chapter 7

Breath, Technology, and the Making of Community Canção Nova in Brazil

Maria José A. de Abreu

Inspiration is wind becoming breath, expiration is breath becoming wind.

—Tim Ingold, *Earth, Sky, Wind and Weather*

In the early months of 1978 a youth group gathering for a "Seminar in the Spirit" in the small town of Areias, State of São Paulo, witnessed an extraordinary event. A priest named Padre Jonas Abib addressed the group by asking them: "which of you would be ready to leave everything behind, family, carrier, hobbies, in order to fulfil a mission God has placed in my heart?" The story goes that exactly 12 people raised their hands as they "were moved by an incredible force." Then Padre Jonas turned to his followers and added three other things. First, the mission would involve working with communication. Second, it was especially addressed to youth and third, the *community* would be called *Comunidade Canção Nova* (New Song Community). This chapter is about the making of Canção Nova Community, a thriving global media network of Catholic Pentecostalism based in Brazil. Communities are often addressed in terms of a social construction around the management of symbols, events, or aspirations that create a sense of bonding and belonging. Anthony Cohen's "The Symbolic Construction of Community" (1975) is a particular case in point in which communities are understood as meaningful constructs that ground the cultural inscription of identity. In so arguing, Cohen implies the existence of a predetermined plane of reference against which construction happens.

Benedict Anderson's (1991) notion of "imagined communities" in turn offers us a much more flexible model for grasping the complex dynamics of community-making. Still, imagination remains dependent on a point of origin or foundation, upon which the community imagines itself. We do not get to know how the real or origin against which imagination evolves is itself already constituted by those imaginations. Alternatively, in what follows, I propose to develop a more circular and interactive approach to community by looking at the material, bodily, and processual mechanisms that signal community are always brought about and implicated through its own making of. Thus, instead of defining a community as an entity bounded to a particular core from which it "constructs" or "imagines" itself, the goal is to expose the very material mechanics or technological existence of the community *as* communication. Rather than conceiving it as a containable entity awaiting signification or as an assemblage of discrete bodies that instrumentally communicate, the aim of the present exercise will be to examine the communal as intrinsic to communication. Shortly put, this chapter argues that communities do not only communicate but that they *are* communication.

More specifically, relying upon the Christian notion of *pneuma*, the Greek word for spirit, breath, or air, we will be invited to ponder the concept of community through the breathing body. Based on the narrative of Pentecost that tells how the Holy Spirit came down upon the apostolic community "in the form of a rushing mighty wind," I will move on to explore how inspirited breath sets the force or mechanism through which the community as communication unfolds. I will then consider the material and motile expressions of breath. That is, by referring to the aspect of reciprocation between inside and outside that is inherent to breathing, I will question the modern separation between inner life and outer expression as we acknowledge that the cycle of breathing in-and-out disallows any prolonged closure as well as any external point whereupon the boundaries of the community could be drawn. What becomes relevant, instead, are the processes and dynamics by which the body is implicated and distributed in the entire natural, human, and technological landscape by means of circulation and a self-regulated balance between inputs and outputs.

I owe my understanding of a breathing body in this discussion to the efforts of media savvy Brazilian Catholic Charismatic Padre Jonas Abib to promote an expanded middle in an era of strong polarization between right and left ideologies. While the 1970s were rich in calls for social mobilization in Brazil and around the world, Padre Jonas's engagement with movement was primarily kinetic. He chose not to be part of a social religious movement but to *be* movement. This meant a leap over the walls of ideological positioning, and landing in a space of sensory modalities.

While the analogy between body and community is not new, I will examine it through the distinctively sensory modality of proprioception. Akin to kinaesthesia, proprioception is the sense responsible for the perception of motion. Sometimes addressed as a sixth sense, it refers to the internal mechanism that enables a body in motion to maintain equilibrium through awareness of the relation of the joints and of body parts to each other. In the same way that proprioceptive awareness keeps track and controls the circulation between different parts of the body, this chapter shows how Canção Nova evolves and maintains itself as a whole community through a circuitry and transmissibility that it manages to establish between different community stations. As we will see, nature, body, architecture, media technology, and economics all enter into a relational field of inter- and intrareferentiality in ways that engage with, and actively configure electronic technology. The goal is to create a structural analogy between the influx of sensory information within the body, and the regime of circularity that connects the important "joints" of the community.

In sum, the purpose of this chapter is threefold: first, to foreground Canção Nova Media Community as a sensuous community in motion or community-in-the-making; second, to reflect on how such a community-in-the-making instantiates the very mechanics of communication; and third, to disclose the constitutive relation between an aesthetic economic regime of transparency and Pentecostal practices of embodied charisma. In line with recent scholarly interest on the relation between the aesthetic and the political, the notion of aesthetics applied here rescues the political power of the sensorial as implied in the Aristotelian concept of *aesthesis* (see also Meyer in this volume). The latter has been defined as a form of organizing experience and knowledge of the senses (Buck-Morss 1992; Verrips 2006; Hirschkind 2006). In order to grasp the making of community in our time we are well advised to take seriously the very discursive practices through which communities produce themselves, and in the case of Canção Nova this inevitably leads us to the sensing body.

The Paths of the CCR

In 1969 two American Jesuit priests arrived in São Paulo State. Their mission was to introduce the CCR movement in Brazil. One was called Father Haroldo Rahm, and the other Father Eduardo Dougherty. Although both priests identified with the ideals of the CCR movement, namely its emphasis on the narrative of Pentecost, once in Brazil, each took very different paths. Whereas Father Rahm opted to live in a farm and do spiritual rehabilitation work among alcoholics and drug addicts, Father Dougherty resolutely mobilized his physical and material capital to start up a Catholic global media network. Very few have ever seen Father Rahm or even know about his activities. Father Dougherty, on the contrary, is renowned as the pioneer of the CCR in Brazil but especially for introducing Catholic televangelism to the country.

The protechnology policies of the ruling regime at the time of the CCR's arrival in Brazil seemed to offer particularly favorable grounds to launch a global media Catholic crusade. It provided the conservative allies of Catholicism with the opportunity to not only counter the surge of American based Protestant televangelism that was spreading all over Latin America but also to break through a deep-seated prejudice against televangelism lodged within the progressive Church of Brazil. One of the reasons why Liberation Theology's militant Catholicism vehemently resisted the importation of Catholic televangelism to Brazil was that it unsettled the assumption that televangelism was a strictly Protestant phenomenon. The fact that the CCR evolved as a predominantly upper middle-class movement among university scholars, affiliated with conservative Catholic groups such as Opus Dei or the Cursilhos, only deepened the rift separating a local progressive left-wing Catholic Church whose alleged "preference for the poor" proved irreconcilable with what they considered CCR's spiritually oriented, Americanized tele-evangelical industry.

Still determined to carry on with his mission, Father Dougherty introduced a strategy based on marketing, technology, and money from America. Later, in the early 1980s, he was chosen to be the entrepreneur responsible for applying the ideals developed by two global media projects to Brazil: the *Lumen Project* financed by Holland and *Evangelization 2000* by the United States, two projects that proved to be groundbreaking. He received a donation of US$ 100,000 and new electronic equipment, with which he further extended his association and TV production center called TV Century XXI (Carranza 2000, 246–265). Subsequently, he hired a team of professionals in the field of communication, independent of their religious affiliations, and a well-known Catholic marketing expert. In reaction, legendary Liberation Theology activist Don Paul Evaristo who presided over the archdioceses of São Paulo, strongly condemned Father Dougherty's attempt to "market Christianity." Furthermore, São Paulo's main broadsheet, *Estado de São Paulo*, denounced the CCR as part of a political maneuver by the Vatican and the conservative elites to eradicate communism and Liberation Theology from the face of the earth (Carranza 2000, 246). Father Dougherty was labeled a "demon from the north" as liberationists often characterized Protestant Pentecostalism (Lima 1987), except that now the demon wore a clerical habit.

As a Catholic Pentecostal movement the CCR was particularly unwelcome because of its hybrid status. It not only distressed progressive Catholics who tended to equate Pentecostalism with North American conservatism in opposition to southern liberalism, but also alerted Protestant Pentecostals who began to accuse Catholics of copying their "methods." Flanked between an antiregime liberationist Catholic majority with a renowned scorn of televangelism and a call to evangelize through the media, Brazilian Padre Jonas realized that he would have to strategize to his own advantage by navigating between the extremes. But instead of dissipating hybridity by taking one of the sides, he thought it better to internalize hybridity and vault over the arched backs of the two main local quarrelsome political forces into a middle zone, eventually, turning this bridge into the strength of his program.

Unlocking the Paths

In 1969, the same year that the CCR arrived in Brazil from the United States, Silesian Padre Jonas Abib (of Lebanese origin and recently ordained) entered a sanatorium in Campos do Jordão—SP due to a serious lung disease. The news about his illness kept him from further participating in the activities of his parish within the region of the Paraiba Valley. Acknowledged as an ambitious and restless person, he rebelled against his chronic pneumonia, just as he did against his superiors who, unable to make sense of his agitations, kept reshuffling him around various parishes within the Valley. In the sanatorium, Padre Jonas started to compose songs, and there he assembled a choir of fellow pneumonic patients bizarrely shaking the walls of the sanatorium. The personnel read into event the expression of an ulterior force that was asking for the release of Padre Jonas. As he describes in one of his books,

> In the next month we had a youth meeting at the sanatorium. Then, not without reason, the doctor called my superior, and told him that if he would want me to be cured he had to let me out. That is what my superior did: he sent me off to Lorena. (Abib 1999, 14)

While in Lorena, one of the Valley's districts, Padre Jonas meets Father Haroldo Rahm, the other CCR pioneer during a "Seminar in the Spirit." During that event in 1971, Padre Jonas was baptized in the Spirit. Many report that the origins of Canção Nova must be found in the baptismal moment of Padre Jonas. That then, and only then, did the pneumonia of

Padre Jonas start to heal; that like an effusion from heaven his unyielding lungs began to inflate, his chest expanded, his chronic fatigue mysteriously disappeared. Padre Jonas spent seven years moving back and forth within and around the green Valley in order to baptize new individuals and organized prayer groups to whom he witnessed his healing and revival experience. With incessant energy, he organized weekly prayer meetings and preaching sessions to Catholic youth. Throughout seven years of meandering in service within and around the Valley, the body of Padre Jonas's body fused with the local landscape. Through the intakes of breathing in and out, his body became dissolved and distributed in it just as it became embedded with him. Then one day, during one of the youth meetings, the wonder aired its call. As words came out of his mouth, Padre Jonas realized how the call he was about to ensue had been building up inside him for all those years; how its spelling out was but the expelling of the last residue of his phlegmatic past along with the outline of a new creation under the pneumatic intervention of the Spirit. Padre Jonas's airways were finally unlocked.

Channeling Proprioception

Unlike Father Dougherty, Padre Jonas lacked financial resources, marketing expertise and technical equipments, as well as, in fact, any experience with televangelism. The only thing he had, he likes to tell, was his faith, and his twelve followers. Such lack, however, was what allowed Padre Jonas to stick closely to the message of Pentecost and, more specifically, to the aesthetic economy of charisma. Having no palpable capital to launch his call, Padre Jonas focused on his *charismatically,* unlocked body in order to tune into his immediate surroundings. It is said, printed, recorded in dozens of Canção Nova media productions that from the very first, nobody in the community knew what the next step would be. The group was primarily an assemblage of individuals baptized in the Spirit. In a vivid reenactment of the apostolic community, they gathered in stables, tents, and other improvised areas, often in open air, in the green Valley of Paraiba River. Words fluttered out of his mouth in ways that, as his followers maintain today, "intoxicated our hearts." It was as if the air that formed his words had the power to carry his listeners into another time, and yet made that language adjustable to the present. One often cited example tells how he recalled Jesus addressing the apostles, exclaiming: "It is now time to launch the nets." Another time, he impersonated St. Mathew's call "to evangelize through the roofs," repeated St. Paul's prophecy on the Second Coming or

The Rapture saying, "we who are left alive will be carried off together with them in the clouds to meet the Lord in the air..." (Thess 4, 15–17). In the words of Nelsinho, one of the early *apostles* of the community,

> The history of Canção Nova has been made from body-to-body with the people. We had no real place... Padre Jonas would walk around with a tape recorder and a bag filled with tapes. He would put on classic music and would ask: Who is God for You? Then, we would start crying, we were touched by the words of the padre. That prepared the sermon. Then the padre would make us travel, he had that kind of language. He worked with our imagination. There and then, the padre *was* DAVI {audiovisual department}, the Radio, the TV and Internet. (Nelsinho 2004)[1]

Then, as now, his followers maintain, everything occurred as if time and space were two units that existed alongside the dynamics of "breathing *in* and *through* the spirit," beyond which there was only "uncertainty." Yet, by perceiving time in line with each singular breath, that is, by living ever more intensively in the here and now of the present, they opened up to the universal. Each singular breath worked as an actualization of creative possibility. The more one inspired, the more one got inspired and thus the higher one's creative potential became.

In the Charismatic sense, to be virtuous (i.e., to be gifted) was and continues to be an opening up to virtuality. As argued, breath-induced virtue stands for the ability to open up to relations with the outside. Insofar that through the dynamic rhythms of breath, the outside is implicated in the inside (and vice versa), any relation is always and necessarily a self-relation (de Abreu 2008). What happens in this process is that the body alternates its objective concreteness with the more abstract dynamism of passage and flow. This alternation between concrete and abstract itself evinces the performative nature of breathing in that, the actual physical activity involved in "the contraction and expansion of breath," also stands for the "least material regime of corporeality" (Sobchack 2008, 202).

Thus, the more Padre Jonas became aware of the proprioceptive aptitudes and fluencies occurring within his body, the more virtuous and virtual his body became. His body became distributed and coimplicated in the physical, human, and technological landscapes. When transposed into the relation between individual and the collective, there was no possible separation between one and the other. Rather these two were interconnected. Just as the physical landscape permeated the body, and the latter was recalibrated to suit the local environment, so too the collective, the community, inhabited—and continues to inhabit—the individual. As long as they breathe, the community and body overlap, expressing what

Brian Massumi when referring to the work of Pierre Levy calls a "collective individuation" (Massumi 2002, 71). As we will see momentarily, technology too enters this process of codependency and mutual modulation between body and space, individual and collective.

The Media Acts of the Apostles

"The Acts of the Apostles," Padre Jonas frequently exhorts, "is the Acts of the Apostles."[2] Often used as a statement of prepositional logic or, alternatively, as a rhetorical strategy, the redundant and symmetrical nature of tautology, literally makes it good to breathe: one inhales while thinking the "Acts of the Apostles" and exhales while thinking "The Acts of the Apostles." Word-bearing symmetries such as this help structure breath, that "art of mechanical reproduction" that for the past three decades has been organizing the life of Canção Nova. Such practice comes after the reformations of Catholic prayer techniques introduced by the CCR, which characteristically uses words and rhythm to structure breath. Bearing in mind media's contemporary efforts to convey a sense of live transmission and directness, Canção Nova's adoption of breath as a dynamic principle allows it to instantiate *liveliness* at the core of the technological, one modulating the other.

The idea, however, is to act according to the teachings of St. Paul to whom communication is inalienably associated with the living body, that is, a body that communicates. As Manfred Schneider notes, St. Paul was "the media specialist of the Apostle's," who "radicalized the difference inaugurated by Jesus and his reporters: namely, that God's power, and the medium of his revelation consisted in spirit" (Schneider 2001, 202–203; see also Sanchez in this volume). Being one of the main protagonists of "The Acts," St. Paul expressed and lived according to the ideal that the body is at once the medium and the message, the singular and the universal. In other words, the body is not an instrument of communication but is itself embodied communication. The breathing body always implicates the world in its inside, just as the latter is distributed in the world.

Essentially, the components of St. Paul's "media theory" comprise the gamut of charismas, gifts, or virtues, which according to the story of Pentecost fell upon the community in the "form of a rushing wind." His well-known dictum, "the body is the temple of the Holy Spirit," is regarded by Catholic Charismatics as an abridgment of the parable of Pentecost as described in Acts 2:4. The parable tells how the Holy Spirit descended upon the apostolic community whereupon their petrified-in-fear bodies—just like the walls in which they were contained—started to open up to the circulation of charisma. Described as the baptism in the Spirit, this event collapses any separation between inner and outer, between body and space. In other words, where previously the body was contained within space, and these two were conceived as discrete entities, the baptism in the Spirit reformulates such state experience by stressing instead the relational and reciprocal nature between body and space that breathing sets in motion: by inhaling the outside moves in, and by exhaling the inside moves out. Breath, in short, instantiates St. Paul's dictum inasmuch as the *body* becomes the *temple* of sacred communication.

What is noteworthy is that such understanding presents a notion of space, which diverts considerably from the one that influenced the standards of modern Western architecture as well as philosophical conceptions of "worldview," which are predicated on the separation between inside and outside. Modern perspective established the need to step outside the world so as to order it on the solid grounds of reason. The Pentecostal abode, on the contrary, does not rest on solid foundations. Indeed, if the ground is the body, then necessarily, the ground is a moving one.

St. Paul's call for direct and transparent communication with the divine has a particular appeal among Catholic Charismatics. This fact signals an attempt to recover the lay-based forms of direct communication prior to the advent of modern Roman Catholicism in Brazil during the second half of the nineteenth century. The new canons and sacraments introduced by the modern Church would lead to what Charismatics refer to as an excessive rationalization of the Church. Charismatics use the figure of St. Peter, the stable rock to comment on this rationalization of the Church and contrast it to St. Paul, the traveler, who made a church, wherever he went.[3]

Furthermore, according to Charismatics, the ideal is to convert the possibility of *seeing* into that of *seeing through*. As they often say, "where the Church (St. Peter) sees, the CCR (St. Paul) sees through." At stake is, once more, the ongoing dispute between the opacities associated with instrumental mediations of the Church that stand between believers and the divine as opposed to CCR's claims for a more direct access. Seeing and seeing through also express divergence in epistemological terms, namely, as the Church that "knows," in opposition to the CCR that "experiences." As we will see, this logic of permeability or seeing through expands into and interconnects the various human and technological aspects that are constitutive of Canção Nova's entire universe, including the economic.

The Netscape of Canção Nova

[He intertwines the fingers of his hands].You have to think of Canção Nova as a network, which is also the work- of- a-net...you see? It *connects* people and it *catches* people. Think of Our Lady of Aparecida, the saint that was found in a fishing net. Think of the apostles, they were fishermen...and now look at that antenna, does it not look like a net? And think of the INPE, the Aerospace Institute over there, what are they doing? Netting!...{*enredando*} Their work is to catch things in the air, that antenna also catches things in the air, it connects but it also catches, converts, transforms, look at my hands now, what is the best way for me to make my hands stronger? It is by interlacing them. Look...your mind, if you listen, my mind is weaving these thoughts and when you see how things are so beautifully related, how can you doubt that there is a greater mind behind all reality?...(Interview with Nuno Carvalho, 8 November 2001)[4]

Canção Nova is situated in Cachoeira Paulista halfway between São Paulo and Rio de Janeiro within the Valley of Paraiba River: a strip of flatlands that border the beautiful Serra da Mantiqueira and Serra do Mar, not far from the Atlantic Ocean. It has a total population of 27.000 inhabitants and an average annual temperature of 26 degrees Celsius. Most of its economy is based on livestock and agriculture. A trip through the region provides one with a fair idea about the dominance of Catholicism, expressed in its many cathedrals and numerous unofficial chapels that have been built by lay believers well back in the colonial days. The event that turned the Valley of Paraiba into a renowned spot, however, is the great miracle of Aparecida, after which the national basilica and sanctuary were built. The legend tells how in 1717 three fishermen found the image of Our Lady of Aparecida on the margins of the River Paraiba. Devotion to the image grew exponentially, and in 1929 Our Lady of Aparecida was crowned as the official patron saint of Brazil. Since then, every year on 12 October, thousands of pilgrims travel from all around Brazil and Latin America to the Sanctuary of Our Lady. The proximity of Canção Nova to the national sanctuary adds to the reputation of the Valley as a privileged spot for religious tourism.

Today, Canção Nova broadcasts on AM, FM, and SW radio, owns four TV generators and 263 retransmitter antennas, is connected to 146 services of cable TV reaching the West of Europe, North Africa and Latin America, Uruguay and Paraguay, and owns the first Catholic WebTV in the world. TV Canção Nova broadcasts in UHF 24 hours a day, and 80 percent of its programs are transmitted live. The main base covers an enormous area of about 20.000 m2 with many subdivisions: the housing

complex where its 300 communitarian members live and thousands circulate every week, the premises of radio Canção Nova and TV Canção
Nova, an audiovisual department called DAVI, a gigantic supermarket
area called Fundação John Paul II that sells Canção Nova's media productions such as tapes, video sermons, CDs, books, magazines, and clothes,
various broadcasting studios, two small chapels, a specific area for intercession and exorcism, and a monastery of the medieval Poor Clares. Apart
from the main mother house, Canção Nova runs 19 other filial houses
called *casas de missão* (mission houses) distributed all over Brazil, four of
which are within the State of São Paulo, and abroad in the United States,
in Fátima (Portugal), Rome, and Israel. In 2005, Canção Nova inaugurated a gigantic gymnasium with a capacity of 70,000. On weekends,
religious and nonreligious holidays (such as carnival) organized excursions arrive in Canção Nova from all parts of Brazil and neighboring
countries. Although Canção Nova is permanently open to visitors, it
charges an entrance fee of *10 Reais* during shows, which normally run
from Thursday to Sunday. Participants are invited to bring a tent and
camp in the large lanes of the site. As a community, Canção Nova fashions, as it were, a town within a town. Apart from the dormitories and the
refectory, it also owns a medical and dentist post, a primary school for the
children of the community, a theology school for lay and vocational members, a hotel, a camping area, and even a hairdresser. In the back part of
the complex, there is a big vegetable garden for the community's own supply extending beyond plain sight toward the Serra.

Especially since the 1990s, there has been a significant change in the
town's human and infrastructure. From a predominantly residential and
rural town, Cachoeira Paulista is now developing a substantial commercial
form of economy. Just outside the grounds there are a good number of
hostels, cafes, and restaurants to cater to the weekly surge of travelers.
Local residents have also made space in their private condominiums to
house last-minute pilgrims. Religious merchandisers set up their stalls,
outside and around the ground's limits.

In general, Cachoeira Paulista is well reputed for its many natural flu-
vial systems. Being one of the countries with the highest use of hydroelec-
tric energy worldwide, electricity supplies in Brazil are highly dependent
on the levels of precipitation provided by seasonal rains. Strikingly, Canção
Nova uses its watery surroundings to foster the relationship between electricity and spirituality, between the energizing power of the "flame of
Pentecost" and a techno-electronic universe. These overlaps rely on
emblematic descriptions used by Catholic Charismatics to account for the
richly somatic experiences of contact with the spirit. They often use
electricity-derived terms such as "warm voltages," "radiances," or "impulses"

to refer to practices of "infusion" and "diffusion," "circuitry" and "conductivity" of spiritual charisma.

Similar juxtapositions between electricity and spirituality became particularly salient in 2001 during my fieldwork period. That year the so-called *Lei do Apagão* ("he Switch-Off Law) was declared, a national energy-saving regime caused by an alarming dry-out of the main barrages resulting from exceptional rain shortage of the previous years. The darkening of the nation in homes, hospitals, institutions, streets, and media stations stirred a major campaign to find alternative resources to keep the country operating against the dark alleys, dimmed public monuments, defrosted fridges, and turned-off devices. As the government went on a frantic search for alternative forms of energy, Canção Nova mined all sorts of metaphors to further conflate the Holy Spirit with media's electrical power. The Holy Spirit was compared to an "electricity generator" that "infuses energies," the bodies of believers were associated with "antennas of retransmission" (de Abreu 2005, 345), and crowds were described in terms of their "good contact" (ibid.). Not infrequently, visitors to Canção Nova expressed that they came to "charge their batteries," or "to obtain good signals," "to galvanize the world." In time, the circuit of analogies between weather, electricity, and spirituality also came to encompass Canção Nova's physical proximity to the national Institute of Spatial Research and Center of Weather Forecast and Climacteric Studies (CPTEC).[5] Curiously, the analogy between electricity and spirituality on the basis of weather conditions was in turn reinscribed in the stock-like economic rhythms of Canção Nova that were being activated as part of its regime of economic transparency and that strikingly resembled the weather maps and real-time screening technologies used by the meteorological broadcast Institute.

Embodying the Midst

Ideas of rejuvenation and renewal form an integral part of CCR's imaginary of an agile and aerate body. These attributes are projected on, and literally embodied by, the thousands of youngsters who assiduously come to Canção Nova. Significant adherence to Canção Nova comes primarily from an upper middle-class and well-educated youth sector. Most travel from within the state of São Paulo in excursions organized via online university networks where the CCR has always had a major presence.[6] Events at Canção Nova are prepared according to certain themes such as "marriage and sexuality," "youth camping," "cure and deliverance," or "seminars in the spirit," many of which show a clear orientation toward young people. Nowhere is this preference as manifest as in the hugely popular *Geração PHN* (PHN Generation). Meaning *No for Today* (Por Hoje Não), PHN Generation primarily concentrates on the daily struggle against sin by teenage and early adult Catholic Charismatics. Among *PHNers* confession happens primarily through the body rather than verbally or through sacrament. The body confesses, and expresses the restorative powers of the Holy Spirit. Religious mega-festivals use songs, prayers, and gestures to structure breath and move the body to confess. Like a form of purification, sins are expelled from the body because as Charismatics reveal, "it is important to improve on the body's potential to retain oil or chrism." The gamut of gifts endowed by the spirit during the Baptism is manifest as an oily fragrant substance; hence the reason why Charismatics refer to one another as "anointed." The premise is that an anointed body will more easily be able to induce the body to expel sin and absorb good.

Frequently described as a kind of "bath immersion in the spirit," the baptism marks, thus, the moment when an individual supposedly attains higher levels of proprioceptive awareness. During prayer, practitioners are called to concentrate on the body internally, and to redirect "oil" to points of tension, closure or ill feeling within the body. The idea is to expand the degrees of freedom within the body, that is, to raise the level of joints mobility, and at the same time, to enter into a relation of permeability with the outside world. As in Pentecost, the body heretofore blocked, starts to open up to the surrounding environment. The aerobic style of Charismatic celebrations sharpens such porosity. Through bodily engagement in breathing exercises, which people learn with the help of recorded technologies, transpiration, and transparency interrelate. Progressively, the perception of the body turns to include and coimplicate, the exterior. The body ceases to be perceived as a self-contained entity, and starts to take on the relational status of a breathing organ predicated on the reciprocal exchange of in and out. Concurrently, a change in the center of gravity seems to occur. From a definable locatable position, the baptized body becomes particularly sensitive to balances in input and output. The body becomes increasingly lighter, fusing with the "electrical life" of the spirit. Thus, repetition and recursivity, agility and fluidity all become qualities shared at once by the aerobic body, the spirit, and electronic technologies across a relational network. Through breathing, Canção Nova is at once the mechanical expression of the apostolic community, as the community is the humanized embodiment of technology.

Religious spaces in Canção Nova, likewise, materialize the logic of openness and transparency. Voids, meshes, or permeable structures have a distinctive presence in Catholic Charismatic architecture (de Abreu, 2008). Iron-grid metal materials are particularly used to intersect the walls of

Canção Nova's spaces of celebration. As prefabricated hangars, these spaces express adapt traditional church furnishing to gym-like arenas. The wired fence that encircles the entire camp adds a new layer to the open-ended architecture of the place as those on both sides are able to see through to the other. In Canção Nova one is never exactly outside or inside. Entering Canção Nova is to enter the province of the middle.[7] Space is delimited by a boundary that is at once everywhere and nowhere. Its beginnings and endings, outsides and insides are interconnected in ways that exclude any foundation upon which a community, imagined or constructed, could be solidly framed.

Navigating through the Field

Padre Jonas was a native priest who, nevertheless, wanted to use televangelism. But he also was baptized in the Spirit who needed to conciliate his peers' objections to televangelism while tuning into the economic aspirations of largely upper middle-class Catholics who felt rejected by Brazilian Catholic liberationists. Well-to-do CCRs strongly resented Liberation Theology's alleged "preference for the poor." It seemed to them a contradiction in terms, and an altogether unchristian attitude, that Liberation Theology fought for the socially excluded while excluding others spiritually.

At the same time, however, the CCR also came out as a critic to the Church's excessive control over sacred means, its hierarchies, and mediations. They argued for a more democratized distribution of charismatic power and proclaimed that the body rather than still imagery ought to be the site of sacred power (de Abreu 2002, 240–258). In order to become a Charismatic one needed to be open and attune oneself to the transparent and unmediated *touch* of the Spirit. Conceived in this way, Padre Jonas envisioned media technology not as a medium that would mediate a certain doctrine—for that would undermine the very attempt to refute mediation in favor of immediacy—but as an entity that could be identified with the direct and immediate claims underscored by the Spirit of Pentecost. As a weak agent in the market, Padre Jonas had to adopt a kind of guerrilla warfare, build flexibility into his moves, so as to be able to quickly change tactics. The issue was less to predict than to be able to absorb change. Especially in the early years, Padre Jonas carefully avoided the possibility of predatory remarks. First, by staying away from a direct confrontation vis-à-vis the main forces of competition; second, by gradually moving *within* the structure toward the more murky zone of a decentered center. That meant finding the fine balance between left and right, and once there, leapfrogging into midair. Thus, even though Padre Jonas would agree that Liberation Theology was way too caught up in ideology and that something had to be done to remove its preponderance in Latin American, he always eschewed overt criticism. On the contrary, despite all the obstacles posed by liberal clerks, he praised Liberation Theology as "a fruit of the will of the spirit" (also implying its gradual decline).[8] He retreated, as though allowing the circumstances to speak for themselves. By withdrawing from the larger political arena to live with his community of disowned, Padre Jonas created an aura around himself that caused some to describe as a "prophet in the times of mass media."[9] By never openly attacking his "enemies," he preserved his energy. This is not to say that he remained apathetic. For example, by tracing his spiritual genealogy to Father Rahm, not to Father Dougherty (as one would expect, considering Padre Jonas's interest in televangelism), he deflected attention from any links to the latter. The fact that Father Rahm chose to do social work among the marginalized in Brazil instead of televangelism destabilized the general argument that Pentecostalism and Catholic conservatives alike do not care for social matters. By stressing his bond to Father Rahm, Padre Jonas was paving the road to linking televangelism with social work. Gradually, Padre Jonas managed to overturn his image in the local mindset toward a possible conciliation between social causes, televangelism, and Brazilian Catholicism, while distancing himself from Father Dougherty, who was after all, his close competitor and most powerful rival.

Father Dougherty's personal ambitions and material funds blinded him from taking a more unassuming way of going beyond the polarized political context of Brazil. Padre Jonas, on the other hand, was able to position himself as the autochthon whose local insight made him extra sensitive to the local political environment. He could wisely sense that the sturdy wall of prejudice against televangelism could only be surmounted, not by going head-on against it, but by strategic navigation. Unlike his American counterpart, Padre Jonas discerned that freedom of action must not necessarily be found outside the local political setting but within it. Being a native, he believed that the paths were already in him. He only needed to unlock these. And so Padre Jonas thought he might as well use televangelism. Yet, contrary to Father Dougherty's evangelical Catholicism, he would not do so with a particular normative ideological content. His project would advance by retreating. While the others would go on weakening each other's energy, he would await his moment to leap forward with a new vigor. His was a politics of ecology, of staying in tune with his environment, and carefully navigating through situations.

There came a moment when Padre Jonas, following Father Dougherty, contacted the local industries in search of publicity revenues, but in prayer, he often says, he realized "he was deviating from the divine path." The prospect of having Canção Nova's existence become exclusively dependent on external publicity seemed incompatible with the principle of immediacy that underpins the pneumatic experience of Pentecost. In addition, reliance on publicity revenues would draw in the opacities of mediation of financial transactions associated with the conventional mechanisms of advertisement. Besides, the risk of regressing into a noncommunitarian based economy was high as a free-ride type of economy is likely to arise when economic transactions take place between entities that are not bound to a particular social network. Not to mention that the marriage between Catholicism and marketing was still highly disapproved of in Brazil. So Padre Jonas had to pull out. After a period of intensive prayer, he decided to rescind all bonds with the local commerce with which he had been in contact, and to turn down all the advertising campaigns and sales promotions in place. He declared that from then on Canção Nova would live exclusively from two sources: selling its own media productions and from charity. Three months later, he created a donators club membership: "The Audio-Club" (*Clube-do- Ouvinte*).

The Audio-Club

The Audio-Club became the heart of the community. Since 1990 Canção Nova transmits a live TV and radio program called "Wednesday Mass of the Audio-Club." The event is supposed to be a ceremony exclusively dedicated to the donors and *Arrecadadores* of Canção Nova. On 7 November 2001, I attended the mass service in the camp. The ceremony was conducted in a hangar with a capacity of about hundred people. On a smaller scale, the building had the same features described earlier of the main hangar *Rincão do Meu Senhor*: a wall intercepted by a rugged tracery of ironwork. The space's inbuilt openness air-conditioned the place. The well-known Padre Edmilson conducted the ceremony, opening the ritual with the sound of an organ that kited the voice of a young female singer. The priest warmly welcomed the audiences and asked them to tune to channel Canção Nova as one "tunes to the Holy Spirit." Padre Edmilson acted like a phone operator switching the flows of spiritual "energy" from one element to another.

> P.E.: I am placing my hands on you [laying his hand toward the TV camera]. Yes, Jesus reaches my brother (...) Now I want you to touch your brother standing next to you with your left arm, while your right hand

touches where it hurts. Cure Lord, Liberate my God [he closes his eyes, while the local audience "prays in tongues"]. The Lord is touching a right leg, the Lord is touching a leprous. Lord, a man is now placing inside You a problem with his stomach (this difficult vital organ) and I ask my Lord also for other causes that are not physical diseases but the others...emotional, adulterous, impossible causes; You who are the God of the impossible, look at the faith of your people, visit now Lord. There is a man who is not a Catholic, he is an evangelic, and the Lord is touching, he will be among us soon, thank you Lord. And now a right leg...thank you Lord because now you are touching someone with ear pain, visit now my Lord. [pause] Now my brothers change your left arm for your right arm and touch the person on your right. If until this moment the words were lacking, now they will be released. You who had a dry stuck tongue, now your tongue is free, thank you Lord. This is now a living Church, not a dead one because the Lord is the same yesterday and tomorrow and we have been obedient with all the members of the Audience Club, all members of C.N...(Mass of the Audio-Club, 7 November 2001)

In media res, Padre Edmilson interrupted his reception of prophecies and started reading e-mails that reached the altar table. The mails had been sent by the audio-viewers who witnessed a miracle foretold by the Padre. This process of sending and receiving spiritual messages was intensified by and associated with terms that pertain to technological interactivity.

Padre Edmilson, you told that we should put the hands where it hurts and that by doing so a person who has a problem with the ears was being cured. I am cured and the pain is gone. I thank the Lord.
     Padre Edmilson, when you spoke about a man being cured of a stomach problem, I touched the screen with my left hand having my right hand on my stomach. My pain is gone thanks to the Lord.

Again, the reading of e-mails was interrupted by the surge of new revelations Padre Edmilson was receiving from the Holy Spirit.

P.E. Yes, Lord a man who is now being cured from a cancer on one of his testicles, thank you Lord for this listener and another who recovered his right vision, My Lord thank you...cure miasma intoxication, cure a heartburn, a tumor on the spine. A forearm needed a prosthesis but today watching the Mass of the Audio Club, he is cured. Let us applaud Jesus, Our Lord!

The voice of Padre Edmilson played a key role in the interchange of "flows" between inner and outer, between "producer(s)" and "audience(s)." Far from being mere spectators, the audiences actively engaged in the framing of communal prayer. Padre Edmilson sanctioned the cures that he himself received from the Spirit, by reading the testimonies that arrived at his altar table via electronic means. "Alleluias" and "Amens" added rhythm to the readings. As the circuit speeded up, a swelling vocalization arose, dramatized by the roaring expression of unintelligible sounds of speaking in tongues. The body partook in the interactive nature of the celebration. The gesture of the laying-on of hands suggested a community of chained bodies integrated into a moving circle of light. The body of the medium, however, did not attempt to pursue a communication between two worlds. Rather, the body—like space, and like the TV medium—was employed as a medium of energy circulation and transmission. In other words, everything in the setting, body, space, media participated in this movement of transmissibility. The laying-on of hands aimed to restore harmony in the body, compensating for some emotional, physical, or spiritual lack. Placing and alternating hands on oneself and another individual, as Padre Edmilson asked his audiences to do, further reinforced the contact established between one's personal body and the collective body where the priest worked as a kind of power source on/off switch. Circulation and relation were, therefore, the terms that worked, literally, as the main conductors of the ceremony. The body of the believer and potential donor extended, and identified with, the technological while inscribing the transactions of charisma ultimately manifested in the form of donations. Insofar as charity is, according to St. Paul the highest charisma—the gift that overflows itself[10]—donations did not refer to a disembodied act of giving but to a condition of being gifted, an aspect that, as we have seen, goes through the body. The act of giving was more a sign of possession than of dispossession. As Charismatics put it, "one exists in charity." Or to recall Mauss, to give is to give oneself, hence to further propel the circulation of the "gift."

Technological Self-Awareness

One would expect that in order to sustain its own mystification in religious as well as economic terms, Canção Nova would go on erasing its technological traces. Yet, at first glance, quite the opposite takes place. Far from concealing, Canção Nova constantly takes us into the back rooms, and the normally invisible off-stage scenery, so that viewers can be aware (on "live transmission") of both its material (technical equipment, new premises, furnishings, etc.) and humanitarian world. Donors, in particular, have a chance to access the flows of capital, that is, the financial balance of transactions in real time as Canção Nova incessantly reveals the percentage level in the race to the 100 percent monthly liquidations.[11] The daily exposure

of the rhythms of the ins and outs of money very much resembles the mer-
curial depictions of weather radars. As we move toward the last days of the
month the emotional investment rises like a temperature. The "generous
downpour" of money, especially toward the end of the month, is often
related to the highly concentrated cloud formed by intense collective
prayer. This idea stems from the perception that prayer is effected through
the breathing and that it affects the surrounding air.

The thing is, side by side with a continual work of mystification of media
(through the disavowal of mediation) there is also at work a logic of economic transparency. Curiously, mediation can be best denied at the moment
of its exposure. Different from Father Dougherty who includes commercials from other religious entities, Canção Nova is totally self-referential in
matters of publicity. Ingeniously, by overtly showing the very means of
mediation—by turning the camera onto itself—those means become themselves the mediated content; the medium quite literally becomes the message. Mediation becomes so full of itself that it performs its own denial in
favor of affective directness (Morris 2000; Taussig 2003). Direct transparency is drawn out from kenotic mediation while absorbed by the rhetoric of
the "live transmission" that such mediation allows in the first place. In
other words, technique partakes in the work of its own denial. Furthermore,
this logic of transparency, which is the counterpart of giving "in charity" in
Canção Nova's moral economic universe, is intrinsic to breathing itself. In
that sense, Canção Nova is not a mere product of Pentecost but rather its
perpetual remaking, renewal, rejuvenation. Simultaneously, Canção Nova
embraces the rules of the global market by operationalizing breath so as to
conflate the material dynamic life of the body with the immaterial and the
volatile aspects of the virtual. It does so by juxtaposing means as ends
through its "aesthetic economy of transparency" (Morris 2000) and through
its self-referential nature that allows it to have control over copyright prop-
erties, ownership of means of communication, people, sounds, and images,
to mention a few, while directing the flow of capital.

Padre Jonas's relative lack of means in relation to Father Dougherty's
abundant resources turned out to benefit Padre Jonas's ability to exploit the
conditions or rules of the global economy. His reliance on the intangible
capital of charisma provided him with the ideal currency to keep the religious and the economic intertwined in the same healthy flow of things.

As Hardt and Negri have expressed, what is distinctive about contemporary labor processes is that they signal a kind of "immateriality." Labor itself
has become a service characterized by the central role of knowledge, information, affect, and communication. In their model concept of "immaterial
labor" they make room for the aspect of "production and manipulation of
affect," which "requires (virtual or actual) human contact, labor in a bodily

mode" (Hardt and Negri 2001, 293). Furthermore, one of the key features of this type of economy via the affect is, according to these authors, its ability to capitalize on the compression between means and ends of production. They also suggest that the reason why it works through the affect is because (like in Canção Nova's self-referential economy) the means of production that mediate the act of manufacturing, have themselves been identified with the ends, and the message with the means. As a result, the state of global capitalism increasingly tends to perform the dispensation of means of mediation involved in the act of production. Products are becoming (like the body) ever more immaterial and lighter so that they can better interface with an increasingly fluctuating relational market, and at the same time, commoditize experience and events more than they accumulate (Massumi 2003). Such fluctuations hold up, thanks to a new exploration of affect through internalized movement fostering transparency. So transparent, in fact, that they stick, becoming adherent. *Adherence*, to be sure, is a good term underpinning Canção Nova's community—in devotion but also in that of being greasy, like a glutinous substance, so that it sticks fast, or the way lungs sometimes stick to the chest wall, during quiet breathing so that chest movements become coupled with the movements of the lungs.

Conclusion

In this chapter, I have addressed the question of community from a bodily, material perspective. Rather than analyzing how a community uses media in order to instrumentally imagine itself, I have tried to identify the very "making of" mechanisms that allow the community to identify with the very materiality of the machinic. In other words, I have chosen to think of communication as a form of community processing. I have analyzed how the Pentecostal/Pauline notion of embodied *pneuma* provide Canção Nova with a kind of religious media theory, and explored how the latter becomes articulated with an economic regime of immediate transparency that is premised on the body's aptitudes to perceive and regulate movement. Once perceived through the mechanics of breathing and circulation, there is no exterior position from which the community can be clearly defined. What matters instead are the cycles and reciprocations between in and out and the need to maintain the proprioceptive-like balance between them.

By focusing on the parable of Pentecost, Padre Jonas targeted different things at the same time. On the one hand, he managed to go beyond Liberation Theology's militant ideology. On the other, he surpassed Father Dougherty's recalcitrance to apply marketing methods to Catholic televangelism against all odds. As a native, Padre Jonas was very mindful of how demonized mass media had been by the internal critical opinion. He knew that before he could start using mass media in order to convert people, mass media had itself to be converted, its demons expelled, the air recycled. And for that he had to start with his most unassailably intimate being: his own wavering body. Instead of joining the forces operating in the polarized political context of Brazilian society, he focused on the motor qualities of the body itself, and from there, in dialogue with his immediate surroundings, he began to open the way toward a balanced expanded middle. While "allowing" Father Dougherty the honor of being a pioneer, Padre Jonas used him as a windbreaker vis-à-vis the local critical mindset. At the same time, in the context of an appealing Pentecostal televangelism, many churchmen knew, if reservedly, that something had to be done to stop the exodus of Catholics to the Protestant and Pentecostal churches. So, the strategic question was how to use mass media and at the same time circumvent the local demonological rhetoric on televangelism? How to use media and disavow mediation? How to go beyond right and left? And the answer to this dilemma came in the form of a community, not in name of an ideology, not another ideology at all, but a community whose power relies on its capacity to perform its own making, ever in motion, ever incomplete: the-community-that-exists-in-the process-of-being-made. Having little means with which to predict successful outcomes in strictly economic terms, Padre Jonas offered instead a well-staged prophetic return of the apostolic community. Rather than offering a set of palpable instruments, or a well-defined scheme, he incorporated a sort of productive precariousness that allowed him to coalesce mediation within the technological while redirecting his own marketing procedures to an open relational field of flows according to the logic of a breathing body. As an engine of circulation and self regeneration, Canção Nova both structures and builds upon the imaginary associated with breathing dynamics. In that sense, it is not a "power-sphere" whereupon discursive meanings are inbuilt as defined by Jürgen Habermas but an *atmosphere* the volatility of which preempts any attempt to clearly define the boundaries of a community-in-the-making. As the saying goes, breathing continuous until it stops.

Notes

This chapter is dedicated to Bonno Thoden van Velzen. I thank Birgit Meyer for inviting me to join the research program on which this volume is based, and all the researchers involved for their stimulating questions and suggestions. Thanks also to David Morgan, Reinhilde König, and Maarten Boekelo for their valuable comments at an earlier stage of this chapter.

1. See www.cancaonova.com/cnova/eventos/coberturas/ (accessed 6 March 2009).
2. The Acts of the Apostles (Greek *Praxeis Apostolon*) is the fifth book of the New Testament. Acts narrates the story of the early Christian church, with especial emphasis on the ministries of the 12 apostles and of Paul of Tarsus.
3. St. Paul was himself a tent maker (Acts 18: 3). I thank David Morgan for calling my attention toward this detail.
4. In 2001 Nuno Carvalho was 27 years old and a follower PHN Generation of Canção Nova, more on which momentarily.
5. The Aerospace Institute of Cachoeira Paulista is a national center that among other functions does research on atmospheric science, technical spatial engineering for remote sensing in the detection, and control of geostationary satellites and satellite images as well as astronomic events. The institute has in the meantime developed a special program connected to the Rainforest (AMZ), and with other distant places like China, and houses a highly sophisticated monitoring system that gives images in real time of deforestation of the Rainforest as well as pollution levels in the main urban centers of Brazil.
6. It is worth recalling that the CCR originated out of a retreat held in February by a group of faculty members and students in one of the headquarters of Duquesne University, in Pittsburgh, Pennsylvania from there spreading to other academia; see Gabriel, Eduardo A. (2005).
7. The Portuguese word for *meio* relates at once to being in the midst, to environment (*meio ambiente*), and to means of communication (*meio de comunicação*), as Michel Serres has also noted about French language; see Connor, Steven "Michel Serre's Milieux," presented in conference on Mediations—Belo Horizonte, 23–26 July 2002. See http://www.bbk.ac.uk/english/skc/milieux/.
8. Press Interview XX National Encounter of the CCR—Aparecida, 2001.
9. See, for example, various opinions about the profile of Padre Jonas in section *O Que Dizem Dele* (What People Say about Him). Http://www.cancaonova.com/portal/canais/pejonas/textos.php?id=34.
10. In his Letters St. Paul enumerates the different charismas in terms of charismas of the word, which include glossolalia, and prophecy; charismas of action, including charity and miraculous cures; charismas of cognition, which include the gift of knowledge, discernment, and science. Charity, however, is the charisma extolled by St. Paul as the foundation for all others. Charisma shares with charity and charm the same etymological root in *charis*.
11. For example, on 30 July 2001 the balance between ins (3.332. 918, 24 Reais), outs (2.336.393.27 Reais) ended up positive (996. 524 97 Reais). Only during the last week of that month did the stream flow of "souls" actually accelerated. See *Revista Canção Nova*, Setembro 2001.

Chapter 8

Modes of Binding, Moments of Bonding. Mediating Divine Touch in Ghanaian Pentecostalism and Traditionalism

Marleen de Witte

Introduction

On a Sunday evening in 2002 a Presbyterian woman in Accra was baptized by the Holy Spirit while watching a charismatic-Pentecostal television broadcast. She had been sweeping the room when *Living Word* came on and caught her attention. As she heard pastor Mensa Otabil preaching on speaking in tongues, she put her broom away and sat down to listen to the message. After the sermon, which was prerecorded in church, Otabil came on to address the viewer at home. His wise and friendly face filled the screen and in his deep voice he said "let's pray together." Suddenly the woman found herself praying in tongues without stopping. For the first time in her life she was filled with the Holy Spirit. That evening she wrote a letter to the church to thank pastor Otabil, telling him how beautiful her experience was and how excited she was, and promising that she would from now on allow God to use him to bless her. Similar testimonies of people who experienced being touched by the Holy Spirit while watching a charismatic TV broadcast abound. What can this tell us about religious bonding in the present age of mass media distraction and about the kinds of religious "communities" that ensue?

Since the deregulation of the media in the 1990s, religious movements in Ghana have increasingly adopted broadcast media to manifest themselves in public, to spread their messages and to attract followers. Charismatic-Pentecostal "media ministries" in particular have become very successful and shape a charismatic-Pentecostal popular culture on Ghana's airwaves and TV screens, in church halls and beyond. This new, mass mediated form of religion is not confined to the particular churches that produce it and their members, but spills over into various forms of popular culture and resonates with a broad audience. One of the most popular charismatic-Pentecostal celebrities operating in the public sphere is pastor Mensa Otabil, whose multichannel "media ministry" made him known as "the teacher of the nation." Confronted with charismatic churches' public influence, other religious groups increasingly feel the need to also enter the media and compete for public presence and for followers. One of them is the neotraditionalist Afrikania Mission, that aims at reforming and rehabilitating Afrikan Traditional Religion (ATR) as a viable alternative to Christianity and a respectable and modern "world religion" in its own right. Mass media and public representation are crucial to this project.

While mass media offer religious leaders new opportunities for reaching and attracting people, they also pose challenges with regard to binding them as followers and congregations. Indeed, the eagerness with which religious leaders employ mass media to reach out comes with a new anxiety about not binding people. Media pastors like Otabil fear that the televisualisation of the gospel "only attracts" people to an "outward religious style" without turning them to Christ. At stake is an insecurity over the new modes of religious attachment that come with reaching new audiences through the airwaves. This chapter examines and compares the ways in which Otabil's International Central Gospel Church (ICGC) and the Afrikania Mission seek to mobilize new forms of religious bonding in Ghana's public sphere.

The entanglement of mass media and religion organizes people into new social formations and modes of attachment that ask for a dynamic approach to "religious community." To capture the dynamics of the imagination and mobilization of bonds between people, and between people and the spiritual, in an age of mass media religion, we need to take into account processes of community making (and unmaking), and possible tensions between techniques of binding and moments of bonding. Although the notion of a religious community as bounded, coherent, and exclusive has long been superseded by more sophisticated approaches that leave room for flexible or porous boundaries, multiple membership, and instability, on an empirical level the model of a church congregation as a bounded, closed, and stable community of members does drive many religious organizations and their ideologies and practices. It is thus to be taken seriously as such. With religious groups making use of mass media, this congregational model has come to exist next to or in tension with social formations and forms of bonding of a much more elusive and momentary nature.

To analyze religious leaders' struggles for binding people, I propose to distinguish between membership, audience, public, and clientele and to examine how these different groups of people relate to, overlap with, or merge into each other. A *membership* is the body of members of an organization. As we shall see, for both the ICGC and Afrikania this notion is less self-evident than it seems. An *audience* comprises the persons within hearing, be they the spectators or listeners assembled at a performance or those attracted by a radio or television program. The notion of audience thus refers to a real group of people watching or listening at a particular moment, independent of whether these people can be known individually or know one another. A *public*, by contrast, is an abstract collective group, regarded as sharing a particular interest and addressed, but not necessarily reached, on the basis of this interest. Finally, a *clientele* is the body of clients, followers or dependants of a (religious) leader. In contrast to a community, which presupposes a certain level of communality between members of the group, the main (if not only) feature shared by the individual clients is their connection to the religious leader. The idea of a religious clientele, important in both traditional African religions and Pentecostalism, acquires new dimensions with religious leaders' employment of commercial mass media. The question that confronts media-active religious leaders, then, is how to turn publics into audiences and audiences into congregations or clienteles.

This chapter discusses the generation of such different modes of binding and moments of bonding by the two religious organizations' use of media. I have found it fruitful to see "media" not as something new and external to religion, but as intrinsic to religion as a practice of mediation (De Vries 2001; De Witte 2008; Meyer 2006a; Stolow 2005). Just as "media" as commonly understood to bridge a distance in space and/or time and call into presence an absent or distant person, religious practices and objects connect to a realm beyond sensory perception and enable religious subjects to experience the presence of "divine" power (see also Meyer in this volume).[1] As a practice of both imagining and engaging with "the metaphysical," religion, in other words, connects people and spirits, or, from a more social-scientific perspective, produces in people a sense of being connected. For this, religion always needs media. Ranging from the bible to the body, from prophets to television, and from compact discs to cowry shells, such media enable people to conceive of and establish, maintain, and renew ties with the presence of spirit beings.

In their capacity of connecting to the divine, modern media technologies such as television or radio are not so different from older or other religious mediations such as holy books, sacred spaces, divine objects, or ritual performance. And yet, modern media cannot be assumed to be unproblematic extensions of older religious mediations. On the contrary, media (old or new) are always possible sources of caution and conflict (cf. Eisenlohr 2006; Engelke 2007; Stolow 2005; Van de Port 2006). They may be taken to counteract an ideal of authentic, immediate religious experience or they may challenge authoritative forms of religious mediation by facilitating new ones. At the same time, the acceptance of particular media and forms of mediation as legitimate often goes together with a denial of mediation (see also de Abreu in this volume). Religious practitioners call upon media to define, construct, and experience their relationship with the spiritual world, but sacralize or naturalize these media so as to authenticate religious experiences as immediate and "real" (cf. Van de Port 2006). An experience of being in touch with the immediate presence of spirit power(s) is fundamental to both charismatic-Pentecostal and traditional modes of religious bonding.[2] For both the ICGC and Afrikania, then, mass mediating a religion that constitutes religious subjectivity through embodiment of spirit power poses challenges with regard to binding people as religious subjects. The question of how to turn publics into audiences and audiences into congregations or clienteles is a question of how to produce in people a sense of immediacy through media representation. Their success in answering this question, I will argue, depends on how the mass media formats they use relate to older, established formats of religious mediation through which believers connect to each other and to spirits.[3]

Religion in Ghana's Public Sphere

Zapping through Ghana's TV channels one cannot miss the energetic, charismatic pastors, who, as professional media entertainers, preach their convictions and communicate their powers to a widespread audience through the airwaves. Some teach their audiences in church and behind the TV screens how to turn failure into success with education, while others teach them how to fight the Devil with continuous prayer. Others again lay their hands on people and cast out demons, or encourage the crowd to praise God in worship. Commercials entice customers to buy sermon tapes and CDs, books and other church products and to attend charismatic conventions and gospel concerts. On radio, an even greater variety of pastors preach their messages, advertise their products, play gospel music, host talk shows and heal listeners through live-on-air prayer.

The proliferation of charismatic-Pentecostal churches in the public sphere was boosted when Ghana returned to democracy in 1992 and the state gradually loosened control over the media. The mushrooming of private TV stations, cable television providers, and especially FM stations in the nineties profoundly changed the Ghanaian media landscape and the place of religion in it. Significantly, it is charismatic churches that have most successfully made use of the new media opportunities to claim public presence and spread the gospel across the nation and abroad. These churches are highly market-oriented and are able to mobilize the financial and human resources needed to produce their own programs and buy airtime on radio and television. Not only do they see the media as an effective channel to evangelize the masses, but also to enhance an image of success, prosperity, and modernity, to boost the charisma of the leader and manage his public personality, and to show God's miracles to an audience outside the churches. Most of them have a "media ministry," a church department devoted to the production, sales and broadcast of radio and TV programs, audio and video tapes and PR material. As a result, mass mediated forms of charismatic-Pentecostal expression and experience have become prominent in the new public sphere and available to a large audience beyond the churches' membership.

The public dominance of charismatic-Pentecostal churches has also reinforced a much older negative Christian attitude towards African traditional religion and caused a shift in the public representation of African traditional religion. In the era of state-controlled media, traditional religion was favored and represented in the media as part of the "national cultural heritage" that was to serve as a basis of national identity. At present the media often sustain and reinforce popular fears of traditional religion generated by Pentecostal representations of traditional religious practices, practitioners, and places as demonic. Sensational images and stories of "juju" priests, shrines, and powers as the dark and evil Other of a morally upright and successful Christian self fill video movies (Meyer 2005a), tabloids, posters, and calendars for sale on the streets. The Afrikania Mission, troubled by this kind of imagery and by people's fear of and hostility towards traditional religion and its adherents, tries to counter such stereotypes with a positive image. Before examining Afrikania's media strategies, let us turn to Mensa Otabil's media ministry.

Mensa Otabil's *Living Word*

As the founder and "general overseer" of the International Central Gospel
Church, with its 4,000-seat Christ Temple in Accra and over 100 branches
elsewhere, Mensa Otabil is a "big shot" in Ghana's charismatic jet set. His
daily radio and weekly television broadcast *Living Word* made him widely
known as "the teacher of the nation." The circulation of his tapes, videos,
VCDs, and books and his frequent travel across the globe have brought
him international fame as well.

   Like most charismatic preachers worldwide, Otabil's focus is on success, achievement, self-development, personal improvement. Likewise,
"transformation" is a central concept in Otabil's sermons, which are
broadcast and marketed as "life-transforming" messages. What is unique
to Otabil, however, is his understanding that transformation on a personal level is intimately connected to transformation on a cultural level
and on a political level and his application of this idea to the challenges
of Africa and Africans. He is well known for his special commitment to
the development of the country and the continent and to the "mental
liberation" of black people in the world. The recurring question around

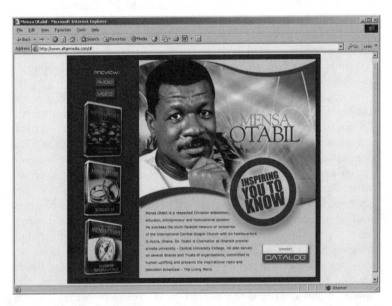

Figure 8.1   Portrait of Mensa Otabil on the ICGC's media department's Web
site (www.altarmedia.com, 2006). Courtesy of the ICGC.

which Otabil builds his messages is: "Why are we in this mess?" His answer is: because of "our inability to modify our culture."[4] Otabil thus pleads for a radical cultural transformation, first of all through education. At the same time, he marks (and markets) his African consciousness with an all-African name and an all-African attire. Otabil thus presents an intriguing mix of born-again ideology, African consciousness, and self-development discourse characteristic of management and consultancy literature.

According to independent audience research (Research International 2003), *Living Word* is among the most popular TV programs. With half of the TV3 audience watching on Sundays at 6 pm, it has an estimated audience of two million in Ghana alone. This media audience is much broader and more diversified than the church membership. As Otabil's message is generally relevant, it is composed not only of born-agains, but of people of various churches and religions, including many Muslims. Otabil's use of English and his appeal to the intellect and scholarly way of preaching limit his "target audience" to the educated middle class. Although in terms of age too the media audience is much broader than the church membership, the public that Otabil addresses with his "life-transforming messages" consists mainly of young, aspiring urbanites, who crave for a charismatic role model who tells them that they have talents to develop and can be successful and rich.

When Otabil preaches on Sundays, he thus at the same time addresses the audience sitting in front of him in the Christ Temple auditorium and the public of the *Living Word* broadcast. He told me that since his messages reach new audiences through radio and TV he has changed his way of preaching: he no longer talks to the Christian crowd in front of him, but to a single person in his mind representing the *Living Word* public, a non-Christian first-time visitor to the church. How do these different audiences and publics and the modes of addressing them relate to each other? Let us first turn to the people in the Christ Temple.

Christ Temple Community

Christ Temple events are much like theatrical performances in which the audience also has a clearly defined part to play. The format of the two-hour Sunday service has several stages and at each stage the communication between the performer and the over 4,000-head audience plays a different role in connecting believers to the divine and in generating a feeling of bonding among the congregation. The first half an hour is filled with "praise and worship," led by the praise and worship song team on stage with backing of the church band. The stirring beat of the first few songs lifts up the people and invokes the Holy Spirit in the auditorium. The crowd claps, dances, and sings along with the song texts projected on the screen. During the slower songs people lift up their hands in surrender to the Lord, singing along, praying aloud, or crying. A few up-beat songs then get people ready for the Word of God and for giving a large "seed" to the church. The main "act" of the service—and the only part that features in the church's media broadcast—is the one-hour sermon by Mensa Otabil. He appears on stage in an elegant and elaborate African lace gown and delivers the Word of God as an experienced lecturer and entertainer. He commands respect and attention with his deep fatherly voice and dignified authority, but also evokes laughter and applause with good jokes and stories, making use of theatrical body movements and storytelling techniques. The audience listens carefully and takes notes of the Bible references and the key points of the sermon, helped by a Power Point projection of the sermon outline. Otabil keeps his audience active by having them look up passages in the Bible, repeat words or phrases after him, or say things to each other. After the sermon, Otabil makes an "altar call," inviting forward all who have not yet given their lives to Christ and want to do so now. He calls upon the congregation to join him in prayer for the new converts. Before closing, Otabil asks everyone to stand up and hold hands while he speaks his benediction over the congregation.

Although the rather "rational" and controlled performance of the Sunday service present a striking contrast to the dramatic bodily performance of the church's (never broadcast) healing and prophecy meetings, during the sermon too, it is a specific bodily way of listening that facilitates the flow of spiritual power. A particular straight up, active, not sprawling way of sitting and paying attention, reacting at the right moment in the right way and for the appropriate lengths of time with clapping, laughter, turning to one's neighbor, lifting up one's hand, or interjecting amens and hallelujahs are all part of a learned, bodily discipline of listening to the Word of God. In order to be fully part of the social and spiritual community of believers and to take part in the blessings bestowed upon this community by God through the pastor, an individual has to participate in the interaction with the man of God according to this gradually embodied format of charismatic mannerisms. The mass character of a church service and the communal participation in such ritual behavior surrounded by the amplified voice of the pastor also generates a feeling of being intimately connected to each other. This experience of community, however, is very momentary and elusive and hardly lasts beyond the temporal and spatial boundaries of the event (cf. de Abreu 2005 and in this volume). The church does try to establish a more stable community, however, through its highly supervised and bureaucratized membership trajectory (De Witte 2008). The effects of this in generating and sustaining a "Christ Temple community" are limited, especially because of the church's mass character. More than by being a member of a strong religious congregation, then, religious subjectivity and bonding is constituted by the personal and momentary experience of Holy Spirit power, mediated by bodies interacting in ritual performance. Whether through the format of the sermon or through the very different format of healing and deliverance, the body of the "anointed man of God" becomes the medium that facilitates a connection between the individual believer and the spiritual. Also, the crowd dynamics generated by the thousands of worshippers filling Christ Temple and jointly participating in a common ritual of worship evokes an experience not only of spiritual presence, but also, if only momentarily, of being one community, one body in the Spirit.

Editing Otabil and His Audience

In the ICGC editing studio the theater of mediating the Holy Spirit is further dramatized by editing the parts both pastor and audience play. Watching this process, I saw how the editors carefully created the image of pastor Otabil and his audience (De Witte 2003). Specific camera angles and editing techniques, close-ups of his face and expressive gestures followed by wide-angle shots showing him elevated on the stage, watching over his large congregation, all add to Otabil's charisma. This focus on the image of the pastor—his face, his dress, his body—connects to the spiritual importance in charismatic churches of the person of the leader (and usually founder). This display of flamboyance on stage, combined with facial close-ups and a personal word to the viewer at once highlight the spiritual power bestowed upon Otabil by God and suggest the possibility of close interaction, and thus of acquiring some of this "anointing."

Just as Otabil's public personality is edited, so is his audience. Shots of Otabil preaching are interspersed with cutaways of the church audience. We see wide-angle shots of the crowd filling the auditorium, moving and being moved almost as one body, simultaneously responding to Otabil with identical gestures and utterances. And we see close-ups of individuals in the audience. From the raw recordings of the moving camera, shots of audience reactions are selected, categorized, and saved in digital folders

Figure 8.2 Series of video stills captured from *Living Word* video tape. Courtesy of the ICGC.

named "opening Bible," "reading Bible," "nod," "lifting of hand," "clap," "smile, laughter," "attention," "writing," and "shout." What we then see on TV are beautifully and decently dressed people taking notes, listening attentively, applauding, and laughing. We see them admiring Otabil, learning from him, and having fun with him. We see close-ups of their faces when the words bring them into a state of exaltation or near trance. Hearing Otabil's deep voice in the background, we can almost see the Holy Spirit flowing into them. But we don't see people sleeping, not paying attention, chewing gum, looking straight into the camera, or not looking decent. As one of the editors explained, people who do not fit the format of bringing across the communication between Otabil and the audience should not appear on screen. By cutting out undesirable behavior as well as empty chairs the *Living Word* editors thus seek to produce a perfect image of the mass of worshippers and of the individual believers. The alternating focus on the image of the individual believer and that of the mass connects to the individual spiritual experience evoked by being in a crowd of believers that characterizes the spectacular mode of charismatic practice.

The *Living Word* format, then, not only constructs a specific public image of Otabil, but also of his audience as the visible embodiment of the "transformation" and "success" he talks about. Moreover, the body language of the people on TV is vital for Otabil's public image. When he speaks, the crowd of thousands is orderly and full of attention and devotion, laughing when it is appropriate to laugh and nodding when it is appropriate to nod. The church audience is shown to admire Otabil and the TV audience is expected to do the same. The *Living Word* TV format thus not only circulates Otabil's teachings, but also visualizes the bodily regimes necessary to appropriately receive them and with them the Holy Spirit. *Living Word* shows that one cannot just listen to the Word of God anyhow; the whole body is involved in a particular way of listening. Bodies that do not listen appropriately and hence do not receive the Spirit, but hear "mere" words, are not shown.

By identifying with the televised bodies of the church audience, the TV audience is expected to similarly subject to "the powerful man of God" and to the Word and experience the power of the Holy Spirit that he transfers onto them. As the physical bodies of the pastor and his followers function as a medium in religious practice, so do the edited and televised images of their bodies function as a medium for the Holy Spirit to "touch" the expectant viewer through the television screen and her "mimetic" relationship with it. Here it is important to stress that audio-visual media address not only the eye and the ear, but involve the whole body and appeal to all senses (Sobschack 2004; Verrips 2002). Watching a religious TV broadcast with an intentional body, "in mimetic sympathy" (Sobschack 2004, 76) with the attentive audience onscreen, may trigger the viewer's embodied sensory memory of live church events and thereby evoke an experience of spirit presence. Note that it was only after the woman in the opening vignette put down her broom and sat down to listen to the whole message that she was touched by the Holy Spirit and started speaking in tongues. The boundary between onscreen and off-screen, between object and subject thus blurs. The Holy Spirit ceases to be an onscreen representation, represented by the interaction between pastor and congregation, but becomes present and able to touch the viewer.

Otabil's media ministry thus creates an audience and evokes religious experiences far beyond church membership. Receiving *Living Word*, and thus being part of the *Living Word* audience, does not necessarily end with the broadcast. People buy or order tapes or CDs, listen to them repeatedly, and give them away or exchange them. Many people respond to Otabil's call to write to him.[5] Some decide to join the ICGC or to convert to (char-ismatic) Christianity after hearing Otabil. As *Living Word* listeners and viewers thus participate in sharing and following up on the church's message, this media audience can be considered as somehow part of the church community. Yet, the church is in no way able to control the persons who make up this fluid and not confined community. As the reception of the ICGC message lacks close supervision and physical interaction, the "inner transformation" that the message is aimed at cannot be monitored as attempted with the community of registered members. The question is whether without this discipline, the media format indeed changes religious experience and sustains bonding.

But also with the registered church members the formation of community is problematic. Not only because of the mass character of church, but also because of its clientele-like character: people are attracted and bound more to Otabil's personality and charisma than to the church as a community. Mass media only reinforce this. But such a "clientelistic" relationship also resonates with the modes of religious bonding between traditional religious specialists and their clients. Despite charismatic churches' doctrinal emphasis on the born-again Christian's direct, unmediated access to the power of the Holy Spirit, in practice a charismatic "Man of God," much like an African shrine priest, functions as a medium through which his followers can, through specific rituals of interaction, get access to the power of the Holy Spirit in order to gain material wealth, physical health, and status (Asamoah-Gyadu 2005; Gifford 2004). In competition with each other, such religious specialists seek to convince people of their powers in order to attract a clientele and make a living. For modern "Men of God" like Otabil, the attraction of clients thrives to a large extent on marketing strategies and personality creation. In the religious marketplace numerous new churches offer a similar "product"—salvation and success—and compete with other churches by trying to appear as more genuine, more powerful, or in one or the other way better than others. They thus try to attract and bind people to the church, or better, to the pastor, as a clientele, despite the presence of so many other churches offering basically the same thing. This fusion of the traditional religious specialist with the figure of the global super star conflicts with the model of the church congregation that the missionaries tried to introduce. This model nevertheless informs church membership procedures, designed to constantly reproduce the Christ Temple "community." Pastors like Otabil criticize people's shallow identification with charismatic Christianity as a style and their clientelistic adherence to the charismatic personalities of pastors rather than to Christ. Yet at the same time this is exactly what they stimulate by the ways they showcase their churches and themselves in the mass mediated religious marketplace.

The Afrikania Mission's Public
Representation of ATR

To counter Ghana's Christian hegemony the Afrikania Mission aims at reconstructing Afrikan Traditional Religion (ATR) as an equally modern religion to serve as a source of African pride and strength and as a religious base for political nationalism and pan-Africanism. Founded in 1982 by an ex-Catholic priest, Kwabena Damuah, as the religious arm of Rawlings' revolution, Afrikania emphasizes cultural renaissance and black emancipation. It believes that Christianity can never sustain the development of the Ghanaian nation and the African continent, because Christianity is "inherently foreign to Afrikans" and "used to oppress and exploit Afrikans." Fighting for the public recognition of ATR as a world religion in its own right, the movement seeks to mobilize and unite all different cults and shrines in the country, and ultimately, the continent.

To unify a variety of spirit cults as one "religion," Afrikania has created new and manipulated old symbols, traditions, and rituals. Paradoxically, for the public representation of ATR, Christianity has, in its changing dominant forms, provided the format for Afrikania in several ways (see De Witte 2004). Afrikania's "creation of a systematic and coherent doctrine for Ghanaians and Afrikans in the diaspora" and its framing of traditional religion in terms of beliefs, symbols, and commandments imply a Christian concept of religion. Its Sunday worship service and its organizational structure are clearly modeled on the Catholic Church. Also, Afrikania has adopted Christian symbols of being established as a religion: a highly visible, huge, and brightly colored building with a copious office for the leader, a signboard, banners announcing events, a church logo (with a globe), a calendar with pictures of the building and the leader, and a printed cloth and head ties for members to buy. At present, charismatic Christianity, being the dominant and most publicly present religion, has become the model for religion as such and also for Afrikania. It now also organizes public conventions, evangelization, camp meetings, all night prayers, and displays a general preoccupation with public visibility and audibility. In competition with spiritual healing offered by these churches, Afrikania also provides "spiritual consultation," a new service that attracts mainly Christians.

From its birth in 1982, the Afrikania Mission has made use of mass media—first radio and print and later audiovisual media—to establish a public presence, to disseminate its message, and to attract followers. During the 1980s Afrikania's friendly rapport with Rawlings's government sustained its constant media presence and made the movement and its leader widely known. Being the only religious group granted airspace on state radio, its weekly radio broadcast, in which Damuah explained Afrikania's objectives and ideologies, reached a large audience throughout the nation. The shifting relations between the media, the state, and religion, however, have complicated Afrikania's access to the media and have altered the frames and formats upon which Afrikania can draw in its efforts at self-representation. Due to Afrikania's loss of government support and the commercialization of the media scene, Afrikania now has to pay for air-time just as any other religious organization, but does not have the means to do so. It thus tries to find other ways into the media, most notably speaking in radio and TV talk shows, inviting the press to newsworthy Afrikania events and press conferences, sending letters to the editors, and being the subject of TV documentaries (De Witte 2005). With these media formats, however, Afrikania depends on the goodwill and interests of journalists and media houses. It has hardly any control over the messages and images they produce, nor over the audiences and possible clienteles that their media productions reach.

Whereas in its early days, Afrikania's representational strategies were mainly to *talk* about ATR as an ideological source, it is now more than ever concerned with public *image*, with making ATR look as nice, clean, and

Figure 8.3 Afrikania Mission altar during the inauguration of the headquarters (March 2002). Photo by the author.

modern as Christianity to counter dominant Christian stereotypes and "make it attractive to the people." In its public representation, then, it is very particular about beautification, hygiene, and orderliness. This implies a focus on, for instance, the white costumes of Afrikania priestesses, beautifully dressed crowds of people and traditional "pomp and pageantry" and the elimination or concealment of practices like bloody animal sacrifices, frenzied spirit possession, or the stinking fermentation of healing herbs in water. The irony of Afrikania's project, however, is that while trying to attract the public to a positive image of ATR, it hardly connects to existing religious traditions and the shrine priests and priestesses whom it claims to represent.

Addressing and Attracting "the People"

The question of Afrikania's audience is complicated, because Afrikania targets very different people at the same time on very different grounds. Moreover, it no longer has its own media audience, as Damuah had and as Otabil has, but depends on the audiences of the programs that feature Afrikania. In this case we can better speak of public then. In this section I discuss Afrikania's imagined publics, its differentiated and often volatile membership, and the clients of its spiritual consultation service. From its very foundation, the notion and awareness of "the public" has been crucial to Afrikania's activities and formats of representation. The recurring concern is to show the goodness of traditional religion and culture to "the people," "the general public," or "the rest of mankind" and Afrikania has developed a strong public voice. Often Afrikania directly and exclusively addresses this abstract, unknown public, as when the leaders speak in a radio or television program or send letters to the editors of newspapers. Sometimes an event is directed both at a physically present audience and "the general public," such as when the press is present to cover the proceedings of a newsworthy Afrikania occasion or when a Sunday service is amplified to the whole neighborhood. And sometimes "the public" is also addressed indirectly, for example, when prospective Afrikania priests are taught how to go about representing their religion or shrine keepers are told to keep their shrines neat and hygienic.

This "general public" Afrikania addresses, however, is very diffuse and differentiated. First of all, "the public" is implicitly envisioned as Christian, urban, and alienated from traditional culture and religion. These are thus more or less the same people as those addressed by Otabil. Afrikania's concern, however, is with changing people's negative attitude toward ATR in order to bring them back to their supposed religious roots. This alienated public is first of all national, but it ultimately includes all (alienated) "Afrikans" in the world, both in Africa and elsewhere, especially in the Americas. But Afrikania's global public also includes non-Africans, whom Afrikania wishes to educate about ATR in order to change global prejudice. In Afrikania's terms, the goal is to teach "the rest of mankind" that "the religion of Afrika" is not "fetish," "voodoo," or "black magic," but a "developed and positive world religion." The call here is not to return to a cultural heritage, but to respect African religion as equal to any other religion. Finally, Afrikania addresses traditional religious practitioners in Ghana and encourages them to be proud of their religion and bring it out into the open. But this aim may clash with the message that "our religion is not fetish or voodoo," as traditional religious practitioners often employ exactly those terms to talk about their gods (Rosenthal 1998, 1). Afrikania also calls on them to join the movement and stand strongly united in an increasingly hostile religious climate. With such differentiated publics that are addressed with different, sometimes conflicting messages, it is not surprising that the membership Afrikania attracts is also very diffuse.

Afrikania claims that all traditional religious practitioners are automatically Afrikania members, but this is of course highly contested. Although membership seems to be fast growing in the rural areas, the question is what Afrikania membership entails. Certainly, Afrikania membership is not exclusive as membership of a Christian church usually is. Afrikania members from a traditional religious background continue to have their spiritual loyalty to a particular shrine and serve a particular god or gods. Afrikania membership is very loosely defined and less elaborate than in the ICGC. In fact, anyone interested can register as a member. While for the ICGC the difficulty of forming a religious community lies mainly in the mass character of the church, for Afrikania, with a membership of only about 150 people in Accra, this difficulty is caused by the variety of backgrounds and interests of its members. In the past the membership of the Accra branch was formed predominantly by ex-Christian, middle-aged men, whose interest in traditional religion was first of all intellectual and political (Boogaard 1993), but at present there are many more women, children, and youth. Some share the militant approach to ATR of the older and leading Afrikanians and have joined the movement out of a combination of a political awareness of Africanness and a personal search for an African religious identity. Others are driven by a personal affinity with traditional healing, an intellectual interest nurtured in school, or certain spiritual experiences or problems that they expect to be addressed by Afrikania. Also, while in the past there was not a single shrine priest or priestess among the Accra

members, now quite some of them attend services and are officially registered members. They are attracted to Afrikania by an urge to also have
a church to go to on Sundays, by the organizational protection Afrikania
offers, or by the recognition Afrikania gives them even if they have not
attained full status by traditional religious laws. With such a diffuse
membership, Afrikania hardly forms a religious community, even more
so because most of its activities are directed more at an outside public
than at its own members.

A last group of people attracted by Afrikania, again on different
grounds, are those patronizing its spiritual consultation and healing service. Interestingly, almost all of them are Christians and come to Afrikania
secretly. They form a clientele in similar ways as the people who are
attracted to charismatic-Pentecostal healing services. In fact, they are part
of one and the same group of people seeking spiritual answers to life's challenges: health problems, infertility, business/money, travel/visa, marriage,
and other thisworldly concerns. Unlike the members—and there is hardly
any overlap between this clientele and Afrikania's membership—these clients do not share Afrikania's goal of publicly promoting ATR or its militant public discourse against Christianity. On the contrary, many of them
will, in other contexts, participate in the widespread denunciation of traditional religion and its practitioners. Instead, what draws them to
Afrikania, in secret, is a conviction that life's problems have spiritual causes
and demand spiritual solutions that Christianity cannot offer, a strong
"belief" in the power of African spirits. They could go to any other shrine
or spiritual healer, and many Christians indeed do so, but for many others
the "civilized" outlook of Afrikania lowers the mental barrier just enough
to make the step.

Between the Public and the Priests

We have seen that Afrikania attracts both people who share its politically
motivated, anti-Christian discourse (as members) and people who seek
spiritual solutions for their problems (as clients). Afrikania's relationship to
the shrine priest(esse)s and devotees it claims to represent and aims to
mobilize, however, remains thoroughly problematic, even though a number of them have joined Afrikania. A major gap separates the intellectualist, Christian-derived reformation of Afrikan Traditional Religion that
Afrikania brings to the attention of the general public and the everyday
spiritual practices and concerns of traditional religious practitioners. In
other words, Afrikania's modes of constituting religious bonding clash

with traditional formats of mediating between people and spirits. First, Afrikania insists on the possibility of "conversion to traditional religion" as a personal decision based on inner conviction. Most Afrikania leaders are "converted" from Catholicism. This understanding of individual religious transformation is founded on a Protestant Christian heritage. In African traditional religious practice religious bonding is generated by very different models, most notably that of "initiation," which suggests a ritual transformation not only of the spirit, but of the body. Moreover, this transformation is not initiated from within, by personal choice, but from outside, by being called by a deity, usually through an illness or other crisis. Initiation as a bodily process of going through affliction and healing and the fusion of human body and deity forms the basis of a person's bond with a particular deity. This is remarkably similar to charismatic-Pentecostal conversion, which, although presented as an individual choice out of inner conviction, also implies a ritual and sensual transformation of the body into the locus of and medium of interaction with the Holy Spirit.

Second, Afrikania's church service, performed according to the rules and conventions of a prescribed and rehearsed liturgy, conflicts with the "uncanny wildness" of spirit possession (Rosenthal 1998, 58). While Afrikania stresses the importance of coming together every Sunday to form a community and worship god in an orderly manner, in traditional religious practice communication with the spirit world requires formats that are very different from the formats of "church service." These formats are instead characterized by a loss of control over the body, which mediates directly in the experience of the presence of gods. Third, Afrikania's beautification of traditional religion and the elimination of anything considered ugly or dirty conflicts with the spiritual power attributed to, for example, animal blood or fermented herbs. Many shrine practices thus do not fit the "civilized" form of religion Afrikania has created. Shrine priests, even those among the membership, therefore perceive the movement as offering at most ideological leadership and organizational protection, but not spiritual leadership.

A fundamental tension thus exists between Afrikania's very project of public representation and the embodied and often secretive character of African religious traditions, that is, between Afrikania's public register of representing gods and traditional religious practitioners' more private registers of dealing with the presence of gods. Afrikania engages primarily in public discourse of talking about spirituality and has developed a strong public voice for the defense of traditional religious practices, but remains very limited in more private registers of engaging with the spiritual. The spiritual consultation it offers now is still a marginal side-activity. Afrikania's symbolization of traditional religion through formats and

Figure 8.4   Afrikania members posing in their shrine (*brekete*) in Accra. Photo by the author.

representations contradicts religious traditions that are not about symbols, formats, and representations, but about embodiment and experience. The division between public and private registers of relating to the spiritual remains strong and points to a difference in the role of the body and the senses in the constitution of religious subjectivity and bonding. While Afrikania's symbolic approach foregrounds the visual and the vocal, it neglects the other sensibilities, notably touch, and the experientiality of practices like initiation and spirit possession. Afrikania's representational modes of addressing and attracting "the people" thus clash with the embodied modes of religious bonding in traditional religious practice.

Conclusion: Bodies, Spirits, and Mediation

This chapter has examined the ways in which a charismatic-Pentecostal and an African traditionalist "church" in Ghana seek to establish religious bonding, that is, to produce in people a sense of being connected to each other as a religious group and to the spiritual realm, both through ritual mediation and through mass media. Taking as a point of departure religion's "problem of mediation," I have approached religious media figures'

challenge of binding people—as audiences, followers, and/or congregations—as a question of how to mediate a sense of divine presence through
media representation. While the two "religions" in case seem at first sight
diametrically opposed, and also position themselves as such, they are
closely connected on a deeper level. Most significant for the present argument is the role of the body as a medium for engaging with the immediate
presence of the divine. In both religions, the formats of spiritual mediation
and modes of religious bonding center on the embodiment of spiritual
power, which can be achieved through specific bodily and sensual "formats." How does this relate to audiovisual mass mediation, that is, to
Otabil's media ministry and Afrikania's public representation of ATR
respectively?

In the first case the formats and modes of address of charismatic ritual
fit those of television. Charismatic churches mediate the experience of spiritual power and community through mass gatherings, serialized spectacle,
and theatrical performance. Their dominant mode of address is a mode of
addressing the masses, or more precisely, the individual as part of a mass of
worshippers. This fits the televisual logic of enchanting the masses with
public spectacle and visual attraction and addressing the spectator as being
part of a mass audience. Indeed, Pentecostalism's evangelical logic of winning as many souls as possible has shaped its authorized modes of transmitting religious knowledge and spiritual power in ways that structurally
connect to television's commercial logic of reaching an audience as wide as
possible. The medium of television thus offers formats and modes of
address that are familiar to those of charismatic events.

I have shown how charismatic media practices extend the role of the
body as a medium for spiritual power and religious bonding through filming and editing techniques that visualize the flow of spirit power in church
and invite the TV audience to participate in this flow. While radically
breaking with Catholic body imagery featuring Christ, Mary and saints as
mediators of the divine, charismatic-Pentecostal imagery stars the bodies
of pastors and worshippers themselves. They become "living icons" mediating the power of the Holy Spirit to the spectators by appealing to their
full sensory being. Charismatic television, then, attempts to connect its
viewers to this power and to one another as a religious audience in similar
ways as happens to the in-church audience during worship service.

By contrast, the Afrikania Mission's media representations lack the spiritual power that occupies the religious practitioners they claim to represent. This has to do with Afrikania's awkward position in between the
public and the shrine priests and the misfit between the formats of mediation of the public sphere and those of spirit cults. In traditional shrines
communication of spiritual power usually takes place in seclusion on a

one-to-one base and many rituals are performed in secret rooms where nobody but the priest may enter. Moreover, access to religious knowledge in traditional cults is restricted by long processes of initiation. This concealment of spiritual practice and restriction of knowledge does not fit the televisual logic of mass enchantment and makes its mass mediation problematic (cf. Van de Port 2006 and in this volume).

As a movement that strives for revaluation of indigenous religious traditions, Afrikania engages in the representation of traditional religious practices and beliefs to the general public, envisioned primarily as Christianized and (thus) alienated. This entails the creation of a new, Christian-derived format for Afrikan Traditional Religion as a world religion. But there is a tension between Afrikania's concern with *representation* of the spiritual to "the general public" and traditional religious concerns with the *presence* of the spiritual in the bodies of practitioners. The embodied, experiential kind of religious bonding generated by practices of spirit possession, initiation, and spiritual healing, finds no place in Afrikania's intellectualist project of addressing and attracting the public in a discursive register. The body only features in Afrikania's representations as an image of beauty and neatness or as a symbol of traditional religion, not as medium for engaging with the spirits. Unlike charismatic media ministries, then, Afrikania's media representations do not connect its audience to the spiritual and thus can hardly play any role in generating religious bonding.

By stressing the difference between charismatic and African traditionalist media practices, I am not arguing that traditional spiritual power cannot be mediated by modern media technologies. On the contrary, the very reason that certain places and activities connected with the presence of spirits may often not be filmed or photographed is that cameras are believed to be able to catch a spirit and take it away or to disturb it and interfere with its operation. Conversely, a spirit can interfere with the camera's operation and prevent the images from appearing. Several "spiritualists" explained to me how they would use a person's photograph to spiritually heal or harm the person depicted over a long distance (see also Behrend 2003). None of them used video for this purpose, but one said it could be possible. In traditional African religiosity, then, the power of vision is closely connected to spiritual power. Images and spirits are not separated by a relation of referentiality, but connected by a relation of presentationality. An image does not represent spiritual power but makes it present (ibid.; Meyer 2006c). It can acquire power of its own and seeing it can affect the seer. In other words, the image is iconic rather than symbolic; it does not symbolize, but it embodies the spiritual reality behind it. Interestingly, then, charismatic-Pentecostal looking practices, in which images can transfer the power of the Holy Spirit to the viewer, are very close to traditional African ideas about seeing and spiritual power (De Witte 2005b; Gordon and Hancock 2005), much closer indeed than Afrikania's representational practices.

In taking on modern media, both charismatic Pentecostalism and African traditional religion struggle with the problem of mediation, but face different challenges. The paradoxical observation is that charismatic Pentecostalism denies mediation, positing the direct access of every born-again Christian to the power of the Holy Spirit, but enthusiastically takes on electronic media technologies, while African traditional religions emphasize the need for mediation, channeling access to spirit powers through various types of religious intermediaries, but find it very difficult to accommodate new media. The difference is that in charismatic Pentecostalism every believer is able and expected to access the power of the Holy Spirit personally, and thus its mass mediation is encouraged, whereas in traditional religious cults, access to the powers of particular divinities is restricted to initiated religious specialists, whose authority (and income) depends on their exclusive access to these powers. The problem for charismatic Pentecostalism, then, is that mass media challenge the ideal of immediacy. This asks for self-concealing media formats that mask mediation and suggest immediate presence. In traditional religion mass media challenge the authorized structures of mediation. This limits media practice to formats that are representational and preclude spirit presence.

In contemporary mass media societies of distraction, the idea of a religious community has come under ever more pressure. This is not to say that community has become impossible, but that the realization of a religious community, or the establishment of bonds between people as believers/religious practitioners and the divine, requires constant work. Nor is it to suggest that the idea or ideal of religious community was unproblematic in the past and only became challenged by the advent of modern mass media. As I have argued, media are intrinsic to religion understood as bonding. Binding people to a religious leader, to each other, and to the divine, always depends on mediating forms that must give people a sense of being connected, but risk being experienced as "mere" forms, be they *perform*ances or media *form*ats. It is perhaps the durability of this sense of being connected that is put under pressure by mass (media) religion. Just like in a mass church like the ICGC's Christ Temple religious bonding needs to be constantly reproduced, the binding of media publics as religious audiences requires media formats that derive their power from a combination of repetition and renewal.

Notes

1. One etymology of the Latin *religio* (first given by Lactantius [*Divinae Institutiones* IV, 28] and made prominent by Augustinus) traces it to the verb *religare*, to bind (again), to reconnect, referring to the bond (*liga*) between man and God.
2. The notion of "bonding," with its connotation of emotional and physical attachment, seems particularly apt to both charismatic Pentecostal and African traditional religiosity.
3. The term format, derived from the context of mass media as a relatively fixed and reproducible set of formal and sequential features applied to organize media content, is taken here to include the more or less fixed and repetitive modes of formal organization of, in this case, religious practice and expression, be they textual, visual, aural, or performative.
4. First Ofori-Atta lecture, quoted in Gifford 2004, 125.
5. The *Living Word* correspondence department files and answers about 400 letters and e-mails a month, mainly from nonmembers.

Chapter 9

Prophecy on Stage: Fame and Celebrities in the Context of the Raelian Movement

Carly Machado

Santa Suzana, Barcelona, August 2005. After a series of train delays, I finally reached the Indalo Hotel where 600 Raelians had convened for the "European Raelian Seminar." I was in a rush, one day late for the conference and worried about arriving on time to take part in the event. When I finally arrived, the first image I saw was Raël himself on stage. Raël is the prophet and leader of the Raelian Movement. It was not the first time I had seen Raël's image, indeed I had often seen the latter projected on stage, but I had never seen Raël in person.[1]

Showing the prophet on stage (whether himself or his image), being on stage, inviting people to come on stage, and enlarging "the stage" to the audience are acts imbued with meaning in the Raelian Movement, whose religious experiences are typically dramatized as mass media performances. After attending various Raelian meetings, I was able to perceive the importance of the stage and its meaning to this movement. Simultaneously invested with mediatic and religious significance, both related to the production and circulation of fame, Raël is omnipresent on Raelian stages, not usually in person, but via mass media forms such as photographs, video clips, and so on. The central concern of this chapter is to analyze how mass mediated performances and the idea of fame making permeate Raelian religious experience, shaping attitudes and ways of being, relating and evolving, while also *creating* values and forms of legitimization.

In the 1970s, Claude Vourilhon, a young Frenchman involved in the worlds of music and motor racing, claimed he had twice encountered extraterrestrial beings, which he called Elohim,[2] who were responsible for creating human life on Earth through "highly developed" biological methods. Claude Vourilhon's message revealed that the Elohim had chosen him as their prophet to spread this truth around the world, simultaneously giving him the name Raël.

Raël's prophecy is presented as a message of evolution and development. Seeking to "free humanity from obscurantism," the prophet's greatest revelation is the power of Science as a path toward social and individual improvement. In the social field, the Raelian message disseminates a high-tech imaginary in which the implementation of technological and biotechnological projects can liberate humanity from the burdens of traditional life, such as work—to be realized in the future by machines and robots—and the family—considered unnecessary given the possibilities afforded by the new reproductive technologies. In the personal field, Raël also adopts a radical stance against any form of traditionalism. Suggesting a new moral technology, the Raelian message incites nonconformism and supports all the more polemical social projects: it is against marriage, supports bisexual and homosexual relations, is in favor of abortion, radically questions the option to have children, suggests open relationships based on "free-love"—in sum, suggests and supports every form of moral action that challenges the standards of traditional Christian morality. The various Raelian projects in support of new social, biological, and moral technologies are seen to be ideally suited to being spread through the mass media, taking advantage of the "polemical" nature of the movement's arguments as the central motif for attracting media interest.

Before becoming the prophet Raël, Vourilhon was involved in various activities linked to communications media: he was a sports journalist, specializing in reports on motor racing, one of his passions.[3] He also worked as a singer in bars, cabaret performances, and on French radio, another form of gaining experience of self-publicity and the pursuit of fame. His earlier relation with the media helped shape his life as the prophet Raël, as well as the religious movement created by him.

The politics of recognition and authenticity predominant in the Raelian Movement are permeated with media values, ranging from a prophet who asserts his recognition within the movement by being always (and only ever) present on stage, sometimes in person but usually through video clips of his appearances on mass media channels. These video clips present Raël around the world, generally in two different situations: first, taking part in Raelian meetings in distant countries, imagery that illustrates the expansion of the movement; and, second, through his appearances on TV programs and at book launches and press conferences covered by the mass media, reaffirming not only the movement's global reach, but also its recognition by the general public and Raël's presumed fame.

The notion of the production of "fame" as a religious value operates in a significant way within this group, and formulates methods of constructing the self and establishing relations with others both inside and outside the movement. The production of fame, which starts with the projection of images of Raël on stage, permeates outward to the audience of followers: experiences at shows and parties provide moments when the stage is shared with the audience, along with the possibility of becoming famous.

Fame making and mass media performances are directly related. Marshall (1997), whose work focuses on the concepts of fame, celebrity, and power in the realm of communication studies, provides a compelling analysis of the "celebrity" and how fame operates as a powerful form of legitimization in contemporary culture. Although his arguments pertain to the field of entertainment, some of his ideas about the power conferred to celebrities through the production of fame help emphasize one of the main points made in this chapter: namely, how fame making becomes a religious form of constructing power within the Raelian Movement, including the way their leaders are present in the public sphere.

However, focusing directly and exclusively on the relationship between fame and media, risks reducing the phenomenon in question to a debate limited to the mass media. The anthropological meaning of "fame," as analyzed by Munn (1992) on the island of Gawa where mass media are largely absent, highlights elements that extend the concept of a "circulation of fame" far beyond the specificities of mass media performance (as pointed by Marshall), expanding its analytic use as a cultural category. Presented as a "circulating dimension of the person" (Munn 1992, 105) beyond his or her physical presence and, as such, as a creator of positive values, this anthropological reading of fame makes the mass media just one of its forms of mediation, without attributing exclusivity to this format.

As Meyer (Meyer and Moors 2006a) suggests, the idea of mediation emphasizes the entanglement of religion and media in two different ways: as well as stressing the presence of modern mass media forms in different religious contexts, it also, and principally, provides us with an insight into how media mediate and thus produce the transcendental and make it tangible. Fame emerges in my own research as a product of mass media models operating as a transcendental category within the Raelian religious movement. In this chapter, therefore, I discuss the production of fame through different media forms both inside and outside the Raelian Movement, as well as its religious meaning within the group's experience.

In so doing, I focus on how this suite of elements composed by mass mediated images—a stage, an audience, and the dynamics of fame making—identifies what Meyer calls "sensational forms" as key elements of the Raelian experience, involving practitioners in particular kinds of worship and playing a central role in the formation of religious subjects (ibid., and in this volume).

This analysis starts out from the figure of Raël who legitimizes his sacred dimension via the values that adhere to him through the circulation of his image in the mass media. In this context, being a "prophet" implies forms of behavior and attitudes like those of a media *celebrity*. By acting in this way, Raël projects himself not only outside but capitally inside the movement created by himself, making up an interesting system of feedback that sustains the strength of his message via the mass mediated acknowledgment of his figure.

Extending and confirming the relationship between the movement and the world of celebrities, I shall also examine the awarding of the title "Honorary Raelian Guide" to high-profile international public personalities. Finally, I conclude this chapter with an analysis of the dynamic of creating celebrities within the Raelian Movement: shows, bodies, and attitudes form the settings for Raelian subjectivity and the multiple forms of being Raelian.

Raël: the "Celebrity" Prophet on Stage

The main event that promoted the global diffusion of Raël's image occurred in December 2002 when he and Brigitte Boissilier[4] announced to the international media the birth of the first human clone, presented to the world with the evidently provocative codename of "Eve." Even for those knowing nothing about Raël and the religious movement he founded, this event was a landmark and any mention of human cloning, even today, means recalling this event in some form.

In *20 ans*, a book describing the history of the movement[5] and providing an important example of the group's official discourse on its own development, one of the key events from 1974, the movement's *inaugural act*, is taken to be Raël's appearance on the French television program Samedi Soir. After this event, identified as an initial landmark, the book proceeds to describe the main actions of the movement's first 20 years: "the pioneer generation." Since the movement's very first actions, Raël has worked to legitimize his status as a prophet through the mass media, exploiting for this purpose events such as appearances on TV programs, book launches, press conferences, and prominent Web sites. Visits to new countries to launch the movement were conducted whenever the local group was able to host a set of activities.[6] These visits used to include speeches and meetings with those interested in Raelian ideas, but also—and perhaps mainly—interviews on radio and TV programs, as well as a book launching event. In *20 ans*, Raël's participation in these kinds of events is repeatedly highlighted as a key part of the movement's progressive development.

The position of the Raelian Movement in the mass media is strategically planned with part of its "Structure" dedicated to developing its media activities.[7] In general, people who have already heard of Raël have done so through his public media appearances. This resonates with Van de Port's (2005c, 46, see also this volume) analysis of the "priests-who-go-public" in the context of Candomblé in Salvador (Brazil), which shows that the credibility of a religious leader in the contemporary world is dependent on his or her media performance, emphasizing the introduction of new parameters into the religious scene—namely, the modes of perception and evaluation cultivated by modern mass media consumers.

Self-styled "prophet of the scientific age,"[8] Raël legitimizes himself as a media age prophet, a "pop star" who uses these mediations to assert his sacred status within the movement and beyond. The media imaginary confers sacredness on the prophet. His religious "aura" is produced through the language of the mass media. During the Raelian Seminars,[9] the RVP (Raël Video Production) team exclusively records all of Raël's steps from his arrival at the airport, including his speeches, walkabouts, and leisure time, presenting clips of these images of the prophet over the course of the event as a way of registering the presence of a "superstar" in a particular city. All of his "tours" are recorded and transformed into video clips, also shown during the meeting, especially the packed airport scenes and the bustling evenings of autograph signing. The prophet status attributed to Raël is reaffirmed through a continual construction of his status as a "celebrity" both within the movement and—especially—beyond.

De Certeau (cited in Van de Port 2005c) argues that the objects and people worthy of our belief and of being invested with our "belief-energy" are found in the cinema, sports, the arts, in general, concert halls, pop festivals, and so on. Thus in Van de Port's application of De Certeau's work, the fact that these entertainment celebrities have become the receptacles of our "belief energy" explains the huge expansion in media performances among specific religious leaders (in his own study, Candomblé priests). Being a religious leader in the media age virtually implies being a celebrity.

According to Marshall's studies (2001), celebrity status gives structure to meanings, crystallizes ideological positions and works to provide sense and coherence to a culture. Being a celebrity provides distinction and confers discursive power to the person: the celebrity is a voice imposed over other voices, a voice channeled by the media systems as legitimately meaningful (Marshall, 2006).[10] The fame acquired by Raël through the mass media, even though relative in quantitative terms,[11] is realized as an extension of his self, a capacity to develop spatiotemporal relations that extend beyond the self (Munn 1992), expanding its dimensions of control. At the start of my ethnographic research, my initial "contact" with Raël was mediated by his online image and his printed word; likewise, others interested in the movement can make contact with "Raël's person" through these same mediations.

Munn (1992, 116) conceives "fame," in the Gawan case, as an extension of a person's immediate influence beyond the minds and actions of his or her partners, reaching others located further away in the network. "Fame" is therefore characterized as the potential to influence the acts of distant third parties: "As iconic and reflexive code, fame is the virtual form of influence" (117). Taking the relation between *fame* and *influence* as a paradigmatic feature of the figure of Raël allows us to pursue a deeper analysis of the effectiveness of the link between the spread of his image through mass communications, associated with the circulation of his person (fame), and the amplification of his influence in creating positive and sacred values associated with his image. The virtual presence of the diffused image, associated with its potential to influence, generates the effect needed to attribute sacredness to the prophet's amplified powers. Circulation of the person, extra-bodily mobility, virtuality, and extended influence are elements held in common by mediatic and sacred effects, and as such can mix to the point where they end up defining the same phenomenon.[12]

Like the category of "fame," the position of "celebrity" confers "otherworldly" qualities to the sacred figure of the prophet. According to Marshall (2001), the celebrity occupies a position without history and without great cultural importance or prior baggage: "Celebrity draws its power from those elements without tradition. This power, however, has a certain liquidity, much like the mobility and exchangeability of capital" (6). Hence, Marshall continues, the celebrity exists above the real world in the domain of symbols that gain and lose values like merchandise on the stock market.

While at first sight the reports produced by the RVP team seem to be targeted toward the outside public, the biggest effect of these images is to feed the internal imaginary of the movement's members who, through *what they see* and *how they see*, legitimate Raël's status as a prophet. The mediation of the camera plays an important role in the way in which Raelians "see" their prophet. As Meyer (2003b) discusses in her analysis of video films in Ghana, the camera, which from a positivist perspective would represent the "mechanical eyes of reason," operates as an "extension of the human eye, showing occult forces in action," mediating forms of the truth-knowledge relation that transcends the boundaries between the visible and the invisible, the physical and the spiritual, and allows people to share this perspective (220). This "occult" dimension and its relation with the camera in Ghana is quite different from the Raelian religious setting, but the question of the audiovisual mediation of the "sacred," highlighted by Meyer, echoes an important analytic theme in the Raelian ethos.

Seeing Raël through the camera, mediated by a telejournalistic audiovisual language that shows, or gives visibility to, his "fame" and recognition in the public sphere is a way of looking that attributes value to this person who declares himself a prophet, and feeds the aura of sacredness surrounding him. In the current context of the Raelian Movement,[13] seeing clips of Raël before seeing him personally functions, therefore, as a form of preparing the gaze for his sacred dimension. Recognizing him—through mediatic means—should precede meeting him personally. This recognition, mediated by the mass media, operates via the logic of celebrity with a two-way effect: publicizing Raël outside the movement and intensifying his image and its value within the group led by himself.

The Celebrity Team and the Formation of a Team of "Celebrities": Raelian Honorary Guides

The Raelian Movement's relation with the "world of celebrities" forms a chapter of the movement's history by itself. Just as its prophet is internally legitimized through his constructed condition of "celebrity," in the public sphere the movement continually strives for legitimacy and recognition by approaching "real" famous people. The desire to capture the famous is an explicit objective of the group's leaders who devote one of the teams of the Movement's Structure to celebrities: The Celebrity Team that is exclusively responsible for spreading the Raelian message among celebrities from the mass media. The most prominent symbol of the relationship between celebrities and new religious movements is without doubt Tom Cruise. Representing Scientology wherever he goes, Cruise personifies the idea of celebrity dreamt of by Raël. Referring to Cruise, Raël praises his attitude of explicitly declaring his allegiance to Scientology, and the form in which, through his public image, he publicizes the movement to which he belongs. Raël dreams and invests much of the Structure's work in search of the movement's own "Tom Cruise."

One of the strategies of the International Raelian Movement is to award the title of Honorary Raelian Guides to international celebrities who demonstrate attitudes considered representative of the movement's generally polemical values. As mentioned earlier, Honorary Raelian Guides include Madonna, Eminem, President Hugo Chávez, Bill Gates, Sean Penn, and others. Being a Guide in the Raelian Movement means taking on responsibilities. For an ordinary member (that is, a nonfamous and therefore non-Honorary member) of the Raelian Movement becoming a guide means taking on activities within the structure and gradually, as a result of the evolution of these responsibilities, raising one's level in the Raelian hierarchy.[14] However, the Honorary Guides are not Raelian and have no responsibilities within the Structure and generally know nothing about Raël's "Message." These celebrities from the artistic, political, or social world are informed about the "honor" awarded by the movement, but very often make no response to receiving the title. On other occasions, the personality awarded the title agrees to take part in a nomination ceremony that normally does not reach the public domain. Awarding the title of Honorary Guide is a form encountered by the Raelian Movement of approaching celebrities and gaining some minutes of their attention. Whether the relationship between the new Guide and the movement later becomes closer is far from certain. So far, in fact, this has never happened. The most interesting image obtained up to now has been a photo of Madonna using a necklace with the movement's symbol,[15] published by the French Magazine *Public* in February 2005 and widely publicized in the group's internal media.

The motives for awarding these titles vary: Nicholas Negroponte received the title for his initiative in creating a computer priced at US$ 100, which for the Raelian Movement signifies an important investment in the technological development of society. The French writer Michel Houellebecq was named an Honorary Guide after turning the Elohim into characters in one of his books. He responded while receiving the award thus: "I am very happy and very proud of this nomination, especially because I am the first and only French citizen to be given this title."[16] Sean Penn was made a Guide after his manifestations against the Iraq War, mirroring the Raelian Movement's values of nonviolence. Hugo Chávez was deemed worthy of the award for his opposition to the American government, another frequent rallying point of Raelian ideas.

The relation between the movement's follows and the Honorary Guides follows two trends: the first is discomfort over the fact that non-Raelians have become Movement Guides. In some more serious cases, the movement's members question the appropriateness of these nominations. Many celebrities receiving this title display behavior condemned by the Raelian Movement, such as the abusive use of drugs, for example, which makes the nomination incompatible with certain elements of the Raelian lifestyle. However, in the official discourse of the movement's leaders, these questions are stifled and the admiration for these public personalities reinforced, repeatedly citing them in the Raelian meetings as examples of ideal behavior, at least those conducts deemed to be iconic of Raelian values.

On one hand, the celebration of Honorary Guides confirms the importance of celebrities in the Raelian Movement's value system. On the other hand, it is presented as a form of strategically reinventing culture, incorporating what is valorized in public space into the movement's religious dimension: whether they want to or not, the celebrity becomes a Guide. The relation between members and Honorary Guides absorbs various aspects of the Celebrity Culture: being a fan—a status taken from the media field—blurs with being a "disciple"—a condition belonging to the religious field. Moreover, the components of scandal and polemic typical of the celebrity culture analyzed by Marshall are also applicable to the image of the Honorary Guides, whose value is identified by precisely these attitudes in the public sphere. As Marshall suggests: "Celebrities are performative texts: They act out" (2006, 11), and these performative acts intrinsic to the scandals surrounding celebrities reinforce the pertinence of their celebration in the Raelian ethos.

Conferring the title of Honorary Guide on a celebrity is a ritual action that blends media objectives with religious objectives to the point of being indistinguishable. Awarding the title to a celebrity produces effects both inside and outside the movement: externally, it corresponds to the pursuit of legitimacy and recognition in public space. Internally, it is defined primarily as a system of religious values on the basis of which particular forms of behavior can be identified as more or less Raelian; above all, the valorization of public recognition and media projection are configured as a means of immediate access to a more Raelian life. Thus the more famous a member of the movement is, the more in accord with Raelian values he or she will be. In this sense, the everyday practice of the Raelian ethos also reflects this quest for notoriety, turning the *spectacle* into a ritual of development continually present in the events experienced during the group's meetings.

Celebrating Religiosity: Shows and Parties as Religious Experiences

Understanding Raelian performances means understanding *celebrities* and *audiences*. These elements represent two levels of reality: the here and now, where the performances of celebrities unfold on the stage of Indalo Park Hotel, and the future that these performances announce and prepare for: a moment when "all of this will be true" and when what today takes place in a hotel auditorium in front of an audience of 600 people will be realized on an international scale with the entire planet as its audience.

The performative acts of Raelian religiosity infuse personal relations with elements typical of the expressions of power inherent to the logic of the spectacle, fame being the principal of these elements. This movement's strongly hierarchical institutional model separates celebrities from the general public: the latter make up the numbers, but do not form the central event in this "show." The smaller the performance, the more prominence each element receives and the more fame becomes diluted. The larger the event, the more the division of these categories is accentuated, meaning that the minority are responsible for the show, while the rest are left to play the role of the audience.

Marshall (2001) stresses the power of the audience as the epicenter of the celebrity's power. Indeed, according to the author, the historical emergence of the idea of celebrity coincides and is correlated with the emergence of the audience as a social category. In his analysis, the author highlights the concept of audience-subject: while the celebrity occupies the scene in a *subjective* position, on the opposite side, rather than a receptive and passive object position as might be anticipated, we find *another* subject position: this gives rise to an *audience-subject*, whose agency participated directly in the constitution of the celebrity. "The celebrity's strength or power as a discourse on the individual is operationalized only in terms of the power and position of the audience that has allowed it to circulate" (65).

The Raelian Seminar is the centre stage of the Raelian experience. Everything that takes place there tends to be replicated in local meetings. In the Seminar, performances are organized to start with the brain and end with the body. In the morning, it's time for meditations and talks: performances of rationality executed on the main stage by the movement's leaders and mostly verbal and, in some cases, audiovisual. Raël is the main performer in these events. Alongside him, Daniel Chabot[17] and Brigitte Boisselier provide the setting of rationality: the former as the one who reveals "the truth" about the brain and its functions through images, confirming the Raelian message; the latter, the spokeswoman for the sciences

on the body, instincts, hormones—chemical aspects of the human leading
to its formation—and, above all, DNA, the centerpiece of her speeches
being the possibilities opened up for humans by science, of which cloning
was (or will be?) merely the beginning.

The afternoons of the first days involve talks too, but gradually experiences led by the speakers are included where the audience begins to take
part more actively in the "rational" argument of the message of Raël,
Daniel, and Brigitte. The audience is rarely allowed to make interventions
or comments to the group as a whole: instead, the interactions are organized in small groups that go beyond conversation to include experiences
that transfer the prophet's words to corporal activities. As preparations,
these experiences anticipate the nighttime performances. Taking the form
of shows and parties, the nocturnal performances directly affect the body,
their main mediations being through music and dance. As performances
organized for an audience, the shows prioritize sensory stimulation, starting with vision and spreading to all the other senses: bodies as images display the model of Raelian sensuality and corporality, lights create
atmosphere, music stimulates the hearing and the overall nonverbal message provokes the whole body. Hence, the main mediation in the shows is
the living body of the performers: music and dance embodied in people
who display themselves in order to develop themselves and provoke the
development of others who watch them.

In the parties, the mediation becomes the body of those who were previously just part of the audience. Music and dance now affect everyone and
become universally accessible. Sensuality finally reaches the bodies of all
the Seminar's participants. The models spoken of in the morning, experi-
mented in the afternoon and seen in the shows can be lived to the full at
night. The typical intentionality and mediation of each activity suggested
at the Seminar create characteristic environments and relations responsible
for different levels of the Raelian experiences.

> The directionality of performance and the media of performance are struc-
> turing the ritual context; together they constitute the meaning of the ritual,
> variously enable the communication of its meaning, and create the possibil-
> ity for the mutual involvement of participants in the one experience, or else
> distance them and lead to their reflection on experience perhaps from a
> structured perspective outside the immediacy of the experience. (Kapferer
> in Turner 1986, 192)

The shows are the highest point of the spectacle while the parties are a
popularization of the performance. In the shows, the design of the spectacle predominates completely—some people present themselves and the
others watch. The split between stage and audience is striking. Those who

present themselves win a place in the hall of fame, while the sequence of presentations is closed with the shows of the most famous and eagerly awaited.

While the shows operate via the logic of the spectacle and fame, the parties provide a conducive environment for everyone to experience the lifestyle promulgated by the movement without a stage separating audience and artists. Generally theme-based, the main function of the parties is to create a climate for experiences of the morally alternative Raelian behavior, diluting the right to the performance in everyone and to everyone—a more "democratized" performance in this context. In the shows, the Raelian models are displayed for some, while in the parties are experienced by everyone.

Raelian shows and parties operate via what Turner (1987) calls the double reflexivity of the performance: the actor may come to know himself better through acting or enactment—experiencing an individual, or singular reflexivity—or one set of human beings may come to know themselves better through observing and/or participating in performances generated and presented by another set of human beings—figuring a group reflexivity. In Raelian shows, reflexivity through observation predominates and, for those on stage, singular reflexivity. In their parties, reflexivity operates as collective participation in its constitution.

The evening spectacles held during the Seminar are the main environments for producing the "famous." The "Raelian show" provides artists seeking fame in show business with a level of recognition and prominence far higher than the level obtained in the official media. Its external micro projection generates an internal macro visibility. Operating on the media model, the Raelian Movement confirms the claim made by Sodré: "At the same time, the media is also taken to stage a new doxa (in the ancient double meaning of 'opinion' and 'celebrity') on the basis of which the value of the other is discussed and recognized" (cited in Burity 2003, 82). The dancer, actor, or singer with some kind of recognition among the general public—however small—becomes someone "famous" within the movement. Hence, the shows containing presentations of music and dance typically culminate in the appearance of these Raelian celebrities. I pick out two of these people from the London group: Robert and Lysa.

Robert is the Guide for the British Isles. An actor and singer in London musicals, the most famous role of his career was playing Jesus Christ in the show "Jesus Christ Superstar." Robert stands out for his double fame: as a guide and as a "famous" actor. So far, Robert is the nearest to being "Tom Cruise" of the Raelian Movement. I met Robert in London at a weekend of activities run by the movement[18] and was able to see that he interacted closely with other members of the London group. At the European Seminar, however, it was difficult to approach Robert. At Level 5 in the Structure—the last level before Raël—the Guide has a range of tasks to perform during the meeting. Moreover, Robert stands out because of his fame. Everyone talks about him. A Raelian from South Korea who had also taken part in the London activities said about the London group when we met again in the Seminar: "I had no idea that our 'friends' from London were so famous!" An outsider in London like myself, he perceived the difference of these 'friends' now they were in their celebrity habitat.

Robert heads a musical project on the Elohim, which Raël dreams of showing in London and in which Robert would play the part of Raël. His compositions for the Elohim entertain the public hugely and his singing is responsible for some of the Seminar's most exciting moments. Robert is a star in the European Raelian Movement and acts as such there on a day-to-day basis. The proximity shown in London disappears during the Seminar. His complete visibility limits his accessibility. The more visible and "famous" a person is, the less accessible he or she is.

The same occurred with Lysa. A Guide, choreographer, and dancer, I also met Lysa in London, at the Gay Parade where she was the person responsible for organizing the participation of the Raelians in the event. Lysa is a vivid example of the Raelian type of woman:[19] beautiful, charming, vane, always well-dressed and striving to be as attractive as possible, she uses her sensuality to stimulate people's interest in the Raelian Movement. In the Gay Parade, she walked with charm and attitude, practically "parading" and catching the eye of spectators, handing them leaflets about the movement. This is a Raelian strategy in action: the attraction toward the person provides the link with the movement's ideas. In this case, the attraction toward Lysa was the form of accessing the leaflet. Lysa's body *expresses* the anticonformist and sexualized attitude of the Raelian Message. Spicing her teasing, erotic sense of humor with sensual gestures and movements, Lysa provoked those who looked at her to respond positively to her behavior.

Over the weekend I spent in London, Lysa was very attentive to all the members of the Raelian group. In the Seminar, she was just as charming, but getting close to her proved much more difficult. Her presence in the meeting's events was invariably striking: during the talks and activities, she stood out through the way she entered the auditorium, wearing a new outfit every day and, especially, every evening in the sensual shows and theme-based parties. In addition, along with Robert, Lysa led a number of activities in English for the group as a whole.[20] Aside from Raël, Daniel, and Brigitte, few leaders climbed on stage, and Robert and Lysa were part of this select group. Lysa is an Angel, Level 5, and consequently represents femininity throughout the duration of the Seminar.[21] She dresses well, always with immaculate makeup, and performs even the smallest movement in sensual fashion.

Being visible and providing visibility to the movement in internal and external interfaces enables people to rise within the Structure, which is why "famous" people occupy high levels in the Raelian hierarchy. This combination of fame and level provokes a range of effects, especially in relation to the Guides: in their home cities, they are close and approachable; at the Seminar, they become difficult to access celebrities. Some degrees of separation are intentionally produced in order to augment the celebrity status of the movement's key people. Without a certain distance, fame becomes banal. Just as Raël walks about the Seminar surrounded by security guards in order to maintain his status as "the biggest celebrity," the creation of a climate of being "difficult to approach" works to valorize those who stand out from a mixture of their artistic talent and their level in the structure. The difference between my experiences of meeting Robert and Lysa in London and later in the Seminar provided me with a demonstration of the close-distant dialectic. The celebrity-audience relationship is fundamental in this context. It is the hope of the audience to one day become a celebrity who feeds this relationship. The media position of being a fan blurs with the religious position of the disciple. In the Raelian religious experience, the audience glimpses models of *selves* that indicate the direction to be taken by their own personal development. Celebrities emerge as icons, "flesh and blood" representations of a religious ideology and project.

Mass Media, Community, and the Raelian Structure

The relationship between the mass media and religion is crucial to any analysis of the Raelian Movement. As we have seen, Raelian performances are modeled by mass media references that turns the *stage* into a significant context for religious experiences and, furthermore, a scope for the production and attribution of fame, conceived as a religious merit. To conclude this chapter, I wish to address the idea of community in the study of the Raelians, given its status as a new kind of religious movement whose members are dissipated into small groups, or even act as isolated individuals, all around the world. Two strategies work together to produce the sense of a Raelian community: regular meetings and mass media mediation. It's important to highlight that media are indispensable in both levels of the Raelian experience: not only in the global circuit of mass media but also—and mainly—in the context of local meetings that become, by this means, virtually global or planetary.

As described earlier, Raelian Guides are responsible for organizing local group meetings at least once a month. These meetings are organized around the stage and screen. Both operate in this specific ethnographic case as *windows* connecting spatially dispersed experiences via the image of a collectivity. Raelian's image of community is planetary in scale. It is not enough for this movement to be local; it has to be global. This explains why the same images of Raelian groups are displayed across the world, while video clips of Raelian Seminars and Raël himself "circulating" in different continents allow people to imagine a planet-wide Raelian community. Indeed, this image is fundamental to shaping a religious experience founded on a project whose very essence is global. The idea of extraterrestrial creators "necessarily" implies a collective congregation of their "creatures" as a holistic group of "terrestrial human beings." Therefore, since the movement's beginnings, mass mediated performances have been the central aspect of its Structure; or, more precisely, the mass media has always been "the" primordial "Structure" that makes the movement possible. Hence, we can conclude that, in the specific case of the Raelian Movement, the mass media is essential to its existence and without it there would be no sense in being Raelian.

Notes

1. The research on which this chapter is based involved multisited fieldwork. During 2004 and 2005, I joined four Raelian groups in different countries, usually during their local meetings: Brazil, Belgium, the Netherlands and England. In addition to these local meetings, the Raelian Movement organizes Annual Seminars, one on each continent. As indicated in the first lines of this chapter, I participated in the European Raelian Seminar, 2005, in Santa Suzana, Barcelona, Spain. I learned about the Raelian Movement through the Internet and the book *The Message Given by Extra-terrestrials*, written by Raël (year). For some months, this ethnographic research—which was initially conducted in Brazil, where the movement has few followers—made intensive use of digital and printed media sources. As the work developed, I realized that these mediations are legitimate and form part of the religious experience of many members of the movement, who first discover Raël through its digital and textual interfaces. This theme was further developed in the full text of my doctoral thesis *Imagine se tudo isso for verdade* ("Imagine if all this were true"), supervised by Professor Patrícia Birman and completed in October 2006 at the State University of Rio de Janeiro.

2. In Raelian cosmology, Elohim means "those who come from the sky," a reference to the extraterrestrial beings who created human life on Earth. The biblical translation of the term as a reference to "God" is claimed to be a mistake in translation that misled humanity to believe in the existence of God. The Raelian Movement claims to be atheist and takes the Elohim to be extraterrestrial human beings, not divine or sacred beings.

3. After becoming leader of the Movement, Raël continued to invest in his career as a motor racing driver; he competed in various events and advertised himself as "the quickest prophet in the world." The financial resources used in this project were subject to intense questioning both inside and outside the Raelian Movement (Palmer 2004).

4. Brigitte Boissilier is one of the main international leaders of the Raelian Movement. A biochemical scientist, Brigitte is the head of CLONAID, a human cloning company created by Raël. She gained fame within the movement for the "courage" shown in publicly defending the project of human cloning, which made her face intense questioning over the project's ethical legitimacy and legality.

5. *20 ans: la générations des pioners.* France: Éditions DIFRA, 1994. Published by the International Raelian Movement, issue no. 286.

6. According to the official figures of the Raelian Movement, the group today has 60,000 members distributed across the five continents, with the highest concentrations in North America, Europe, and Asia.

7. The Raelian Movement's structure is formed by those responsible for spreading the message of the extra-terrestrials and all the Raelian projects. Composed of regional, national, and planetary leaders, it is also divided into teams with specific tasks. The Raelian leaders are called guides and are organized in levels (from 0 to 6) according to the responsibilities assumed within the structure. Raël is the "Guide's Guide" and the only person at Level 6 in the Structure.

8. Raël presents himself as the prophet capable of using Science to explain all the mysteries misinterpreted by religions. In this sense, he calls himself the prophet of the scientific age, an age in which his attempt to explain can be understood, since human beings are now able the comprehend scientific explanations, in contrast to what happened in earlier times with other prophets such as Jesus, Buddha, and Muhammad, whose societies were not sufficiently evolved to understand them.

9. These Raelian Seminars are organized every year on each continent. I took part in the European Raelian Seminar in 2005, held in Barcelona, Spain, in the first week in August. The Seminars are the main activity of the Raelian groups, serving as a moment of congregation and, most of the time, direct contact with the prophet Raël. The Seminar activities will be described in more detail below.

10. Marshall (2006) points to the existence of a "celebrity culture" in contemporary Western societies, analyzed from different angles in the reader edited by himself on the topic. In this book, identity and individuality combine in the image of the celebrity, which presents the essential components of the structure of a consumer culture—in the case of celebrities, a mixed consumption

of persons and things—as well as the aspirations engendered by the possibilities provided to people in a democratic society, represented iconically in these celebrities and their success.

11. Despite all the media campaigning of its leaders, the Raelian Movement is still unknown to many people.

12. Here it is worth recalling various studies on the sacred aura attributed to media personalities, such as the research into fan clubs and even churches built around figures whose fame is converted into divinity. I would single out the work of Eloísa Martin on the Argentinean singer Gilda: "No me arrepiento de este amor. Fan's clubs y devoción a Gilda, una cantante Argentina" (I do not regret this love. Fan Clubs and devotion for Gilda, an Argentine singer). In *XII Jornadas sobre Alternativas Religiosas na América Latina (XII Latin American Seminar on Religious Alternative)s*, São Paulo, 2003.

13. The history of the Raelian Movement provides numerous indications that the relation between followers and Raël has changed significantly over the movement's more than 30 years of existence (see *20 ans* and Palmer 2004). Consequently, this reading of audiovisual mediation is undertaken within the current context of the Raelian Movement posterior to these transformations and their incorporation into the Raelian ethos.

14. At Level 3 in the Structure, the member of the movement becomes an Assistant Guide, while at Level 4 and 5, the member becomes a Full Guide, acquiring even more responsibilities and status within the movement. Level 6 is occupied by Raël alone. If persons fail to perform their tasks as a Guide, their level is downgraded. If they resume these tasks, they can be repromoted. Being a Guide represents an honor in the movement and indicates involvement with the Message and its spreading across the planet. It should be stressed that the Raelian Guide is not attributed divine qualities. Guides are defined by their responsibilities, not their personal attributes.

15. The original symbol of the Raelian Movement is extremely polemical: a Swastika within a Star of David. Over the years, this symbol was transformed into an image that dissolves the Swastika into a spiral form, set within the same Star of David. This model was the one used by Madonna in the cited photo. The earlier symbol is still used by various Raelian groups and the movement's official argument is that it recuperates the Swastika's original religious symbology, aiming to liberate it from the Nazi distortion of the image. However, despite the Raelian interpretation, the symbol containing the Swastika has been the target of intense reprisals throughout the Raelian Movement's history.

16. "Contact." Issue No. 286. 11 October 1960 A. H. (Raelian Official Press). It should be explained that the Raelian Movement is the target of intense rejection by that part of French society that generally works to combat the existence and dissemination of new religious movements understood as "sects" that manipulate the country's young people. For this reason, Houellebecq stresses the fact that he is the only French person with the title of Honorary Guide. Although French, Raël left France due to the intensity of the criticism

and reprisals aimed at his religious movement. On the antisect movements in France, see Birman (2005) and Giumbelli (2002).

17. Daniel Chabot is a psychologist, the planetary Raelian leader responsible for psychological teachings related to Raël's Message. His main aim is to place Raelian ideas in dialogue with discoveries from the scientific field, showing their relevance.

18. I took part in the 2005 Gay Parade with the London group and also went to a meeting with members of the movement.

19. The Raelian Movement has its own determinant conception of what constitute "feminine" characteristics. Sensuality, beauty, and delicacy are prominent on the list and these "typically feminine" attributes are valued and developed in the group as paradigmatic examples of more evolved behavior for men and women alike.

20. The official language of the European Seminar is French, the language spoken by the majority of participants. There is a team responsible for providing simultaneous translation into various other languages, including Italian, Spanish, German, and English. However, a large part of the group is Anglophone and Raël's aim is to make English the movement's official language in response to its globalization. Consequently, some of the activities at the 2005 Seminar were already conducted by Robert and Lysa in English.

21. The Raelian Movement has an order formed exclusively by women called "The Order of Angels of Raël." Its objective is to develop "femininity" and prepare these women to look after Raël and the Elohim. Its existence intensifies the controversy surrounding the Raelian Movement since part of this group of women is dedicated sexually to the prophet. Although the issue of the role of women and representations of the "feminine" are not the focal point of this chapter, they make up part of the wider field of debates found in the global context of this research.

Chapter 10

Seized by the Spirit. The Mystical Foundation of Squatting among Pentecostals in Caracas (Venezuela) Today

Rafael Sánchez

> Democracy is always a matter of temporizing. It cannot be conceived of without this continual obligation to take the time—to develop proposals, to discuss the possible outcomes, to persuade, to implement decisions. Democratic power is always exercised more slowly than individual authoritarian power. Thus democracy must remain patient. even at those times when it encounters, more or less fortunately, the media's haste.
>
> —Sylviane Agacinski, Time Passing: Modernity and Nostalgia

"Our God is a Living God," or "we do not believe *in* God, we believe God." The Pentecostal squatters in Venezuela's capital city, Caracas, among whom I have recently done fieldwork, voice these and other related statements often to distinguish their own brand of spirituality from that of other religious communities across Venezuela. Although I originally found what the squatters said somewhat puzzling, their statements soon began to resonate powerfully with what I had first observed during the initial moments of fieldwork, namely, the strange (at least to me), unexpected spectacle of these squatters illegally occupying—in the name, and on the behalf, of the Holy Ghost—an empty 12-story building located in what was once a relatively posh, bohemian part of the city now teeming with informal commerce and all sorts of criminality.

A few initial encounters with the squatters sufficed for me to grasp the connection between the squatters' phenomenal spatial avarice and the notion of a "living God" instantaneously conveying His dictates to His squatter-people. This is a God, moreover, that one does not so much believe *in,* as if He was forever installed in some distant, invisible realm mediated by some visible image or authority. Rather, one believes *Him* as much as one believes or ought to believe a figure of authority that in the here and now tells you what to expect and what to do. If the Pentecostal squatters assert that you must "believe God" this is, indeed, simply because He, as a living, present deity, addresses you right now as a believer who, as such, is part of the community of the chosen, you better not merely believe *in* Him but *believe Him,* paying close attention to all that he tells you in the very moment that he speaks and you hear him. In what follows I hope to make clear that, at least in Venezuela, much of Pentecostal spirituality is precisely about obliterating the gap between God and his own creation so that, presumably, representation may give way to forms of religious presencing pregnant with all sorts of far-reaching, devastatingly efficacious worldly social and cultural effects.[1] Before, however, I simply will note that, given the connection between the squatters' spirituality and their spatial orientations, it is not all that surprising if the image of a hungry Holy Ghost gobbling vast stretches of the cityscape by means of the squatters' docile agency eventually seized my imagination. Such a ghostly apparition presides over much of what I write here.

Spirit Seizures

I credit the rapidity with which I gained some preliminary insight into the squatters' behavior to the very insistence with which they accounted for their actions in terms of the Holy Spirit's agency. A few examples will suffice to give an idea of the extent to which it is the Pentecostal squatters themselves who reflexively assume the link between the Holy Ghost's innermost designs and their own spatial agency.

One inheres in the insistence with which the squatters legitimate their illegal operations through appeal to transcendental grounds, claiming that whatever they seize is theirs "because God has given it to us." I cannot think of any more effective means to circumvent worldly property rights than the claim, drawn from the Bible, that "God is the owner of the entire world's silver and gold." Voiced constantly by the squatters, with syllogistic necessity such a claim neatly assigns divine origins to all worldly property while rendering the squatters' rights to whatever they seize ever more unassailable. After all, if it is the Divine owner himself who hands something to *me*, a member of the community of the chosen, is then not such a thing *mine*—at least in trust? What could be a more compelling property right than one that originates in such a direct heavenly transmission from God to his People and away from the undeserving?[2] Given such premises, it is no wonder that the Pentecostal squatters inhabit a thoroughly miraculous economy, a sort of parallel universe where all sorts of portentous signs—from dreams, to uncanny voices and visions—impinge on believers as so many divine injunctions continuously tell them what to do.[3]

That it is a matter of doing, of a supremely action-oriented deity seizing across history His very own spatiotemporal creation through the agency of His third person Trinity filling like electricity the bodies of the faithful—the squatters speak of themselves as "vessels" to be filled by Spirit—should be clear from my second, final example. One day as I was driving Hermana Juana,[4] the squatters' irresistibly charismatic leader, through the streets of Caracas, suddenly she turned away from the empty buildings she had been gazing at through her window and, briefly catching my eye, said: "You know, if we do not occupy spaces we do not receive blessings from the Holy Spirit." What better indication of a divinely inspired logic of spatial occupation spiraling out of all possible control in a limitless series of seizures, acts of more or less violent appropriation, to which there is no foreseeable limit? Does not this statement insinuate a religiously imbued, unbridled logic of consumption that posits the space of the city, the nation, and even the world as fair game, an ever-expanding field for this logic's limitless self-extension? Lest anyone find fault with mentioning the Holy Ghost and such logic of spatial occupation in the same breath, so to speak, let me say that none other than Hegel himself once spoke of the relation between the three persons of the Trinity as the mode whereby God dialectically seizes or spatiotemporally takes hold of his own creation across history. Thesis, antithesis, and synthesis: according to Hegel it is through these persons' interactions that God self-relates by constantly bringing back to Himself, the originating source of all things, His own creation that had become detached from Him throughout history.[5]

If the Holy Ghosts' ongoing, active reclamation, for and on behalf of God, of the spaces of His own creation may be characterized as limitless, then this is due to the limitlessness of the spatiotemporal flight whereby, since the Fall and on account of their sinfulness, men and women detach the world away from the Father. Ultimately extending to the whole of creation, it is due to such a postlapsarian metonymic flight from one object and space to the next that the third person Trinity has His task cut out for

Himself. Faced with such a predicament, Spirit, in other words, cannot but intervene *in* the world or, what comes to the same, in the spatiotemporal manifold so as to constantly reclaim and return it to its originating source and foundation.

When Hermana Juana told me that in order to "receive blessings" from the Holy Spirit she and the other Pentecostal squatters must "occupy spaces," she was simply voicing the extent to which her own and the other Pentecostal squatters' agencies overlap with that of the Holy Ghost to the point, indeed, of both being one and the same. It is precisely such an overlap that the squatters have in mind when, in line with all other Pentecostals, they insist on their self-proclaimed status as mere "vessels" or conduits of the Holy Spirit, with no independent will or agency of their own. Given such a folk theory of the person as a sheer empty medium available to the designs of the deity,[6] it is little wonder that such expressions as "I was used by the Holy Spirit" or "the Father used me" are uttered so often among the squatters. They use such phrases to signal God's exclusive hand in some singularly momentous or delicate matter over which they claim no special responsibility, for example, a miraculous healing or, as happens to be the case, the occupation of the Yaracuy building followed in short succession by the seizure from its Portuguese owner of a relatively large shoe factory in the building's basement or garage. Such expressions unambiguously convey how much the squatters view their illegal activities not as "theirs" but the Father's. In other words, in the squatters' understanding, they are merely the docile instruments that the Holy Spirit "uses" to occupy and repossess those spaces away from the undeserving.

But the peculiarly aggressive spatiotemporal tendency of the squatters' religious practices as forms of seizure and occupation of spaces hitherto held by others is not only present in these *invasiones* or *tomas*, as they are called in Venezuela, although these disclose such a tendency in a singularly dramatic fashion. It is, for example, evident in the processions that Hermana Juana orchestrated on several occasions with the aim of reclaiming, in all its filth, messiness, and chaos, the Boulevard of Sabana Grande for Christ. I remember catching my breath while trying to keep up with her, single-mindedly walking straight ahead of me on one of the long avenues parallel to the boulevard with a small group of Pentecostal sisters lagging a few steps behind. With their long, colorful skirts adding a somewhat anachronistic touch to the surrounding cityscape of street vendors, dilapidated storefronts, occasional manic honking, and slightly amused passersby, Hermana Juana and the other sisters made a remarkable sight.[7] Seemingly oblivious to anything going on around her, she accompanied her walking with the staccato recitation of a series of barely inaudible formulas. These amounted to so many invocations of the Father to "take out" the Evil One from one object or place to the next so that He could repossess them all. Every once in a while Hermana Juana would rapidly extend either her left or right hand to touch one or another object, briefly pausing while slightly inclining her whole body forward as if to use her weight to push her powerful words right into the wall, phone booth, or lamp post she was passing.

In line with the belligerent overtones of Pentecostalism everywhere, for which the Manichaean battle between God and the Devil is a structuring force immanent in the most diverse religious practices, what Hermana Juana and the sisters sought to accomplish with this kind of procession was straightforward enough: namely, chasing the Devil from the boulevard while turning it into "Christian territory" freed from all the un-Christian practices and commodities so prevalent in the area.

"Blessed, Prosperous, and Victorious"

The sheer excitement and energy that filled the air each time the possibility of a new seizure arose give an idea of the consuming desires that render the squatters as subjects of a certain lack—one that can be filled only momentarily by adding yet another space to a list that keeps serially expanding. Discernible in the many frantic comings and goings, and in the mischievous smiles, quick glances, knowing looks, and hushed words the squatters hastily traded among themselves, such outbursts of enthusiasm were clearly in excess of any utilitarian calculation of needs. Indeed, they betrayed a subjective disposition for which ceaselessly seizing or occupying space after space is clearly an end in itself.

The places the squatters considered seizing ranged from the small businesses located on the ground floor of the Yaracuy building, including a relatively large restaurant, a pub, and an electric appliance shop, to a series of unoccupied buildings, private homes, and, even an abandoned hospital on the coast far away from Caracas filled with bats and hundreds of rusting metal beds. As for those other spaces that Hermana Juana and her daughter Nivea had already seized with the help of the other squatters before I arrived among them, the list includes part of the ground floor of what at some point was a bank in another part of the city away from Sabana Grande, the Yaracuy building itself, and a shoe factory located in what used to be this building's garage. The latter the squatters occupied with the purpose of turning it into a storage place where, for a price, the informal merchants of Sabana Grande could store their goods at night.

Highlighting how much a capitalist logic of increase is, from the start, intrinsic to the economic relations between the Three Divine Persons there is a strictly Hegelian way of talking about the quintessential Christian mystery of the Trinity that throws light on how the squatters' religiosity possibly relates to their ceaselessly seizing proclivities. Thus, according to Mark Taylor, Hegel's speculative system—for whom the Incarnation prefigures "the self-reflexive structure of the Absolute Idea"—"prepares the way" for later accounts of capitalism, such as Marx's, where the structural parallels between God and money are distinctly brought out. This is so because, already in Hegel and very much in line with the "economic" structure of his system, Spirit behaves as a universal currency or equivalent that, much like money for Marx, mediates between thoroughly heterogeneous dimensions. Thus, while Spirit mediates between the Son and the Father or the "particular" and the "individual" throughout history, continuously bringing a fallen creation back to its originating source, so too, as their universal equivalent, does money for Marx mediate among heterogeneous commodities. Furthermore, it does so within an economic circuit that, much as in the case of religion or speculative philosophy, amounts to a circle always closing or returning to itself. In line with such an understanding, if God, as both "interior" to and "outside" every system of exchange and hence "omnipresent," is "money in more than a trivial sense," then money, and, by extension, capitalism are quite metaphysical entities. It is precisely on account of such a momentous convergence between religious and economic structures that, as much in capitalism as in Christianity, "immaterial structures are constitutive of ostensibly material realities" (Taylor 1999, 157–158).

It is important to realize here that whether in the case of God, the Absolute, or Money, the universal equivalent embodies excess. To stay with the economy for a moment, it is clear that money can only behave as the universal equivalent of a welter of heterogeneous commodities on the basis of a "surplus" that, beyond the production of use values or the mere satisfaction of immediate needs, calls for the realization of exchange (ibid., 158). In turn, when money evolves historically into its "most developed form" of capital, with exchange value taking off from use value, "growing wealth" becomes "an end in itself." In other words, as "the self-reflexivity of the exchange process becomes clear," "exchange value posits itself" as such "only by realizing itself [that is], increasing its value" in a process that is, in principle, limitless (160). It is at this point that the Spirit of Christianity and that of capitalism fuse into a single, spectral agency poised to take over the world.

One night in the summer of 2006, Hermana Juana asked me if I could drive her and two sisters from the building to inspect some abandoned dwellings in an upper middle-class residential area of the city. With her and the two other sisters intently gazing through the windows at one relatively lightless house after another, trying to identify whether or not they were actually abandoned, I remember slowly cruising in my jeep through the dark, quiet streets and avenues of the upper middle-class neighborhood thinking to myself that a taboo was being broken in my presence. It was as if, seized by the (neoliberal) spirit of a certain capitalism, I was about to witness the sisters moving into a brave new world that, thus far, had eluded the grasp of the Prosperity Gospel to which, in all of its incremental possibilities, they are so religiously devoted—a Gospel, I might add, for which endlessly consuming commodities, accumulating wealth, or seizing territory are nothing less than "ends in itself."[8]

A Haunted Landscape

At this point one may wonder about the kind of circumstances under which these events can be possibly happening. Because even if it is true that Spirit has a tendency to wander, unimpeded by any material obstacles, when it is no longer a matter of simply moving about with supine disregard for all worldly partitions but of actually seizing vast chunks of space the material and the spiritual can no longer be separate. They must, that is, once again enter into a mutually contaminating commerce where neither can be said to emerge unscathed. Here this means mostly two things. One, it means that, eager to carry out its designs while obviating all "religious" mediations, under such circumstances Spirit passes directly into matter, availing itself of a wide panoply of bodies and other material implements— guns, crowbars, or hammers—capable of bringing down whatever obstacles crosses its path. It also means that when this occurs, the material world itself fills with Spirit swelling with the powerful, aggressive winds that swiftly course through it, blowing right from above.

As Michel de Certeau has argued for Reformation and Counterreformation Europe, for Spirit to be able to so thoroughly do away with all religious and political institutional mediations these must have already been considerably weakened by debilitating circumstances. Only then, in all of its power, can Spirit blow right through the living, directly imprinting itself on the body of the believers (de Certeau 1995). If in the sixteenth and seventeenth centuries it was the melting away of the world's institutions and partitions that paved the way for the Spirit's coming, something similar happened recently in Venezuela. Briefly, it all has to do with the establishment of the Chávez regime in 1999 following an acute economic crisis made more critical by the implementation, 10 years earlier, of a program of neoliberal structural adjustment imposed by the International Monetary Fund that issued in the delegitimation of most forms of cultural and political representation. Finally, bereft of all credibility, under the impact of President Chávez's polarizing rhetoric as well as the policies of his administration, which were bent on replacing what is left of the country's liberal institutions with a direct democracy focused on the President, such representational forms have in recent years almost thoroughly washed away. In retrospect such an outcome was something of a foregone conclusion considering the extent to which Venezuelan representative institutions relied upon the paternalistic ability of political parties and other institutional instances to clientelistically channel resources to the poor in exchange for loyalty and various forms of support. Given such cultural and institutional premises, it is not surprising that, precipitated if not necessarily caused by the imposition of the International Monetary Fund program, the nation's dire predicament eventually resulted in the thorough delegitimation and virtual collapse of Venezuela's representative democracy.

Avatars of the One

These were auspicious circumstances for the emergence of both a political outsider like Chávez and the kind of Pentecostal spirituality that concerns me here. Armed with a new constitution and informed by a virulently totalizing Bolivarian political theology, since it came into power in 1998 in the wake of general elections that President Chávez unexpectedly won by a devastating margin, his regime seeks to make tabula rasa of every existing circumstance while founding anew all aspects of the nation, from the national assembly to workers' unions, neighborhood organizations, and the universities. Permeated by a fundamentalist nationalist ideology, Chávez's secret organization, the MBR200, sought to regenerate the nation's decay by returning the nation to the teachings of its founding fathers, especially those of Simón Bolívar, father of the fatherland. So much so, indeed, that collapsing time and space while obviating all representative instances, Chávez often parades as the medium through which, in "real time," the Spirit of Bolívar instantaneously reaches, so to speak, "live" Venezuelans from the past.

With its born-again emphasis, Pentecostal spirituality aims for no less radical beginnings: a primeval condition in which, with all mediating, representative religious instances gone, Spirit may once again directly seize the body of the believers and, through them, the larger world that has temporarily become detached from the deity. Through aggressive processes of recentralization, in both intimately related cases it is all a matter of bringing a stranded world back to the One as its single originating source and foundation, regardless of whether such a One is called the Holy Ghost or Bolívar with Chávez parading as mouthpiece.

A History of Violence

As for the world that such a morphing One so jealously and, ultimately, I believe, hopelessly reclaims, constantly "negating itself... either... by limitlessly multiplying itself, or... by turning itself into nothing" (Nancy 2004, 110),[9] let me return to the beginning to give a sense of just how ravaged it is—that is, to the double set of doors of the Yaracuy building, which I repeatedly ran up against during the first few days of fieldwork before being allowed inside. Passing through these doors into the building is not in any way akin to entering some reclusive "inside"; rather than any hidden depths, what one meets "inside" is the most unflinching "outside." Indeed, whatever lies "inside," from broken elevator in the lobby to the stairs leading through the mezzanine and a series of floors all the way up to the "penthouse," bears the unmistakable traces of the "outside" reality that one presumably leaves behind, in the streets, when entering the building.

Simply climbing the main stairs of the building all the way up to the "penthouse" suffices to confirm what I say. Everywhere the heavily locked doors of the apartments, often secured with thick chains or reinforced with heavy metal planks, bear testimony to how fragile the boundaries between "inside" and "outside" are within the building. The same can be said of the groups of apartments barricaded behind some impromptu common gate that blocks the corridor and that one must necessarily trespass before reaching any one of them. All of this mutely yet eloquently speaks to a recent history of violence, of forced entries, sieges, and seizures, and to the corresponding countermeasures undertaken to set the balance straight.

Indeed, as I eventually found out, during the months immediately preceding my arrival, a true reign of terror had taken hold of the building, leading to several violent deaths and the temporary forceful eviction of the squatters by the police. It all had to do with warfare between rival squatter bands, one of which forced itself into the building armed with guns, machine guns, and other deadly weapons only minutes after Hermana Juana and her largely evangelical following had seized the place.[10] Such rivalries are not unprecedented in a city and nation that in recent decades have experienced a dramatic informalization not just of the economy, with over more than half of the available jobs going to the informal commercial sector, but also of all forms of social intercourse, which increasingly overflow the normative channels and forms of authority that, in the past, had more or less precariously contained them. If to all this one adds a housing crisis of terrifying proportions, made worse by the geologic instability of the lands around Caracas, then the scene is set for the kind of confrontation I have been describing.

To see why it suffices to focus briefly on Sabana Grande, where the Yaracuy building stands, an urban area where informal commerce and all sorts of criminality coexist. Picture this area as a long boulevard fed by parallel streets covered by an unimaginable profusion of precariously erected stalls packed against each other with only the barest space for pedestrians to fight their way through a labyrinth of paths, and where day in and day out, rain or shine, myriad street vendors peddle a bewildering variety of services and goods amidst the enveloping soundscape—a deafening roar where evangelical sermons and songs, rap and salsa music are synchronously blasted from loudspeakers everywhere—and you will have an idea of the place. To say that such a sea of informality is largely beyond the reach of most representative institutions or institutionalized forms of authority is to immediately conjure a shady world where an array of criminal or semicriminal elements and networks fill the void partially left vacant by older forms of ordering. Bribing their way with different officials, it is these criminal elements that, especially in the boulevard's most profitable areas, discharge some of the functions hitherto incumbent on the state; among these, maintaining a modicum of peace among the different vendors or, through intimidation and beatings, keeping a tight control over large numbers of stalls, charging the individual vendors for their daily use while adjudicating over who at any time does or does not have the right to occupy a given spot on the boulevard.

Anyone's ability to wrest an ever meager subsistence from these deteriorating circumstances, marked by a relentless even if not always overt struggle over territory, is continuously lessened by the increasing competition provoked by the growing numbers of those swelling the economy's informal sector. But beyond economic considerations, I do not think that one even begins to take stock of the lives of this people other than through some kind of empathetic understanding that allows one to somehow sense or imagine what it is to go on fending off dispossession without ever letting go of the need to watch over one's place of work, which at any time may be gone, occupied by another, or, in what amounts to a constant search for an ever-elusive dwelling, without worrying sick about keeping a roof over one's head at night. A true crossing of the desert, as witnessed by the many stories, signs, uncanny voices, or visions that proliferate among the Pentecostal squatters around this traumatic absence of home, such a quest raises the whole issue of the dwelling from physical to metaphysical proportions.

It is from such a world and otherworldly visions that Hermana Juana rose as some Moses-like figure ready to lead her squatter-people into the Promised Land of the building. The comparison with Moses is entirely hers, not mine, as well as the insistence on assimilating the building to a Promised Land overflowing with rivers of milk and honey. Her life before seizing the Yaracuy as the quasi-millenarian leader of a relatively large following of mostly Pentecostal squatters is not unlike that of many living in Caracas' poor neighborhoods: a continuous struggle to merely stay afloat where charm, cunning, hard work, or, in the case of Hermana Juana, an obvious native intelligence along with considerable entrepreneurial skills barely suffice to keep the head above water.[11]

When Hermana Juana seized the Yaracuy, she did so as the hub of a concentric network of alliances among individuals and families formed over time, mostly around the many Pentecostal churches that increasingly dot the poorer neighborhoods of Caracas. Such groupings are what spontaneously forms in a sociality like Venezuela's that, in the wake of a failing institutional network, increasingly looks like a landscape of new tribes. It is not, therefore, surprising if minutes after Hermana Juana and her Pentecostal following seized the building, a rival band of heavily armed squatters showed up at the gates, threatening to shoot everyone in sight unless immediately allowed into the building. From the squatters' many retellings of this incident and its aftermath, a disturbing scenario emerges of two rival "peoples" crashing head on, each more or less fleetingly summoned into being by rival forms of sovereignty or alternative politico-theological regimes—a phenomenon that is highly symptomatic of the fates of sovereignty in Caracas today as well as of the mutations that a construct like "the people" is presently undergoing there.

What followed the two consecutive seizures by the rival bands of squatters were months of intense fear and uncertainty, of clandestine meetings in the Pentecostals' apartments with members of this camp secretly fabricating weapons, including rudimentary hand guns, in order to fight their oppressors, something that they eventually did, as well as plotting in hushed voices about what to do next; and armed patrols coursing the corridors throughout the night, often banging in deafening succession on their doors, awakening them with the occasional gun to the head, all to summon such a godly bunch at godless hours to perform the most menial of tasks, for example, washing the building's main stairway clean as rivers of water released by the armed thugs from the penthouse flowed downward through the Yaracuy's stairs. And all of this punctuated by rumors, shouting, or the string of ominous threats, say, of point blank execution or rape confronted by the occasional "hallelujah" or "Christ loves you" from the Pentecostal camp that, occasionally, some of them cannily shouted at their oppressors in the theatrical attempt to, momentarily, turn the tables around until some more conclusive means were mustered to permanently redress the situation in their favor.

The leadership of the building never directly incriminated themselves with regard to the killings, yet widespread talk of "Christian warriors" brought by the Pentecostals themselves into the building from far away *barrios* during the worst moments of the conflict between the rival camps intimate God's hand in the matter, as well as the extent to which, in all of what happened, the Pentecostal squatters were not so much believing *in* Him as heeding His commands. In case there were any doubts about the killings' Christianity, the frequency and conviction with which Hermana Juana and the rest appealed to the Bible, either invoking the text's canonical beheadings or, if not, reveling in those passages where, trumpets in hand, Joshua and his followers bring the walls of Jericho down, surely served to dispel them. In yet another indication of the Bible's prodigious encoding capacities, not the least due to its condition as a vast repository of many gory deeds, Hermana Juana and the other Pentecostals seamlessly linked the building's bloody killings to God's overall design to repossess His creation. Or, as they often put it while significantly drawing a finger across their throats, "you know what happens when anyone messes with a Pentecostal."

Nor is it as if in and of themselves the killings were devoid of all Christian pathos or significance. One of the stories that the squatters like to tell is of one of the *sicarios*—as hired killers are called in Venezuela—refusing to die while being shot at one, two, three, many times from above. All along, according to the squatters, this *sicario* simply stayed seated in the pool of his blood while twitchingly taking the bullets that, one after the other, someone fired at him in succession. The bloody mess did not, however, get in the way of Hermana Juana's daughter trying to discharge her Christian duties. In one more manifestation of the logic of increase inherent in the Prosperity Gospel practiced by the squatters, all throughout the event she greedily urged the dying man to surrender to Christ, thus adding yet one more soul to His Harvest. As one would expect, with all the twitching involved, to do so was farthest from the man's mind, or that, in any case, is what not without some perverse humor several of the squatters told me, clearly attuned to the slapstick comedy possibilities of the incident.

Mystical Foundations

This, then, is the kind of reality to which in recent years both the Holy Ghost and Chávez have arrived; ever since these two related arrivals occurred, it has definitely been show time in Venezuela. Leaving aside for the moment both the media and Chávez, what I wish to underscore here is that it is from the very depths of the squatters' dispossession that the most extreme form of possession, that is, by God Almighty himself, is insistently called forth. As the Pentecostal squatters put it while not always convincingly insisting in their total fearlessness amidst their utter vulnerability, it is all a matter of "standing firm on the rock of Christ" allowing Him amidst all of the world's sinfulness and fears to do battle for oneself. Such a dramatic turnaround brings to mind Racine's play *Athalie,* where the character Abner exchanges the dangers and fears of this world for "fear of God" as that "supplemental fear" that is "more frightening than all earthly fear." According to Slavoj Žižek, in Lacan's understanding such an exchange retroactively renders these "fears into a perfect courage" while turning Abner from an "unreliable zealot" into "a firm, faithful adherent sure of himself and of divine power" (1991, 16–17).

What Lacan says about Abner may also be said about the Pentecostal squatters who, by standing firm on Christ's unmovable rock, land on the very "mystical foundation of authority." As analyzed by Derrida, it is on such grounding that every higher authority rests as an originary "violence," a "mystical foundation" that cannot be legitimized. This is just to say that lawlessness lies at the very source of the law as a violent, ineffable origin that, while inaugurating the law, nevertheless exceeds both the law and the logos itself. (Derrida 2002, 228–298). Silently trapped inside the law, it is such an unaccountable, embarrassing excess that nonetheless enables the law to be the law or legislate the world's manifold, hybrid realities, the myriad disappropriations of the proper, as so many seemingly self-possessed, self-identical entities, an outcome to which violence, of one or another sort and of a greater or lesser degree, is by no means irrelevant.[12] Given the depth of the Pentecostal squatters' disappropriation, it is not surprising if it is not just violence but its highest form, Divine Violence, which they enlist in their attempt to repossess the world in the name and on behalf of the Holy Ghost.

Even if their circumstances may seem dramatically different, the squatters nevertheless live in the same fallen world as we do. Much as in any other, in such a world "the religious" names the ineradicable trace of ideality and transcendence that, always in excess of the world, must nevertheless intervene *in* the world if some enduring experiences and entities are, through repetition, to be temporarily wrested away from this world's many losses and disappearances. While the violence of such a religious force may be more or less, amounting as it does to the sovereignty of the Holy Ghost seizing or repossessing through them the fallen world that has become stranded from the Godhead, the religious force that takes hold of the squatters' minds and bodies could not be more excessive and violent. In its excessiveness, such a force is minimally equal to the squatter's equally excessive, radical disappropriation.

It is not just, then, that as a result of such a possession the squatters are seized by the Spirit; through them, such a Spirit literally seizes everything on which these squatters have either put their hands or fantasize so doing, from buildings and shoe factories to beer pubs, restaurants, abandoned hotels, shops for electric and electronic appliances, and so on, in a list that is potentially infinite. Even if I might have suggested otherwise it is not, however, as if a recalcitrant world no longer posed any limits to the Holy Spirit's repossessing designs so that, availed of this Ghost's founding power and authority, the squatters were free to possess whatever they wished without any worldly obstacles ever crossing their path. If that were so, the Pentecostal squatters would be some kind of superpower irrepressibly swallowing all of reality, which clearly they are not. In their repossessing spatial practices the squatters constantly brush against the law. This is just to say, first, that no matter how weakened, the Venezuelan state still has some coercive powers of its own, and, second, that regardless of their ambitions, as God's chosen people the squatters have yet to step out of the desert like some self-sufficient, sovereign power; far from such a Leviathan-like condition, as exposed and vulnerable as ever, they rather insist on their harsh circumstances, ignorant for the most part of what such a Promised Land would be like.

Ghostly Possessions

If there were any doubts about the squatters' vulnerability, these were dispelled in the wake of the murders when, sweeping through all the apartments, police forces temporarily evicted them from the building while stealing all of their possessions, from TVs, radios, and VCRs to refrigerators, beds, and other household appliances. When a few days later the squatters were officially authorized to reenter their apartments, they returned to empty floors and walls, stripped bare of what was there before an experience that, dramatically so, made once again explicit the very dispossession that, in their inability to hold to anything for too long, is endemic to their existence. Albeit in a more extreme police register, such an experience simply replayed the myriad humiliations, dispossessions, and losses, the sense of constantly having to start anew from scratch, which forms the fabric of their every day.[13]

This, I suppose, is one of the reasons why the squatters repeat so often that "even if we are in this world, we're not of this world." Because, including the seizure of the Yaracuy, which, given its illegality, at any time may be undone by the state, the sovereign acts that the Holy Ghost perpetrates through the mediation of the squatters unfold in a kind of parallel universe. A phantasmatic double of the "real" world as it is defined by normative expectations, symbolic affiliations, and existing power relations, from movies to rap songs, ideally, at least, in such a religiously inflected realm everything that is of this world must have its "spiritual" counterpart in the other, hence the profusion of "Christian" CDs and DVDs that one can find serially displayed in the stalls of informal traders or *buhoneros* specializing in this kind of commodities. Trying to attract a clientele these *buhoneros* often blast the music of their religious CDs through loudspeakers or, if not, show their Christian DVDs to an absorbed audience of onlookers on the TV sets that they often keep in theirs stalls. I submit that doubleness is an attribute not just of the "Christian" commodities that the squatters endlessly acquire; it marks everything that they do or seize on behalf of the Holy Ghost or, better yet, that such a Ghost seizes through them, imbuing with spectrality, as not quite of this world, every worldly thing, good, place, or space on which they put their hands.

Showtime

Given how promiscuous the exchanges between "religion" and the "electronic media" are in our times, it is not surprising that whenever the Holy Ghost arrives through the squatters to such a radically dispossessed world, He does so in fully televisual terms (see also de Abreu in this volume). Arriving to the bodies of the Pentecostal squatters, so to speak, in "real time," such a televisual possession goes a long way to account for these squatters' sense that, as opposed, for example, to the Catholics' "dead" deity, theirs is a "living God" instantaneously conveying His messages and dictates to His squatter-people.[14] Indeed, swiftly seizing the bodies of the believers as "vessels" through which to reconnect with the living, whether in tongues or the vernacular, the Holy Ghost's messages and dictates directly erupt in broad daylight to more or less sensationalist effects, and often in the television studio-like stage of the various Pentecostal churches that the squatters attend every Sunday. To give a sense of the televisually inflected character of the public sphere that is so sensationally brought about through the intimations of Spirit, it suffices to cast a brief glance at any of these Sunday services in downtown Caracas' Monarchical Church. Attended by crowds of believers, these services are part of the "Prosperity Gospel" that, more and more throughout Venezuela, places spirituality and material gain in a strict means-end relationship, so much so that, among the squatters, the question "how are you?" is often answered with a resounding "blessed, prosperous, and victorious," a set phrase that poignantly conveys the acquisitive and belligerent overtones of their brand of Christianity.

Something noticeable about the services is how little they respect the separation between audience and stage that authors like Lyotard and others regard as requisite to the constitution of representation or the representative relation.[15] In the Monarchical Church, no one really represents anything; there is seemingly no gap or temporal delay separating the representative from the represented, safely kept at a distance in their place, patiently waiting for the proceedings to end. Instead, in this televisual context everyone is bent on directly presenting live the power of Spirit bursting among those present through their talking, singing, laughing, trembling, jumping, or uncontrollable sobbing. It begins with the audience on their feet, their arms raised high like a forest of swaying, vibrating antennas, thus ready to receive the gift of the Holy Ghost descending among them right from the stage where, clad in black, the pastor thunderously preaches. From that moment on, all precarious distinctions start to break down. As a large part of the "audience" moves onto the stage, a ritual battle unfolds there in which, from demons to deity, everything that once was either distant or hidden is instantaneously revealed. In principle invisible, such hitherto unavailable dimensions break into the open through forms of disclosure or revelation that unceremoniously break down any separations between "private" and "public" domains or the "represented" and the "representative" that formerly were more or less precariously in place.

"Everything that is hidden must be revealed;" this is how Hermana Juana responded this past June to my horrified reaction to the Venezuelan attorney general's words on national television concerning a prominent priest found killed in his hotel room in Caracas. Insisting that the priest had "participated in his own death," the government official publicly disclosed the state of the priest's most intimate viscera, revealing to a national audience that his "rectum had been mistreated" and that a "condom was found stuck in his anus." These horrific homophobic words are part of the Chávez regime's attempt to discredit one of its most staunch

internal enemies, the Catholic Church. But beyond this contingent political motivation, such a public explosion of viscerality is, I believe, closely
related to similar instances where President Chávez and members of his
government have introduced into public discourse references and expressions that hitherto had been rigorously confined to the realm of the private. Such "intimate publicities," as I call them elsewhere, have become
routine in Venezuela (Sánchez 2006, 401–426). One could cite a number
of these nefarious, homophobic, or misogynous instances, rich with
exposed viscerality, such as statements by President Chávez on national
television joking about sodomizing his enemies in the upcoming general
elections. One, however, stands out: the words by one government official on a television program who, asked to comment on a female politician who at the time Chávez had just named his vice president, answered
by jokingly cautioning his audience about never trusting "an animal that
bleeds monthly and does not die" (*El Nacional,* 11 October 2000).

One does not begin to grasp these instances in their significance as public explosions of viscerality, bodiliness, and, generally, the hidden and the
intimate unless one takes stock of the breakdown of representation and the
representative relation as it, for example, takes place in the Pentecostal service that I have alluded to before. As I argue elsewhere in reference to
Venezuela, a sealed bourgeois sphere of political representation gathered
around specularity and the eye and protected by protocol and secrecy was
erected in both Europe and North, Central, and South America in the late
eighteenth and early nineteenth century as an inherently violent means to
defuse the violence and terror of the revolutionary wars then raging on
both sides of the Atlantic (Sánchez 2004).

Fuelled by universal skepticism and subjected to the kind of "media's
haste" of which Sylviane Agacinski speaks in the epigraph to this chapter,
the current withdrawal of such a separate, relatively self-contained sphere
of political representation, no longer protected by secrecy, signals the
blurring of the demarcation between "private" and "public" domains, a
return of bodiliness, viscerality, and the senses to center stage and, along
with these, the generalization of violence that now colors all of sociality.
Drawn into a globalized avalanche of digitally and electronically reproduced images and texts, with their penchant for obliterating any temporal
gap or delay between events and their "live" presentation to the public,
such a bourgeois sphere begins to give in, no longer is allowed the "tem-
porizing" that, again according to Agacinski, is needed in order "to
develop proposals, to discuss the possible outcomes, to persuade, to imple-
ment decisions" within a domain that is somewhat protected from the
urgent demands, pressures, and instigations of the public (Agacinski
2003, 139).

Under such a relentless exposition and exposure, politicians must put their bodies—now increasingly rendered in all of their idiosyncrasies and quirks as sites of government in their own right—on the line and govern through constant polling, focus groups, plebiscites, and other such means that make them directly answerable to the whims and desires of the public. As celebrities and politicians are increasingly exchangeable, so too, the distinctions between "present" and "past," "here" and "there," or "private" and "public" domains become increasingly blurred in a media-saturated environment that renders the body into the tremulous site where, in all of its passionate immediacy, the intimations of a ghostly elsewhere are immediately registered and sensed. No longer protected by a series of representative instances that are either gone or currently undergoing a severe crisis, such a sentient, haunted body is, in other words, returned to the center of sociality and, much like that of the Pentecostals in the service that I briefly evoked a few pages ago, is increasingly delivered to a battle against demons. No wonder, then, if more and more around the globe, social life increasingly dissolves into mortal bodily combat, with a series of antagonistic interests and aspirations directly expressed and registered through the medium of the human body.

As witnessed by President Clinton's cigar, the Abu Ghraib photographs, the Mark Foley scandal, or, even more recently and ominously, the digitally reproduced execution of Iraq's Saddam Hussein, which bespeak the catastrophic intrusion of the "private" into the very heart of quintessential "public" institutions, recently all over the world such a protected bourgeois sphere has been emitting signs of a severe malaise. Occasioned by globalization and the proliferation of media of all kinds, from small to mass, one may detect in such a malaise signs of a universal withdrawal of the politico-theological, hounded by a bunch of dirty little secrets digitally reproduced and nearly uncontrollably disseminated by the media, a situation that, as with the Pentecostal squatters, does not come without both the wholesale spectralization of sociality and widespread violence[16]—this, along with the viscerality and bodiliness inherent in a collective life increasingly reduced to a sweaty hand-to-hand combat with politics dissolving into a series of discreet issues, all viscerally fought out on behalf of one or another "mystical" instance or authority. Dangerously bereft of those representational protective instances that in the past introduced a postponement or delay between the immediate expression of a series of conflicting passions and interests, focalized in the body, and their properly *political* negotiation in a sphere away from such a turbulent setting, such a collective life, in other words, increasingly looks like a series of disjointed battlefields where bodies meet and clash with one another.

One can learn something about how, and with what effects, such an uncanny mix of viscerality and religious violence happens by briefly focusing on what goes on during possession among the Pentecostal squatters. Much as in television with which such a spectral being is so conspicuously entangled, when the Holy Ghost seizes the body of one or another squatter, He arrives "live," something that is evident from the profuse tears, singing, frothing, praising, shaking, and dancing that his invisible yet overwhelming presence *sensuously* draws from the believers. Coursing through what remains of the institutional assemblage, now hardly capable of representing or mediating the numinous, in His crusade to repossess the world such a living God places the body and bodiliness at the crossroads of a thunderous clash of forces on a mobile terrain where all territorial and social boundaries constantly shift. Bereft of all mediating institutional protections, in all of its vulnerability such a tremulous body is, in other words, increasingly delivered to a battle against demons. This, by the way, is one possible meaning of the return of bodiliness, not only to our academic attention but to the center of sociality, as well.

As the character of electoral campaigns all over the world increasingly shows, with most markers of distinction between the "public" and the "private" blurred, much of collective life increasingly looks like such a bodily spiritual battle. One good example is the poisonous campaign ads and right-wing blogs in the United States with their unmediated appeal to and exposure of a series of "lowly" bodily passions; another is the latest elections in Venezuela, troped by Chávez as a battle of the people against an opposition cast as the devil: posters figuring a wholesome people's representative overwhelming a squeamish, stereotypically homosexual devil starkly made the point that, more and more, with the theologico-political retreating, politics is all a matter of filling one's mouth with ugly, filthy words so as to momentarily recollect one's dispersed forces to, yet again, go and demolish the enemy. The extreme polarization and extraordinarily close results of many elections around the world are, I believe, sure symptoms of such a widespread reduction of sociality to mortal bodily combat. Whether from the left or from the right, if something good is ever to come out from such an unsettling state of affairs, so redolent with viscerality, I simply do not know.

Notes

This is a reduced version of an essay published in Public Culture 20, no. 2 (2008). The research on which this chapter is based was carried out while I was a postdoctoral fellow in the research program on which this volume is based. Earlier versions were presented at a conference at the Wits Institute for Social and Economic Research at the University of Witwatersrand in Johannesburg, South Africa, at the Anthropology Department of New York University, as a BOAS Lecture at Columbia University, at the Graduate Workshop of Anthropology of Latin America and the Caribbean (WALAC) at the University of Chicago, at the Anthropology Department of The Johns Hopkins University and at the Center for Contemporary Theory at the University of Chicago. I would like to thank the members of these audiences for their comments and questions. Adam Becker, Deborah Kapcham, Webb Keane, John Kelly Brian Larkin, Claudio Lomnitz, Birgit Meyer, Rosalind Morris, Nancy Munn, Emilio Spadola, Rupert Stash, and Paula Vásquez have generously read and commented on the paper at different stages of its development, for which I am most grateful. I also wish to thank here my wonderful research assistant Isabela Luján. Much of the paper was developed at New York University's Center for Religion and Media, where I was a Fellow in 2006, and completed while I was a Faculty Fellow at NYU's Center for Latin American and Caribbean Studies. I would like to thank the directors of these two centers, Faye Ginsburg and Angela Zito, and Thomas Abercrombie, respectively, for their generosity and intellectual stimulation. As always, Patricia Spyer has provided invaluable intellectual and personal companionship. Finally, I owe an immense debt to the Pentecostal sisters, their families and followers with whom I work in Caracas.

1. Needless to say, what I have here in mind is not any "real" presence but the effect of such presence brought about by a wide range of digital and electronic technologies, especially television, that seemingly obliterate the difference between so-called real presence and its representation. See Samuel Weber 1996, 121, 161.

2. In line with the squatter's understanding, by "the undeserving," I mean all those *mundanos* or worldly, mundane beings that have not been baptized or "born again" in the Holy Spirit; that is, virtually everyone who is not a Pentecostal.

3. The literature on Pentecostalism grows at a pace that is hard to keep up with. I have found especially useful Corten and Marshall, 2001; Robbins 2004; Meyer 2004b; Stoll 1990; DeWitte 2005b; Oosterbaan 2005. In general, for Venezuela the essays on Pentecostalism by David Smilde are especially insightful. For the bearings it has on some of the arguments in this chapter see especially Smilde 1998.

4. In order to protect the confidentiality of the Pentecostal squatters among whom I have done fieldwork during the past two years, all proper names have been changed.

5. For Hegel's treatment of the Christian Trinity see Hodgson 1988, 111–198, 417–432.

6. If that is what it is, given the squatters' borrowing in order to formulate their self-understanding of both person and agency from a globalized repertoire largely shared by Pentecostals everywhere.

7. For an illuminating study on this connection see Meyer 1999.

8. For a fascinating account of the connections between, on the one hand, Christian Fundamentalism generally, and, on the other, neoliberal globalization see Comaroff 2006. For a stimulating consideration of these issues see also Meyer 2005b.

9. Indeed, I believe that the intensity with which such a morphing One nowadays recurrently dissipates along a metonymic chain where images and things constantly slide from one to the next, without easily lending themselves to be comprehended by any totalizing instance, is key to understanding why it increasingly exhibits such extreme hyperbolic tendencies. In other words, the tendency with which, as a greedy "Holy Ghost," as "Bolívar" or, for that matter, as Bush's "Crusading Mission" such a One becomes monstrous, turned into an oversized spook agonically striving to swallow all of reality is, in my view, directly proportional to its helplessness vis-à-vis a globalized world that is ever more resilient to any and all such totalizing ambitions. In this respect, it is highly significant that the quintessential demonic, pagan "other" of Pentecostal Christianity in Venezuela is the Maria Lionza possession cult. Elsewhere I have written about this cult as a site where, possessed by television, the mediums irrepressibly slide along metonymic chains where, in any one session, they may become possessed by literally dozens of globalized spirits from "Vikings" and "Barbarians" to "Egyptian Pharaohs," "wild Indians," dead movie stars, and heroes from the Venezuelan Wars of Independence. See Sánchez 2001.

10. When Hermana Juana seized the Yaracuy building, sometime in 2003, she did so as the head of some 65 families, of which roughly half were Pentecostals. Calculating an average of 4 or 5 members per family, this would amount to somewhere between 100 and 150 Pentecostals in the building.

11. The image is not only metaphorical. Both the zone where Sister Juana used to live before seizing the Yaracuy building and the nearby Vargas state suffered in 1999 massive landslides, resulting in 1,000 officially confirmed dead, thousands disappeared, and 150.000 people displaced. For a fascinating account of the emergency generated by the 1999 mudslides and its management by the military, see Fassin and Vasquez 2005. See also Vásquez 2005, 2006.

12. For an insightful discussion of Derrida's "economy of violence" and its implications for the understanding of both political processes and the reformulation of cultural and political identities see Beardsworth 2000, 1–46.

13. This has been made quite evident in recent months when, at least for the time being, the Boulevard of Sabana Grande has been retaken by the state, clearing the whole area from informal merchants. Given how crucial the support from this informal sector is to the Chávez administration the long-term repercussions from such a state intervention still remain to be seen.

14. On televisual possession see Sánchez 2001.

15. For an insightful consideration of Lyotard's understanding of the notion of representation see Bennington 1988.

16. On the withdrawal of the Theologico-Political see Lacoue-Labarthe and Nancy 1997, 122–142. In line with Lacoue-Labarthe and Nancy's arguments,

the chapter here should not be read as a nostalgic plea for the return of a theologico-political formation that nowadays seems irrevocably compromised. In the hope of aiding the search for democratic solutions to the current crisis of political representation, it merely aims to call attention to some of the more traumatic aspects and consequences of such a global crisis.

Bibliography

Abib, Jonas. *Canção Nova: Uma Obra de Deus. Nossa História e Missão*. São Paulo: Edições Loyola, 1999.

Agacinski, Sylviane. *Time Passing: Modernity and Nostalgia*. New York: Columbia University Press, 2003.

Ahmed, Rahnuma. "'Women's Awakening': The Construction of Modern Gender Differences in Bengali Muslim Society." In *Shamprotik Nribigyan* [Contemporary Anthropology], edited by S. M. Nurul Alam, Ainoon Naher, and Manas Chowdhury, 109–130. Dhaka: Department of Anthropology, Jahangirnagar University, 1999.

Aiyar, S. Devasankar. "The Indian Cinematograph Committee Evidence, 1927–1928." Written Statement, New Delhi, *Government of India Press* 3 (1928): 388.

Altman, Rick. *Sound Theory, Sound Practice*. London and New York: Routledge, 1992.

Amin, Sonia Nishat. "The Orthodox Discourse and the Emergence of the Muslim Bhadromohila in Early Twentieth Century Bengal." In *Mind Body and Society: Life and Mentality in Colonial Bengal*, edited by Rajat Kanta Ray, 391–422. Delhi: Oxford University Press, 1995.

Anderson, Benedict. *Imagined Communities: Reflections on the Origin and Spread of the Nationalism*. Rev. ed. London: Verso, 1991.

Anonymous. "Putting the Indian Film on the Market: Its limitations and Exploitation, a Survey of the Present Position." *The Hindu*, 17 July 1931.

———. "Our Kino Talks—Madras at Last." *Funny Magzin*, 20 May 1933.

Antoniazzi, Alberto. "A Igreja Católica face a expansão do Pentecostalismo." In *Nem Anjos nem Demonios*, edited by A. Antoniazzi, R.C. Fernandes, W. Gomes, P. Sanchis, R. Valle, and I. Sarti, 17–23. Petrópolis: Editora Vozes, 1994.

Anwar, Auwalu. "The Struggle for Influence and Identity: The Ulama in Kano, 1937–1987." PhD diss., University of Maiduguri, 1989.

Appadurai, Arjun. *Modernity at Large. Cultural Dimensions of Globalization*. Minneapolis: University of Minnesota Press, 1996.

Arnold, David. *The Congress in Tamilnad: National Politics in South India 1919–1937*. London: Curzon Press, 1977.

Arora, Poonam. "'Imperilling the Prestige of the White Woman': Colonial Anxiety and Film Censorship in British India." *Visual Anthropology Review: Journal of the Society for Visual Anthropology* 11, no. 2 (Fall 1995): 36–50.

Asad, Talal. *Genealogies of Religion: Discipline and Reasons of Power in Christianity and Islam*. Baltimore and London: Johns Hopkins University Press, 1993.
———. *Formations of the Secular: Christianity, Islam, Modernity*. Stanford: Stanford University Press, 2003.
Asamoah-Gyadu, Kwabena. "Anointing through the Screen. Neo-Pentecostalism and Televised Christianity in Ghana." *Studies in World Christianity* 11, no. 1 (2005): 10–28.
Ayyah, Sesha. "Indian Talkies—A General View." *Filmland*, 19 November 1932.
Azevedo Santos, Maria Stella de. *Meu Tempo é Agora*. São Paolo: Editoria Oduduwa, 1993.
Azevedo Santos, Maria Stella de, and Cleo Martins. "Manifesto. Para que o Candomblé Sobreviva". Planeta 201, (June 1989): 19–22.
Babb, Lawrence, and Susan Wadley, eds. *Media and the Transformation of Religion in South Asia*. Philadelphia: University of Pennsylvania Press, 1995.
Bakker, André. "God, Devil and the Work of Television: Modern Mass Media and Pentecostal Christianity in an Evangelical Community in Brazil." Masters Thesis, VU University, Amsterdam, 2007.
Bannerjee, Himani. "Attired in Virtue: The Discourse of Shame (*lajja*) and the Clothing of the *Bhadramahila* in Colonial Bengal." In *From the Seams of History: Essays on Indian Women*, edited by Bharati Ray, 67–106. New Delhi: Oxford University Press, 1997.
Barkindo, Bawuro M. "Growing Islamism in Kano City since 1970: Causes, Forms and Implications." In *Muslim Identity and Social Change in Sub-Saharan Africa*, edited by Louis Brenner, 91–105. Bloomington: Indiana University Press, 1993.
Barthes, Roland. *The Responsibility of Forms: Critical Essays on Music, Art, and representation*. Berkeley and Los Angeles: University of California Press, 1991 [1982].
Baskaran, S. Theodore. *The Message Bearers: The Nationalist Politics and the Entertainment Media in South India, 1880–1945*. Madras: Cre-A, 1981.
———. *Eye of the Serpent: An Introduction to Tamil Cinema*. Madras: East-West Books, 1996.
Baudrillard, Jean. *Selected Writings*. London: Polity, 2000.
———. *Impossible Exchange*, translated by Chris Turner. London: Verso, 2001.
Bauman, Zygmunt. *Liquid Modernity*. Cambridge: Polity Press, 2000.
———. *Community. Seeking Safety and Security in an Insecure World*. New York: Polity Press, 2001.
Beardsworth, Richard. *Derrida and the Political*. London: Routledge, 2000.
Beasley-Murray, Jon. "On Posthegemony." *Bulletin of Latin American Research* 22, no.2 (2003): 117–125.
Beckford, George L. *The George Beckford Papers*. Selected and introduced by Kari Levitt. Kinston: Canoe Press, 2000.
Behrend, Heike. "Photo Magic. Practices of Healing and Harming in East Africa." *Journal of Religion in Africa* 33, no. 2 (2003): 129–145.
Belton, John. "Technology and Aesthetics of Film Sound." In *Film Theory and Criticism, Sixth Edition*, edited by Leo Braudy and Marshall Cohen, 386–394. New York and Oxford: Oxford University Press, 2004.

Benjamin, Andrew. *Style and Time. Essays on the Politics of Appearance.* Evanston: Northwestern University Press, 2006.

Benjamin, Walter. "The Work of Art in the Age of Mechanical Reproduction." In *Illuminations*, edited by Hannah Arendt, 211–244. London: Pimlico, 1999 [1936].

Bennington, Geoffrey. *Lyotard: Writing the Event.* New York: Columbia University Press, 1988.

Benitez-Rojo, Antonio. *The Repeating Island: The Caribbean and the Postmodern Condition*, translated by James Maraniss. Durham: Duke University Press, 1996.

Bhattacharya, Rimli, trans. *Binodini Dasi—My Story and My Life as an Actress.* Delhi: Kali for Women, 1998.

Birman, Patrícia. "Entre França e Brasil: Viagens Antropológicas num campo (religioso) minado." *Horizontes Antropológicos* 5, no. 10 (1999): 35–60.

———. "Futilidades levadas à sério: o candomblé como uma linguagem religiosa do sexo e do exótico." In *Galeras Cariocas: territórios de conflitos e encontros culturais*, edited by Hermano Vianna, 224–242. Rio de Janeiro: Editora UFRJ, 2003.

———. "Fronteiras espirituais e fronteiras nacionais: o combate às seitas na França." *Mana* 11, no. 1 (2005): 7–39.

———. "Future in the Mirror: The Media, Evangelicals and Politics in Rio de Janeiro." In *Religion, Media and the Public Sphere*, edited by Birgit Meyer and Annelies Moors, 52–72. Bloomington: Indiana University Press, 2006.

Birman, Patrícia, and David Lehmann. "Religion and the Media in a Battle for Ideological Hegemony: The Universal Church of the Kingdom of God and TV Globo in Brazil." *Bulletin of Latin American Research* 18, no. 2 (1999): 145–164.

Birman, Patrícia, and Marcia Pereira Leite. "'Whatever Happened to What Used to Be the Largest Catholic Country in the World?'" *Daedalus* 129, no. 2 (2000): 271–291.

B. N. R. "Cinema and Stage: How Does One Reform." *Cinema Ulagam*, May 1935. English translation from selected readings prepared for the Workshop on Tamil Cinema: History, Culture, Theory, 15–19 August 1997. Chennai: Madras Institute of Development Studies.

Bolter, Jay David, and Richard Grusin. *Remediation: Understanding New Media.* Cambridge, MA: The MIT Press, 1999.

Boogaard, Paulien. "Afrikania. of: hervormde traditionele religie. Een politiek-religieuze beweging in Ghana." Master's Thesis, University of Amsterdam, 1993.

Brenner, Louis, and Murray Last. "The Role of Language in West African Islam." *Africa* 55, no. 4 (1985): 432–446.

Brigaglia, Andrea. "The Radio Kaduna Tafsir (1978–1992) and the Construction of Muslim Scholars in the Nigerian Media." *Journal for Islamic Studies* 27 (2007): 173–210.

Briggs, Asa, and Peter Burke. *Uma história social da mídia: de Gutenberg à Internet.* Rio de Janeiro: Jorge Zahar Editora, 2004.

Brown, Judith. *Gandhi and Civil Disobedience: The Mahatma in Indian Politics, 1928–1934*. Cambridge: Cambridge University Press, 1977.

Buck-Morss, Susan. "Aesthetics and Anaesthetics: Walter Benjamin's Art Works Essay Reconsidered." *October* 62 (1992): 3–41.

Burity, Joanildo. "Mídia e Religião: regimes do real entre o mistério, o aparente e o virtual." *Religião e Sociedade* 23, no. 2 (2003): 77–91.

Butler, Judith. *Gender Trouble: Feminism and the Subversion of Identity*. New York: Routledge, 1999.

Campos, Leonildo Silveira. *Teatro, templo e mercado: Organização e marketing de um empreendimento neopentecostal*. Rio de Janeiro: Vozes, 1997.

Campos, Vera Felicidade de Almeida. *Mãe Stella de Oxossi. Perfil de uma Liderança Religiosa*. Rio de Janeiro: Jorge Zahar, 2003.

Capone, Stefania. *La quête de l'Afrique dans le candomblé: pouvoir et tradition au Brésil*. Paris: Éditions Karthala, 1999.

Carranza, Brenda. *Renovação Carismática. Origens, Mudanças e Tendências*. São Paulo: Editora Santuário, 2000.

Castells, Manuel. *The Information Age: Economy, Society and Culture*. 3 Vols. Oxford: Blackwell, 1996–1998.

Castillo, Lisa Earl. "Entre a oralidade e a escrita: percepções e usos do discurso etnográfico no candomblé da Bahia." PhD diss., Instituto de Letras, Universidade Federal da Bahia, Salvador, 2005.

Chettiar, P. S. "Mothers Younger than Sons, Electric Fans in Puranic Films." *Madras Mail*, 15 August 1936.

Chidester, David. "Material Terms for the Study of Religion." *Journal of the American Academy of Religion* 68, no. 2 (2000): 367–380.

———. *Authentic Fakes: Religion and American Popular Culture*. Berkeley: University of California Press, 2005.

———. "Zulu Dreamscapes: Senses, Media, and Authentication in Contemporary Neo-Shamanism." *Material Religion* 4, no. 2 (2008): 135–158.

Chowdhury, Manosh. "Politics of Secularism in Bangladesh: On the Success of Reducing Political Vocabularies into 'Evil' Islamism." *The Journal of Social Studies* 109 (2006): 1–14.

Clegg, Peter. "The UK Caribbean Overseas Territories: Extended Statehood and the Process of Policy Convergence." In *Extended Statehood in the Caribbean: Paradoxes of Quasicolonialism, Local Autonomy and Extended Statehood in the USA, French, Dutch and British Caribbean*, edited by Lammert de Jong and Dirk Kruijt, 125–156. Amsterdam: Rozenberg, 2006.

Cohen, Anthony P. *The Symbolic Construction of Community*. London: Tovistock, 1985.

Comaroff, Jean. "The Force That Is Faith." *Wiser Review*, no. 2 (2006): 6–7.

Comaroff, Jean, and Comaroff, John, eds. "Millenial Capitalism and the Culture of Neo-liberalism." Special Issue of *Public Culture* 12, no. 2 (2000).

Conrado, Flávio Cesar. "Política e Mídia: a Igreja Universal do Reino de Deus nas Eleições." *Religião & Sociedade* 21, no. 2 (2001): 85–111.

Cooper, Carolyn. *Sound Clash: Jamaican Dancehall Culture at Large*. New York: Palgrave Macmillan, 2004.

Correia, Luis Gustavo. "Axé; a força vital do candomblé e o mundo dinámico da física moderna." *Caos. Revista Electrônica das Sciencas Socias*, 1999. http://www.cchla.ufpb.br/caos/00-correia.html (accessed 25 July 2008).

Corten, André. "Transnationalised Religious Needs and Political Delegitimisation in Latin America." In *Between Babel and Pentecost: Transnational Pentecostalism in Africa and Latin America*, edited by André Corten and Ruth Marshall-Fratani, 106–123. London: Hurst, 2001.

Corten, André, and Ruth Marshall, eds. *Between Babel and Pentecost. Transnational Pentecostalism in Africa and Latin America*. Bloomington: Indiana University Press, 2001.

Cousins, Margaret. *Music of Orient and Occident: Essays towards Mutual Understanding*. Madras: B. G. Paul, 1935.

Crary, Jonathan. *Suspensions of Perception. Attention, Spectacle, and Modern Culture*. Boston, MA: MIT Press, 2001.

Cravo Neto, Mario. *O Tigre do Dahomey—A Serpente de Whydah*. Salvador: Galeria de Arte Paulo Darzé, 2004.

Csordas, Thomas. "Asymptote of the Ineffable. Embodiment, Alterity, and the Theory of Religion." *Current Anthropology* 45, no. 2 (2004): 163–184.

———. "Introduction: Modalities of Transnational Transcendence." *Anthropological Theory* 7, no. 3 (2007): 259–272.

Cunha, Christina Vital da. "'Ocupação evangélica': efeitos do crescimento pentecostal na favela de Acari." Masters Thesis, Federal University of Rio de Janeiro, 2002.

Daniel, Justin. "The French Departments d'Outre Mer: Guadeloupe and Martinique." In *Extended Statehood in the Caribbean: Paradoxes of Quasi Colonialism, Local Autonomy and Extended Statehood in the USA, French, Dutch and British Caribbean*, edited by Lammert de Jong and Dirk Kruijt, 59–84. Amsterdam: Rozenberg, 2006.

Dantas, Beatriz Góis. *Vovó Nagô e Papai Branco. Usos e abusos da África no Brasil*. Rio de Janeiro: Editora Graal, 1988.

De Abreu, Maria José Alves. "Charisma, Media and Broken Screens." *Etnofoor* 15, no. 1/2 (2002): 240–258.

———. "Breathing Into the Heart of the Matter: Why Padre Marcelo Needs No Wings." *Postscripts* 1, no. 2/3 (2005): 325–349.

———. "Goose Bumps All Over: Voice, Media and Tremor." *Social Text* 25, no. 3 (2008): 59–78.

———. "In Midair: Breath, Media, Body, Space. A Study of the Catholic Charismatic Renewal Movement in Brazil." PhD diss., University of Amsterdam, 2009.

De Certeau, Michel. *The Practice of Everyday Life*. Berkeley: University of California Press, 1984.

———. *The Mystic Fable. Volume One. The Sixteenth and Seventeenth Centuries*, translated by Michael B. Smith. Chicago: University of Chicago Press, 1999.

De Vries, Hent. "In Media Res. Global Religion, Public Spheres, and the Task of Contemporary Comparative Religious Studies." In *Religion and Media*, edited by Hent de Vries and Samuel Weber, 3–42. Stanford: Stanford University Press, 2001.

De Vries, Hent., ed. *Religion: Beyond a Concept*. New York: Fordham University Press, 2008.

De Witte, Marleen. "Altar Media's *Living Word*. Televised Charismatic Christianity in Ghana." *Journal of Religion in Africa* 33, no. 2 (2003): 172–202.

———. "Afrikania's Dilemma. Reframing African Authenticity in a Christian Public Sphere." *Etnofoor* 17, no. 1/2 (2004): 133–155.

———. " 'Insight,' Secrecy, Beasts, and Beauty. Struggles Over the Making of a Ghanaian Documentary on African Traditional Religion." *Postscripts* 1, no. 2/3 (2005a): 277–300.

———. "The Spectacular and the Spirits. Charismatics and Neo-Traditionalists on Ghanaian Television." *Material Religion* 1, no. 3 (2005b): 314–335.

———. "Spirit Media. Charismatics, Traditionalists, and Mediation Practices in Ghana." PhD diss., University of Amsterdam, 2008.

Derrida, Jacques. "Above All, No Journalists!" In *Religion and Media*, edited by Hent de Vries and Samuel Weber, 56–93. Stanford: Stanford University Press, 2001.

———. "Force of Law: The 'Mystical Foundation of Authority.' " In *Acts of Religion*, edited by Gil Anidjar, 228–298. New York: Routledge, 2002.

Doane, Mary Ann. "The Voice in the Cinema: The Articulation of Body and Space." *Yale French Studies* 60 (1980): 35–50.

Douglas, Mary. *Purity and Danger: An Analysis of Concept of Pollution and Taboo*. New York: Routledge, 2002 [1966].

Durkheim, Emile. *The Division of Labour in Society*. New York: Free Press, 1984 [1893].

Dwyer, Rachel. *Filming the Gods: Religion and Indian Cinema*. London: Routledge, 2006.

Eickelman, Dale, and Jon Anderson. *New Media in the Muslim World. The Emerging Public Sphere*. Bloomington: Indiana University Press, 1999.

Eisenlohr, Patrick. "As Makkah Is Sweet and Beloved, So Is Madina. Islam, Devotional Genres, and Electronic Mediation in Mauritius." *American Ethnologist* 33, no. 2 (2006): 230–245.

———. Technologies of the Spirit: Devotional Islam, Sound Reproduction, and the Dialectics of Mediation and Immediacy in Mauritius. Unpublished Manuscript, n.d.

Eisenstein, Elizabeth. *The Printing Press as an Agent of Change. Communications and Cultural Transformations in Early-Modern Europe*. 2 Vols. Cambridge: Cambridge University Press, 1979.

Eliade, Mircea. *The Sacred and the Profane: The Nature of Religion*. New York: Harcourt Brace Jovanovich, 1959.

Engelke, Matthew. *A Problem of Presence. Beyond Scripture in an African Church*. Berkeley: University of California Press, 2007.

Engelke, Matthew, and Matt Tomlinson, eds. *The Limits of Meaning: Case Studies in the Anthropology of Christianity*. New York: Berghahn, 2006.

Erlmann, Veit. "How Beautiful Is Small? Music, Globalization and the Aesthetics of the Local." *Yearbook for Traditional Music* 30 (1998): 12–21.

Fassin, Didier, and Paula Vasquez. "Humanitarian Exception as the Rule: The Political Theology of the 1999 Tragedia in Venezuela." *American Ethnologist* 32 (2005): 389–405.

Featherstone, Mike. *Cultura Global: nacionalismo, globalização e modernidade.* Petrópolis, Rio de Janeiro: Editora Vozes, 1999.

Ferguson, James. *Global Shadows: Africa in the Neoliberal World Order.* Durham: Duke University Press, 2006.

Fonseca, Alexandre. *Evangélicos e a mídia no Brasil.* Rio de Janeiro: IFCS/UFRJ, 1997.

———. "Lideranças evangélicas na mídia: Trajetorias na política e na sociedade civil." *Religião & Sociedade* 19, no. 1 (1998): 85–111.

———. "Fé na tela: características e ênfases de duas estratégias evangélicas na televisão." *Religião & Sociedade* 23, no. 2 (2003): 33–53.

Foucault, Michel. "Of Other Spaces." In *The Visual Culture Reader*, edited by Nicholas Mirzoeff, 227–236. New York: Routledge, 2002 [1984].

Frankl, R. "Transformation of Televangelism, Repackaging Christian Family Values." In *Culture, Media and the Religious Right*, edited by J. Lesage and K. Kintz, 161–190. Minneapolis: University of Minnesota Press, 1997.

Freedberg, David. *The Power of Images. Studies in the History and Theory of Response.* Chicago: University of Chicago Press, 1989.

Freston, Paul. "Popular Protestants in Brazilian Politics: A Novel Turn in Sect-State Relations." *Social Compass* 41, no. 4 (1994): 537–570.

———. "Protestantismo e Democracia no Brasil." *Lusotopie* (1999): 329–340.

———. "Os evangélicos e a nova realidade política." *Editora Ultimato* 280 (2003), published online, http://www.ultimato.com.br/?pg=show_artigos&secMestre= 481&sec=506&num_edicao=280.

Funkenstein, Amos. *Theology and the Scientific Imagination from the Middle Ages to the Seventeenth Century.* Princeton: Princeton University Press, 1989.

Gabriel, Eduardo A. "Evangelização Carismática Católica na Universidade: O 'Sonho' do Grupo de Oração." MA Thesis, UFSCarlos, São Carlos, 2005.

Garnham, Nicholas. "The Media and the Public Sphere." In *Habermas and the Public Sphere,* edited by Craig Calhoun., 359–376 Cambridge, MA: MIT Press, 1992.

Geertz, Clifford. "Religion as a Cultural System." In *The Interpretation of Cultures*, 87–125. New York: Basic Books, 1973.

Gennep, Arnold van. *The Rites of Passage.* Chicago: University of Chicago Press, 1960 [1909].

Geschiere, Peter. *The Perils of Belonging: Autochthony, Citizenship, and Exclusion in Africa and Europe.* Chicago: University of Chicago Press, 2009.

Gifford, Paul. *Ghana's New Christianity. Pentecostalism in a Globalising African Economy.* London: Hurst and Company, 2004.

Ginsburg, Faye. "Rethinking the 'Voice of God' in Indigenous Australia; Secrecy, Exposure, and the Efficacy of Media." In *Religion, Media and the Public Sphere*, edited by Birgit Meyer and Annelies Moors, 188–204. Bloomington: Indiana University Press, 2006.

Ginsburg, Faye, Lila Abu-Lughod, and Brian Larkin, eds. *Media Worlds: Anthropology on New Terrain.* Berkeley: University of California Press, 2002.

Gitelman, Lisa. *Always Already New: Media, History and the Data of Culture.* Cambridge, MA: MIT Press, 2006.

Giumbelli, Emerson. *O fim da religião: dilemas da liberdade religiosa no Brasil e na França.* São Paulo: Attar Editorial, 2002.

Gordon, Tamar, and Mary Hancock. "The Crusade Is the Vision. Branding Charisma in a Global Pentecostal Ministry." *Material Religion* 1, no. 3 (2005): 386–403.

Gormly, Eric Kevin. "Evangelizing Through Appropriation: Toward a Cultural Theory on the Growth of Contemporary Christian Music." *Journal of Media and Religion* 2, no. 4 (2003): 251–265.

Guadeloupe, Francio. "Chanting Down the New Jerusalem. The Politics of Belonging on Sint Maarten and Saint Martin." PhD diss., University of Amsterdam, 2006a.

———. "Carmelita's Impossible Dance: Another Style of Christianity in the Capitalist Ridden Caribbean." *Journal for the Study of Religion* 19, no. 1 (2006b): 5–22.

Gumbi, Muhammad Sanusi. *Tarihin Sheikh Abubakar Mahmoud Gumi.* Kaduna: Sanusi Gumbi Enterprises, 1986.

Gumi, Sheikh Abubakar Mahmoud. *Al-Aqidah Al-Sahihah Bi Muwafiqah Al-Shari'a.* [The Right Belief Is Based on the Shari'a]. Kaduna, 1972.

Gumi, Sheikh Abubakar Mahmoud, with Ismaila A. Tsiga. *Where I Stand.* Ibadan: Spectrum Books, 1992.

Habermas, Jürgen. *The Structural Transformation of the Public Sphere: Inquiring Into a Category of Bourgeois Society.* Boston: MIT Press, 1989.

———. *Strukturwandel der Öffentlichkeit: Untersuchungen zu einer Kategorie der bürgerlichen Gesellschaft.* Frankfurt: Suhrkamp, 1990 [1962].

Harding, Susan. "The Born-Again Telescandals." In *Culture/Power/History: A Reader in Contemporary Social History,* edited by Nicholas B Dirks, Geoff Elley, and Sherry B. Ortner, 539–556. Princeton: Princeton University Press, 1993.

———. *The Book of Jerry Falwell: Fundamentalist Language and Politics.* Princeton: Princeton University Press, 2001.

Hardt, Michael, and Antonio Negri. *Empire.* Cambridge, MA and London: Harvard University Press, 2001.

Heidegger, Martin. *The Question Concerning Technology and Other Essays.* New York: Harper Perennial, 1982.

Hervieu-Léger, Daniele. "Space and Religion: New Approaches to Religious Spatiality in Modernity." *International Journal of Urban and Regional Research* 26, no. 1 (2002): 99–105.

Hirschkind, Charles. "The Ethics of Listening: Cassette-Sermon Auditioning in Contemporary Egypt." *American Ethnologist* 28, no. 3 (2001): 623–649.

———. *The Ethical Soundscape: Cassette Sermons and the Islamic Counter Public.* New York: Columbia University Press, 2007.

Hirschkind, Charles, and Brian Larkin, eds. "Media and the Political Forms of Religion." Special Issue of *Social Text* 26, no. 3 (Fall 2008).

Hodgson, Peter C., ed. *Lectures on the Philosophy of Religion. One-volume Edition.* Berkeley: University of California Press, 1988.

Hoek, Lotte. "The Mysterious Whereabouts of the Cut-Pieces: Dodging the Film Censors in Bangladesh." *IIAS Newsletter* 42 (2006): 18–19.

———. "Cut-Pieces: Obscenity and the Cinema in Bangladesh." PhD diss., University of Amsterdam, 2008.

Hofmeyr, Isabel. "Books in Heaven: Dreams, Texts and Conspicuous Circulation." *Current Writing* 18, no. 2 (2006): 136–149.

Houtman, Dick. "Op jacht naar de echte werkelijkheid: Dromen over authenticiteit in een wereld zonder fundamenten." Inaugural Lecture, Eurasmus University Rotterdam, June 2008.

Hoover, Stewart M. *Religion in the Media Age.* London and New York: Routledge, 2006.

Howes, David. *Sensual Relations. Engaging the Senses in Culture & Social Theory.* Ann Arbor: University of Michigan Press, 2003.

Hughes, Stephen Putnam. "The 'Music Boom' in Tamil South India: Gramophone, Radio and the Making of Mass Culture." *Historical Journal of Film, Radio and Television* 22, no. 4 (2003): 445–473.

———. "Mythologicals and Modernity: Contesting Silent Cinema in South India." *Postscripts: The Journal of Scared Texts and Contemporary Worlds* 1, no. 2–3 (August/November 2005): 207–235.

———. "House Full: Film Genre, Exhibition and Audiences in South India." *Indian Economic and Social History Review* 43, no. 1 (March 2006): 31–62.

———. "Music in the Age of Mechanical Reproduction: Drama, Gramophone and the Beginnings of Tamil Cinema." *Journal of Asian Studies* 66, no. 1 (February 2007): 3–34.

Hughes, Stephen, and Birgit Meyer. "Mediating Film and Religion in a Postsecular World." Special Issue, *Postscripts* 1, no. 2/3 (2005): 149–153.

Hume, David. *An Enquiry Concerning Human Understanding and Concerning the Principles of Morals.* Oxford: Clarendon Press, 1975 [1758].

Irschick, Eugene. *Tamil Revivalism in the 1930s.* Madras: Cre-A, 1986.

James, C. L. R. *The Black Jacobins: Toussaint L'Ouverture and the San Domingo Revolution.* New York: Vintage Books, 1963 [1938].

James, Liz. "Senses and Sensibility in Byzantium." *Art History* 27, no. 4 (2004): 523–537.

James, William. *The Varieties of Religious Experience.* Plain Label Books, 1904. http://etext.lib.virginia.edu/toc/moding/public/Jamvari.html (accessed on 6 April 2009).

Jeffery, Patricia. *Frogs in a Well: Indian Women in Purdah.* London and New Jersey: Zed Books, 1979.

Johnson, Paul Christopher. *Secrets, Gossip, and Gods. The Transformation of Brazilian Candomblé.* Oxford: Oxford University Press, 2002.

Kane, Ousmane. *Muslim Modernity in Postcolonial Nigeria: A Study of the Society for the Removal of Tradition and Reinstatement of Tradition.* Leiden: Brill, 2003.

Kant, Immanuel. *Kritik der Urteilskraft.* Hamburg: Felix Meiner Verlag, 2001 [1790].

Kapur, Geeta. "Revelation and Doubt in *Sant Tukaram* and *Devi*." In *When Was Modernism: Essays on Contemporary Cultural Practice in India*, edited by Geetha Kapur, 233–264. New Delhi: Tulika Books, 2000.

Kaul, Gautam. *Cinema and the Indian Freedom Struggle*. New Delhi: Sterling, 1998.

Keane, Webb. *Christian Moderns. Freedom & Fetish in the Mission Encounter*. Berkeley: University of California Press, 2007.

Khan, Fawzia. "Cholochhitre Naribad [Feminism in Film]." *Drishorup* 2–3 (2005–2006): 65–100.

Kirsch, Thomas G. "Ways of Reading as Religious Power in Print Globalization." *American Ethnologist* 34, no. 3 (2007): 509–520.

Kittler, Friedrich. *Discourse Networks 1800/1900*, translated by Michael Metteer, with Chris Cullens. Stanford: Stanford University Press, 1990.

Kramer, Eric W. "Possessing Faith. Commodification, Religious Subjectivity, and Collectivity in a Brazilian Neo-Pentecostal Church." PhD Diss., University of Chicago, 2001.

———. "Spectacle and the Staging of Power in Brazilian Neo-Pentecostalism." *Latin American Perspectives* 32, no. 1 (2005): 95–120.

Krings, Matthias. "Muslim Martyrs and Pagan Vampires: Popular Video Films and the Propagation of Religion in Northern Nigeria." *Postscripts* 1, no. 2/3 (2005): 183–205.

Lacoue-Labarthe, Philippe, and Jean-Luc Nancy. *Retreating the Political*. London: Routledge, 1997.

Lakshmi Pathi, A. R. "Indian Cinematograph Committee Evidence, 1927–1928." Written Statement, New Delhi, *Government of India Press* 3 (1928): 165.

Larkin, Brian. *Signal and Noise. Media, Infrastructure, and Urban Culture in Nigeria*. Durham: Duke University Press, 2008.

Larkin, Brian, and Birgit Meyer. "Pentecostalism, Islam and Culture. New Religious Movements in West Africa." In *Themes in West African History*, edited by Emmanuel Akyeampong, 286–312. Oxford: James Currey, 2006.

Lastra, James. *Sound Technology and the American Cinema: Perception, Representation, Modernity*. New York: Columbia University Press, 2000.

Latour, Bruno. *Reassembling the Social. An Introduction to Actor-Network-Theory*. Oxford: Oxford University Press, 2005.

Lima, Délcio Monteiro de. *Os Demónios Descem do Norte*. Rio De Janeiro: Editora Francisco Alves, 1987.

Lima, Vivaldo da Costa. "Os Obás de Xângo." *Afro-Ásia* 2–3 (1966): 5–37.

Lindholm, Charles. *Culture and Authenticity*. Oxford: Blackwell, 2008.

Lody, Raul, and Vagner Gonçalves da Silva. "Joãozinho da Goméia. O lúdico e o sagrado na exaltação ao candomblé." In *Caminhos da alma. Memória afro-brasileira*, edited by Vagner Gonçalves da Silva, 153–182. São Paulo: Selo Negro, 2000.

Loimeier, Roman. *Islamic Reform and Political Change in Northern Nigeria*. Evanston: Northwestern University Press, 1997.

Lutgendorf, Philip. "*Jai Santoshi Maa* Revisited: On Seeing a Hindu 'Mythological' Film." In *Representing Religion in World Cinema*, edited by S. Brent Plate, 19–42. New York: Palgrave Macmillan, 2003.

Lyotard, Jean-François, and Eberhard Gruber. *The Hyphen between Judaism and Christianity*. New York: Humanity Books, 1999.

Machado, Carly. "Religião na Ciberculura: navegando entre novos ícones e antigos comandos." *Religião e Sociedade* 23, no. 2 (2003): 133–145.

Maffesoli, Michel. *The Contemplation of the World. Figures of Community Style.* Minneapolis & London: University of Minnesota Press, 1996.

Maggie, Yvonne. *Medo do feitiço: Relações entre magia e poder no Brasil.* Rio de Janeiro: Arquivo Nacional, 1992.

Mahabir, Joy A. "Rhythm & Class Struggle: The Calypoes of David Rudder." *Jouvert* 6, no. 3 (2002): 1–22.

Mahmood, Saba. "Rehearsed Spontaneity and the Conventionality of Ritual: Disciplines of Salāt." *American Ethnologist* 28, no. 4 (2001): 827–853.

———. *Politics of Piety. The Islamic Revival and the Feminist Subject.* Princeton: Princeton University Press, 2005.

Mandeville, Bernard. *The Fable of the Bees,* edited by F. B. Kaye. Oxford: Clarendon Press, 1924 [1732].

Mankekar, Purnima. *Screening Culture, Viewing Politics: An Ethnography of Television, Womanhood and Nation in Postcolonial India.* Durham: Duke University Press, 1999.

Mariano, Ricardo. *Neopentecostais: Sociologia do novo Pentecostalismo no Brasil.* São Paulo: Loyola, 1999.

———. "Expansão pentecostal no Brasil: O caso da Igreja Universal." *Estudos Avançados* 18, no. 52 (2004): 121–138.

Mariz, Cecília Loreto. *Coping with Poverty. Pentecostals and Christian Base Communities in Brazil.* Philadelphia: Temple University Press, 1994.

Marshall, P. David. *Celebrity and Power: Fame in Contemporary Culture.* Minneapolis: University of Minnesota Press, 2001.

———, ed. *The Celebrity Culture Reader.* New York and London: Routledge, 2006.

Martin, David. *Tongues of Fire. The Explosion of Protestantism in Latin America.* Oxford: Basil Blackwell, 1990.

Massumi, Brian. *Parables of the Virtual: Movement, Affect, Sensation.* Durham: Duke University Press, 2002.

———. "Navigating Movements." Interview published in *Hope: New Philosophies for Change,* edited by Mary Zournazi, 210–242. New York: Routledge; London. Lawrence and Wishart; Sydney: Pluto Press, 2003.

Matory, J. Lorand. *Black Atlantic Religion. Tradition, Transnationalism and Matriarchy in the Afro-Brazilian Candomblé.* Princeton: Princeton University Press, 2005.

Mazzarella, William. "Culture, Globalization, Mediation." *Annual Review of Anthropology* 33 (2004): 345–367.

———. "Internet X-Ray: E-Governance, Transparency, and the Politics of Immediation in India." *Public Culture* 18, no. 3 (2006): 473–505.

McDannel, Colleen. *Material Christianity. Religion and Popular Culture in America.* New Haven: Yale University Press, 1995.

McLuhan, Marshall. *Understanding Media: The Extensions of Man. Critical Edition,* edited by Terrence Gordon. Corta Madera, CA: Gingko Press, 1994 [1964].

Meyer, Birgit. *Translating the Devil. Religion and Modernity Among the Ewe in Ghana*. Edinburgh: Edinburgh University Press, 1999.

———. "Visions of Blood, Sex and Money. Fantasy Spaces in Popular Ghanaian Cinema." *Visual Anthropology* 16, no. 1 (2003a): 15–41.

———. "Ghanaian Popular Cinema and the Magic of Film." In *Magic and Modernity. Interfaces of Revelation and Concealment*, edited by Birgit Meyer and Peter Pels, 200–222. Stanford: Stanford University Press, 2003b.

———. "Praise the Lord: Popular Cinema and the Pentecostalite Style in Ghana's New Public Sphere." *American Ethnologist* 31, no. 1 (2004a): 92–110.

———. "Christianity in Africa: From African Independent to Pentecostal-Charismatic Churches." *Anthropology* 33 (2004b): 447–474.

———. "Mediating Tradition: Pentecostal Pastors, African Priests, and Chiefs in Ghanaian Popular Films." In *Christianity and Social Change in Africa. Essays in Honor of J. D. Y. Peel*, edited by T. Falola, 275–306. Durham, NC: Carolina Academic Press, 2005a.

———. "Religious Remediations. Pentecostal Views in Ghanaian Video-Movies." *Postscripts* 1, no. 2/3 (2005b): 155–181.

———. "Religious Sensations. Why Media, Aesthetics and Power Matter in the Study of Contemporary Religion." Inaugural Lecture, VU University, Amsterdam, 6 October 2006a.

———. "Impossible Representations. Pentecostalism, Vision, and Video Technology in Ghana." In *Religion, Media and the Public Sphere*, edited by Birgit Meyer and Annelies Moors, 290–312. Bloomington: Indiana University Press, 2006b.

———. "Religious Revelation, Secrecy, and the Limits of Visual Representation." *Anthropological Theory* 6, no. 4 (2006c): 431–453.

———. "Pentecostal and Neo-liberal Capitalism: Faith, Prosperity and Vision in African Pentecostal-Charismatic Churches." *Journal for the Study of Religion* 20, no. 2 (2007): 5–28.

———. "Powerful Pictures: Popular Christian Aesthetics in Southern Ghana." *Journal of the American Academy of Religion* 76, no. 1 (2008a): 82–110.

———. "Media and the Senses in the Making of Religious Experience." Special Issue *Material Religion* 4, no. 2 (2008b): 124–134.

Meyer, Birgit, and Annelies Moors, eds. *Religion, Media and the Public Sphere*. Bloomington: Indiana University Press, 2006a.

———. Introduction to *Religion, Media and the Public Sphere*, 1–25. Bloomington: Indiana University Press, 2006b.

Meyer, Birgit, and Jojada Verrips. "Aesthetics." In *Key Words in Religion, Media and Culture*, edited by David Morgan, 20–30. New York: Routledge, 2008.

Mintz, Sidney W. *Sweetness and Power: The Place of Sugar in Modern History*. New York: Viking, 1985.

———. "Enduring Substances, Trying Theories: the Caribbean as Oikoumene." *Journal of the Royal Anthropological Institute* 2, no. 2 (1996): 289–311.

Mitchell, W. J. T. *What Do Pictures Want? The Lives and Loves of Images*. Chicago and London: University of Chicago Press, 2005.

Montes, Maria Lúcia. "As Figuras do sagrado: Entre o público e o privado." In *História da vida privada no Brasil 4*, edited by L. Schwarz, 63–172. São Paulo: Companhia das Letras, 1998.

Moore, R. Lawrence. *Selling God: American Religion in the Marketplace of Culture.* Oxford: Oxford University Press, 1994.

Morgan, David. *Visual Piety. A History and Theory of Popular Religious Images.* Berkeley and Los Angeles: University of California Press, 1998.

———. *The Sacred Gaze. Religious Visual Culture in Theory and Practice.* Berkeley and Los Angeles: University of California Press, 2005.

———. *The Lure of Images: A History of Religion and Visual Media in America.* New York: Routledge, 2007.

Morris, C. Rosalind. "Modernity's Media and the End of Mediumship. On the Aesthetic Economy of Transparency in Thailand." *Public Culture* 12, no. 2 (2000): 457–475.

Mumford, Lewis. *Technics and Civilization.* New York: Harvest Books, 1963.

Munn, Nancy. *The Fame of Gawa: A Symbolic Study of Value Transformation in a Massim (Papua New Guinea) Society.* Cambridge: Cambridge University Press, 1992.

Muthu. "Cinema in Madras." *Cine Art Review*, Deepavali Special, November 1936.

Nambi Arooran, K. *Tamil Renaissance and Dravidian Nationalism, 1904–1944.* Madurai: Koodal Publishers, 1980.

Nancy, Jean-Luc. "Of the One and Hierarchy." *Cultural Critique* 57 (2004): 110.

Nasreen, Gitiara, and Fahmidul Haq. *Bangladesher Cholochhitro Shilpo: Shongkote Jonoshongshkriti* [The Film Industry of Bangladesh: Popular Culture in Crisis]. Dhaka: Shrabon Prokashoni, 2008.

Novaes, Regina Reyes. "Crenças religiosas e convicções politicas: Fronteiras e passagens." In *Política e cultura: Século XXI*, edited by Luis Carlos Fridman, 63–98. Rio de Janeiro: Relume Dumará, 2002.

Ong, Walter. *The Presence of the Word. Some Prologemena for Social and Cultural History.* New Haven: Yale University Press, 1967.

Oosterbaan, Martijn. "'Escrito pelo Diabo', interpretações pentecostais das telenovelas." *Religião & Sociedade* 23, no. 2 (2003): 53–76.

———. "Mass Mediating the Spiritual Battle: Pentecostal Appropriations of Mass Mediated Violence in Rio de Janeiro." *Material Religion* 1, no. 3 (2005): 358–385.

———. "Divine Mediations: Pentecostalism, Politics and Mass Media in a Favela in Rio de Janeiro." PhD diss., University of Amsterdam, 2006.

———. "Spiritual Attunement: Pentecostal Radio in the Soundscape of a Favela in Rio de Janeiro." *Social Text* 26, no. 3 (2008): 123–145.

———, "Sonic Supremacy: Sound, Space and Charisma in a Favela in Rio de Janeiro." *Critique of Anthropology* 29, no. 1 (2009): 59–82.

Oostindie, Gert. "Dependence and Autonomy in Subnational Island Jurisdictions: The Case of the Kingdom of the Netherlands." *Round Table* 95, no. 386 (2006): 609–626.

Oostindie, Gert, and Inge Klinkers. *Decolonising the Caribbean: Dutch Policies in a Comparative Perspective*. Amsterdam: Amsterdam University Press, 2003.

Oro, Ari Pedro. "A política da Igreja Universal e seus reflexos nos campos religioso e político Brasileiros." *Revista Brasileira de Ciências Sociais* 18, no. 53 (2003): 53–69.

Oro, Ari Pedro, and Seman, Pablo. "Neopentecostalismo e Conflitos Éticos." *Religião & Sociedade* 20, no. 1 (1999): 39–54.

Paden, John N. *Religion and Political Culture in Kano*. Berkeley: University of California Press, 1973.

———. *Ahmadu Bello, Sardauna of Sokoto: Values and Leadership*. Zaria: Hudahuda, 1986.

Palmer, Susan. *Aliens Adored: Raël's UFO religion*. New Brunswick, New Jersey, and London: Rutgers University Press, 2004.

———. "The Raël Deal." *Religion in the News* 4, no. 2 (2001). http://www.trincoll.edu/depts/csrpl/RINVol4No2/Raël.htm (accessed on 11 July 2004).

Parés, Luis Nicolau. "The Phenomenology of Spirit Possession in the Tambor de Mina. An Ethnographic and Audio-Visual Study." Unpublished PhD diss., SOAS, London, 1997.

———. *A Formação do Candomblé. História e ritual da nação jeje na Bahia*. Campinas: Editora Unicamp, 2006.

Pels, Peter, and Birgit Meyer. *Magic and Modernity: Interfaces of Revelation and Concealment*. Stanford: Stanford University Press, 2003.

Perrone, Charles A., and Christopher Dunn, eds. *Brazilian Popular Music and Globalization*. Gainesville: University Press of Florida, 2001.

Pinney, Christopher. *"Photos of the Gods": The Printed Image and Political Struggle in India*. London: Reaktion Press, 2003.

Poewe, Karla. "On the Metonymic Structure of Religious Experiences: The Example of Charismatic Christianity." *Cultural Dynamics* 2, no. 4 (1989): 361–380.

Plate, S. Brent. "Introduction: Filmmaking, Mythmaking, Culture Making." In *Representing Religion in World Cinema. Filmmaking, Mythmaking, Culture Making*, 1–15. New York: Palgrave, 2003.

Pretto, Nelson de Luca, and Luiz Felippe Peret Serpa. *Expressões de Sabedoria. Educação, Vida e Saberes*. Salvador: Edufba, 2003.

Quijano, Anibal. "Coloniality of Power, Eurocentrity, Latin America." *Nepantla* 1, no. 3 (2000): 533–548.

Raël. *A Mensagem transmitida pelos Extra Terrestres*. Porto Alegre: Imprensa Livre, 2003a.

———. *Sim, clonagem humana!* Porto Alegre: Imprensa Livre, 2003b.

———, *Intelligent Design. Message from the Designers*. E-book, 1998. http://www.rael.org/ (accessed on 9 April 2005).

Raghavan, V. "Methods of Popular Religious Instruction in South India." In *Traditional India: Structure and Change*, edited by M. Singer, 130–138. Philadelphia: American Folklore Society, 1959.

Rajagopal, Arvind. *Politics after Television: Hindu Nationalism and the Reshaping of the Public in India*. Cambridge: Cambridge University Press, 2001.

Raju, Lakshmana. "Indian Films in South India." *Varieties Weekly*, 9 December 1933.

Raju, Zakir Hossain. "National Cinema and the Beginning of Film History in/ of Bangladesh." *Screening the Past* 11 (2000). http://www.latrobe.edu.au/ screeningthepast/firstrelease/fr1100/rzfr11d.htm.

———. "Bangladesh: A Defiant Survivor." In *Being and Becoming: The Cinemas of Asia*, edited by Aruna Vasudev, Latika Padgaonkar, and Rashmi Doraiswamy, 1–25. Delhi: Macmillan, 2002.

Rancière, Jacques. *The Politics of Aesthetics*. London: Continuum, 2006.

Ranganathan, A. "South Indian Films: Suggestions for Improvement." *The Hindu*, 30 October 1936.

Richman, Paula. *Many Ramayanas: The Diversity of a Narrative Tradition in South Asia*. Berkeley: University of California Press, 1991.

Robbins, Joel. "The Globalization of Pentecostal and Charismatic Christianity." *Anthropology* 33 (2004): 117–143.

Rosario, Santi. *Purity and Communal Boundaries: Women and Social Change in a Bangladeshi Village*. London and New Jersey, 1992.

Rosenthal, Judy. *Possession, Ecstasy, and Law in Ewe Voodoo*. Charlottesville: University of Virginia Press, 1998.

Rosenthal, Michele. *American Protestants and TV in the 1950s. Responses to a New Medium*. New York: Palgrave MacMillan, 2007.

Ryerson, Charles. *Regionalism and Religion: The Tamil Renaissance and Popular Hinduism*. Madras: Christian Literature Society, 1988.

Salvatore, Armando. *The Public Sphere: Liberal Modernity, Catholicism, and Islam*. New York: Palgrave Macmillan, 2007.

Sá Martino, Luís Mauro. "Mercado político e capital religioso." In *Comunicação na pólis. Ensaios sobre mídia e política*, edited by Clóvis de Barros Filho, 312–331. Petropolis: Vozes, 2002.

Samy, G. V. "Indian Films." *Oozhian*, 17 May 1935.

Sánchez, Rafael. "Channel Surfing. Media, Mediumship and State Authority in the María Lionza Possession Cult (Venezuela)." In *Religion and Media*, edited by Hent de Vries and Samuel Weber, 388–434. Stanford: Stanford University Press, 2001.

———. "Dancing Jacobins. A Genealogy of Latin American Populism (Venezuela)." PhD dissertation, University of Amsterdam, 2004.

———. "Intimate Publicities: Retreating the Theologico-Political in the Chávez Regime." In *Political Theologies: Public Religions in a Post-secular World,* edited by Hent de Vries and Lawrence Sullivan, 401–426. New York: Fordham University Press, 2006.

Sanchis, Pierre. "O repto Pentecostal à cultura Católico-Brasileira." In *Nem Anjos nem Demonios*, edited by A. Antoniazzi, R.C. Fernandes, W. Gomes, P. Sanchis, R. Valle, and I. Sarti, 34–63. Petrópolis: Editora Vozes, 1994.

Santos, Jocélio Teles dos. *O dono da terra. O caboclo nos candomblés da Bahia*. Salvador, Brazil: Sarah Letras, 1995.

———, *O poder da cultura e a cultura no poder. A disputa simbólica da herança cultural negra no Brasil*. Salvador, Brazil: Edufba, 2005.

Santos, Juana Elbein dos. *Os nagô e a morte*. Petrópolis, Brazil: Vozes, 1998.

Santos, Maria Stella de Azevedo. *Meu tempo é agora*. São Paulo: Editora Oduduwa, 1993.

Santos, Stella de Azevedo, and Cleo Martins. "Manifesto. Para que o Candomblé Sobreviva." *Planeta* 201 (1989): 19–22.

Sarkar, Mahua. "Muslim Women and the Politics of (In)visibility in Late Colonial Bengal." *Journal of Historical Sociology* 14, no. 2 (2001): 226–250.

Sarkar, Sumit. *Modern India, 1885–1947*. Madras: MacMillan India, 1983.

Scannel, Paddy. *Radio, Television and Modern Life: A Phenomenological Approach*. Oxford: Blackwell, 1996.

Schneider, Manfred. "Luther with McLuhan." In *Religion and Media*, edited by Hent de Vries and Samuel Weber, 198–215. Stanford: Stanford University Press, 2001.

Schofield Clark, Lynn. *From Angels to Aliens. Teenagers, the Media and the Supernatural*. New York: Oxford University Press, 2003.

Schulz, Dorothea A. "Charisma and Brotherhood Revisited: Mass-Mediated Forms of Spirituality in Urban Mali." *Journal of Religion in Africa* 33, no. 2 (2003): 146–171.

———. "Promises of (Im)mediate Salvation: Islam, Broadcast Media, and the Remaking of Religious Experience in Mali." *American Ethnologist* 33, no. 2 (2006a): 210–229.

———, "Morality, Community, Publicness: Shifting terms of Public Debate in Mali." In *Religion, Media and the Public Sphere*, edited by Birgit Meyer and Annelies Moors, 132–151. Bloomington and Indianapolis: Indiana University Press, 2006b.

Schulze, Gerhard. *Die Erlebnisgesellschaft—Kultursoziologie der Gegenwart*. Frankfurt: Campus, 1993.

Schultze, Quentin J. *Televangelism and American Culture: The Business of Popular Religion*. Grand Rapids: Baker Book House, 1991.

Schwartz, Vanessa R. "Cinematic Spectatorship Before the Apparatus: The Public Taste for Reality in Fin-de-Siècle Paris." In *Cinema and the Invention of Modern Life*, edited by L. Charney and V. R. Schwartz, 297–319. Berkeley: University of California Press, 1995.

Shusterman, Richard. "Somaesthetics and the Body/Media Issue." *Body & Society* 3 (1997): 33–49.

———. "Wittgenstein's Somaesthetics: Body Feeling in Philosophy of Mind, Art, and Ethics." *Revue Internationale de Philosophie* 219 (2002): 91–108.

Silva, Vagner Gonçalves da. *Orixás da Metrópole*. Petrópolis: Vozes, 1995.

———. *O antropólogo e sua magia. Trabalho de campo e texto etnográfico nas pesquisas antropológicas sobre religiões afro-brasileiras*. São Paulo: Editora da Universidade de São Paulo, 2001.

Silverman, Kaja. *The Acoustic Mirror: The Female Voice in Psychoanalysis and Cinema*. Bloomington and Indianapolis: Indiana University Press, 1998.

Silverstone, Roger. "Complicity and Collusion in the Mediation of Everyday Life." *New Literary History* 33 (2002): 761–780.

Singer, Milton. *When a Great Tradition Modernizes*. Chicago: University of Chicago Press, 1972.

Smilde, David. "'Letting God Govern': Supernatural Agency in the Venezuelan Approach to Social Change." *Sociology of Religion* 59, no. 3 (1998): 287–303.

Smith, Jeff. "Black Faces, White Voices: The Politics of Dubbing in Carmen Jones." *Velvet Light Trap* 51 (spring 2003): 29–42.

Sobchack, Vivian. *Carnal Thoughts: Embodiment and Moving Image Culture.* Berkeley: University of California Press, 2004.

———. "Embodying Transcendence: On the Literal, the Material, and the Cinematic Sublime." *Material Religion* 4, no. 2 (2008): 194–203.

Souza, Eunice de. *Purdah: An Anthology.* New Delhi: Oxford University Press, 2004.

Spyer, Patricia. "The Cassowary Will Not Be Photographed." *Religion and Media*, edited by Hent de Vries and Samuel Weber, 304–320. Stanford: Stanford University Press, 2001.

———. "Christ At Large: Iconography and Territoriality in Postwar Ambon." In *Religion. Beyond a Concept*, edited by Hent de Vries, 524–549. New York: Fordham University Press, 2008.

Stoll, David. *Is Latin America Turning Protestant? The Politics of Evangelical Growth.* Berkeley: University of California Press, 1990.

Stolow, Jeremy. "Religion and/as Media." *Theory, Culture and Society* 22, no. 4 (2005): 119–145.

———. "Holy Pleather: Materializing Authority in Contemporary Orthodox Jewish Publishing." *Material Religion* 3, no. 3 (2007): 314–335.

———. "Salvation by Electricity." In *Religion and Media*, edited by Hent de Vries and Samuel Weber, 668–686. Stanford: Stanford University Press, 2008.

———. *Orthodoxy by Design.* Berkeley: Stanford University Press, forthcoming.

Sumiala, Johanna. "Circulation." In *Key Words in Religion, Media and Culture*, edited by David Morgan, 44–55. New York: Routledge, 2008.

Taussig, Michael. *Mimesis and Alterity: A particular History of the Senses.* London and New York: Routledge, 1993.

———. "Viscerality, Faith and Skepticism: Another Theory of Magic." In *Magic and Modernity: Interfaces of Revelation and Concealment*, edited by Peter Pels and Birgit Meyer, 272–306. Stanford: Stanford University Press, 2001.

Taylor, Charles. *Sources of the Self. The Making of the Modern Identity.* Cambridge, MA: Harvard University Press, 1989.

———. *A Secular Age.* Cambridge, MA: Belkamp Press of Harvard University Press, 2007.

Taylor, Marc. *About Religion: Economies of Faith in Virtual Culture.* Chicago: University of Chicago Press, 1999.

Thangam, B. "Music in Films." *Film News* 1, no. 10 (January 1937): 11–12.

Tolson, Andrew. *Mediations. Text and Discourse in Media Studies.* London: Arnold, 1996.

Turner, Victor. *The Anthropology of Performance.* New York: PAJ, 1987.

Turner, Victor, and Edward Bruner. *The Anthropology of Experience.* Urbana: University of Illinois Press. 1986.

Umar, Muhammad Sani. "Sufism and Anti-sufism in Nigeria." Master's Thesis, Bayero University, Kano, 1988.

Umar, Muhammad Sani. "Changing Islamic Identity in Nigeria from the 1960s to the 1980s: From Sufism to Anti-sufism." In *Muslim Identity and Social Change in Sub-Saharan Africa*, edited by Louis Brenner, 154–178. Bloomington: Indiana University Press, 1993.

————. "Education and Islamic Trends in Northern Nigeria: 1970s–1990s." *Africa Today* 48, no. 2 (2001): 127–150.

Van de Port, Mattijs. "Registers of Incontestability. The Quest for Authenticity in Academia and Beyond." *Etnofoor* 17, no. 1/2 (2004): 7–22.

————. "Candomblé in Pink, Green and Black. Re-scripting the Afro-Brazilian Religious Heritage in the Public Sphere of Salvador, Bahia." *Social Anthropology* 13, no. 1 (2005a): 3–26.

————. "Circling around the Really Real. Spirit Possession Ceremonies and the Search for Authenticity in Bahian Candomblé." *Ethos* 33, no. 2 (2005b): 149–179.

————. "Sacerdotes Midiáticos. O candomblé, discursos de celebridade e a legitimação da autoridade religiosa na esfera pública baiana." *Religião e Sociedade* 25, no. 2 (2005c): 32–61.

————. "Priests and Stars: Candomblé, Celebrity Postscripts: Discourses, and the Authentication of Religious Authority in Bahia's Public Sphere." *Postscripts. The Journal of Sacred Texts and Contemporary Worlds* 1, no. 2–3 (2005d): 301–324.

————. "Visualizing the Sacred. Video Technology, 'Televisual Style,' and the Religious Imagination in Bahian Candomblé." *American Ethnologist* 33, no. 3 (2006): 444–461.

————. "Bahian White. The Dispersion of Candomblé Imagery in the Public Sphere of Bahia." *Material Religion* 3, no. 2 (2007): 242–273.

Van der Veer, Peter. "Religious Mediation." In *Media and Social Perception*, edited by E. R. Larreta, 345–356. Rio de Janeiro: UNESCO/ISSC/Educam, 1999.

Van Well, Michiel, ed. *Deus et Machina, de verwevenheid van technologie en religie*. Utrecht: Stichting Toekomstbeeld der Techniek, 2008.

Vásquez, Paula. "Sufrir Para Ser Dignos. Antropología Política de la Asistencia a los Damnificados." *El Nacional*, 2 April 2005.

————. "Los Damnificados y la Ilusión de Alteridad." *Veintiuno*, February–March, 2006.

Vasudevan, Ravi. "Devotional Transformation: Miracles, Mechanical Artifice, and Spectatorship in Indian Cinema." *Postscripts: The Journal of Scared Texts and Contemporary Worlds* 1, no. 2–3 (August/November 2005): 237–257.

Verbeek, Peter-Paul. *What Things Do. Philosophical Reflections on Technology, Agency, and Design*. Penn State: Penn State University Press, 2005.

Vergari, Silvia Constant, and Helio Arthur Reis Itagaray. "Os Orixás da Administração." *RAP* 34, no. 2 (2000): 7–24.

Verrips, Jojada. " 'Haptic Screens' and Our 'Corporeal Eye.' " *Etnofoor* 15, no. 1/2 (2002): 21–46.

————, "Aisthesis and An-aesthesia." *Ethnologia Europea* 35, no. 1/2 (2006): 27–33.

Wafer, Jim. *The Taste of Blood: Spirit Possession in Brazilian Candomblé*. Philadelphia: University of Pennsylvania Press, 1991.

Warner, Michael. *Letters of the Republic: Publication and the Public Sphere in Eighteenth Century America.* Cambridge, MA: Harvard University Press, 1990.

———. "The Mass Public and the Mass Subject." In *Habermas and the Public Sphere,* edited by C. Calhoun, 377–401. Cambridge, MA and London: MIT Press, 1992.

———. "Publics and Counterpublics." *Public Culture* 14, no. 1 (2002): 97–114.

Weber, Samuel. *Mass Mediauras. Form, Technics, Media.* Stanford: Stanford University Press, 1996.

Weiner, Norbert. *Cybernetics, or, the Control and Communication in the Animal and Machine.* Cambridge, MA: MIT Press, 1961.

Wilce, James. *Eloquence in Trouble: The Poetics and Politics of Complaint in Rural Bangladesh.* New York and Oxford: Oxford University Press, 1998.

Willford, Andrew, and Kenneth George. *Spirited Politics. Religion and Public Life in Contemporary South-East Asia.* Ithaca, NY: Southeast Asian Publications Series, 2004.

Williams, Linda. *Hard Core. Power, Pleasure, and the "Frenzy of the Visible."* Berkeley: University of California Press, 1988.

———. "Film Bodies: Gender, Genre and Excess." *Film Quarterly* 44, no. 4 (1991): 2–13.

Yakubu, Mahmood. *An Aristocracy in Political Crisis. The End of Indirect Rule & the Emergence of Party Politics in the Emirates of Northern Nigeria.* Aldershot: Avebury Press, 1996.

Zito, Angela. "Culture." In *Key Words in Religion, Media and Culture,* edited by David Morgan, 69–82. New York: Routledge, 2008.

Žižek, Slavoj. *For They Know Not What They Do. Enjoyment as a Political Factor.* London: Verso, 1991.

Zvelebil, Kamil. *The Smile of Murugan.* Leiden: Brill, 1973.

Contributors

Maria José A. de Abreu just finished her dissertation PhD-thesis titled "In Midair: Breath, Media, Body, Space. A Study of the Catholic Charismatic Renewal Movement in Brazil" at the Amsterdam School for Social Science Research (University of Amsterdam). In the past she has worked in the fields of physical anthropology, museum studies, and material culture, and studied the political receptions of Indian Cinema in the Portuguese post-dictatorship period. Her present research interests deal with the versatile articulations of media technologies, body, space, and ethics applied to the Catholic Charismatic Renewal in Brazil.

Marleen de Witte is a postdoctoral researcher at VU University Amsterdam, where she works on a project on the dynamics of cultural heritage in Ghana. Her research interests include religion and media, anthropology of death, popular culture, and Africa. She has published *Long Live the Dead! Changing Funeral Celebrations in Asante, Ghana* (Aksant, 2001) and several articles in journals and volumes. Her dissertation "Spirit Media: Charismatics, Traditionalists, and Mediation Practices in Ghana" deals with public manifestations of Pentecostalism and African traditional religion in Ghana's new mediascape and the relationship between mass media and religious practice.

Francio Guadeloupe's roots and routes connect the French, Dutch, English, and Spanish Caribbean, and he lived most of his life in Europe. Currently he holds the position of Assistant Professor of Cultural Anthropology at the Radboud University Nijmegen (RUN). He is also attached to the Royal Netherlands Institute for Southeast Asian and Caribbean Studies (KITLV) as a postdoctoral Research Fellow, and associated to the University of St. Martin (USM in the Dutch Antilles) as extraordinary Research Fellow. His full-length study on the politics of belonging on Saint Martin & Sint Maarten entitled *Chanting Down the New Jerusalem: Calypso, Christianity, and Capitalism in the Caribbean* was published by the University of California Press in 2009.

Lotte Hoek is lecturer in Anthropology at the University of Amsterdam. Her research interests include gender and sexuality, visual culture, cinema, and popular culture in South Asia, especially Bangladesh. Her PhD dissertation *Cut-Pieces: Obscenity and the Cinema in Bangladesh* is an ethnography of the Bangladesh film industry and focuses on the common practice of inserting sexually explicit imagery into B-quality action movies.

Stephen Putnam Hughes completed both MA and PhD in Social and Cultural Anthropology at the University of Chicago, where he specialized in media history and visual anthropology with special reference to cinema in south India. He currently teaches Anthropology and Sociology at the School of Oriental and African Studies, University of London, where he is the Director of Studies for the MA program in the Anthropology of Media. Having lived and worked in Tamil-speaking south India on and off over the course of the past 22 years, he has published articles and chapters on various topics related to media history.

Brian Larkin is the author of *Signal and Noise: Media, Infrastructure and Urban Culture in Nigeria* (Duke University Press, 2008), and a coeditor of *Media Worlds: Anthropology on New Terrain* (California University Press, 2002). With Charles Hirschkind he coedited a special issue of the journal *Social Text* on media and the politics of religion. His recent research is on religion and media theory. He teaches at Barnard College, Columbia University.

Carly Machado (PhD, 2006, Faculty of Social Science, University of the State of Rio de Janeiro, Brazil) conducts research in the field of religion and media, with a particular focus on new technologies, cyberculture, and the contemporary religious imaginary, both in Brazil and in transnational contexts. Her doctoral dissertation Imagine *If It All Were True: The Raelian Movement Among Truths, Fictions and Religions of Modernity* dealt with the Raelian Movement, a controversial new religious movement concerned with questions about human cloning, bioethics, and the existence of extra-terrestrials. Machado teaches at two universities in Rio de Janeiro: Estacio de Sá University and Candido Mendes University. In 2007 she was a visiting postdoctoral research fellow at the Institute on Globalization and the Human Condition, McMaster University.

Birgit Meyer is professor of Cultural Anthropology at the Department of Social and Cultural Anthropology at VU University Amsterdam. She has conducted research on missions and local appropriations of Christianity, Pentecostalism, popular culture and video-films in Ghana. Her publications include *Translating the Devil. Religion and Modernity Among the Ewe in Ghana* (Edinburgh University Press, 1999), *Globalization and Identity. Dialectics of Flow and Closure* (edited with Peter Geschiere, Blackwell,

1999), *Magic and Modernity. Interfaces of Revelation and Concealment* (edited with Peter Pels, Stanford University Press, 2003), and *Religion, Media and the Public Sphere* (edited with Annelies Moors, Indiana University Press, 2006). She is vice chair of the *International African Institute* (London), a member of the Royal Dutch Academy of Sciences, and one of the editors of the journal *Material Religion.*

Martijn Oosterbaan studied Cultural Anthropology at the University of Amsterdam, where he submitted his dissertation titled *Divine Mediations: Pentecostalism, Politics and Mass Media in a Favela in Rio de Janeiro.* Currently he is postdoctoral fellow at the Faculty of Philosophy, University of Groningen, a researcher in the NWO research project *New Media, Public Sphere and Urban Culture* and a lecturer in the Department of Anthropology at Utrecht University.

Rafael Sánchez teaches at the Center for Latin American and Caribbean Studies, New York University. His publications focus on media, politics, populism, and spirit mediumship. His book *Dancing Jacobins. A Genealogy of Latin American Populism* is forthcoming from Stanford University Press. His current project, "The Fate of Sovereignty in the Landscape of the City," focuses on urban imaginaries and territorializing practices under the current Chávez regime in Venezuela.

Mattijs van de Port is lecturer and researcher at the Research Center for Religion and Society at the University of Amsterdam and professor of popular religiosity at VU University Amsterdam. He is author of *Gypsies, Wars & Other Instances of the Wild. Civilization and Its Discontents in a Serbian Town* (Amsterdam University Press, 1998) and *Geliquideerd. Criminele Afrekeningen in Nederland* (Meulenhoff, 2001) as well as several articles in journals and edited volumes. Currently he is writing a book on the divulgation of Candomblé imagery in Bahia, Brazil.

Index